CEYLON AND THE CINGALESE

CEYLON AND THE CINGALESE

HENRY CHARLES SIRR

VOL (I)

Published by

FacsiMile Publisher
12 Pragati Market
Ashok Vihar, Ph-2
Delhi - 110052, India
Phone: 011-47034999
Email: www.facsimilepublishers.com
info@facsimilepublishers.com

Distribution Network
gyanbooks.com
India, USA, Canada, UK, Australia

ISBN: 978-93-753-9490-7 (Set)
978-93-687-8668-9 (PB)
First Published, 1850

2nd Impression 2025

Printed at: Gyan Press, Delhi.

CEYLON AND THE CINGALESE
VOL (I)
Author: Henry Charles Sirr

CEYLON

AND

THE CINGALESE.

"——— It is a goodly sight to see
What Heaven hath done for this delicious land!
What fruits of fragrance blush on every tree!
What goodly prospects o'er the hills expand!"

BYRON.

COLOMBO

CEYLON AND THE CINGALESE;

THEIR

HISTORY, GOVERNMENT, AND RELIGION,

THE

ANTIQUITIES, INSTITUTIONS, PRODUCE, REVENUE, AND CAPABILITIES

OF THE ISLAND;

WITH

ANECDOTES ILLUSTRATING

THE

MANNERS AND CUSTOMS

OF THE

PEOPLE.

BY

HENRY CHARLES SIRR, M.A.,

OF

LINCOLN'S INN, BARRISTER-AT-LAW,

AND

LATE DEPUTY QUEEN'S ADVOCATE

FOR THE

SOUTHERN CIRCUIT IN THE ISLAND OF CEYLON.

VOL. I.

LONDON:

WILLIAM SHOBERL, PUBLISHER,

20, GREAT MARLBOROUGH STREET.

1850.

TO

THE MOST NOBLE AND RIGHT HONORABLE

JAMES BROWNLOW WILLIAM GASCOIGNE CECIL,

MARQUIS OF SALISBURY, K.G , D.C.L.,

LORD LIEUTENANT OF THE COUNTY OF MIDDLESEX,

&c. &c. &c.

This Work is, by permission, respectfully dedicated,

BY HIS LORDSHIP'S

MOST OBEDIENT,

HUMBLE SERVANT,

THE AUTHOR.

PREFACE.

From the extraordinary interest created by recent events in Ceylon, and the desire for information evinced by all classes upon the subject of the late Rebellion, we have been induced to prepare the following pages for the press, some portion of which appeared in a leading periodical shortly after our return from the Colony.

Our object has been to unfold the capabilities of this beautiful island, and call attention to its undeveloped resources: amongst the former may be classed the proposed emigration to Newera-Ellia, and amongst the latter the long talked of, and essential undertaking—the restoration of the ancient tanks—the whole credit of which last-named proposition, a recent writer, who has never visited the Colony, has most unjustly claimed for himself, although the greater number of, *if not all*, authors who have sojourned in the "Cinnamon Isle" have referred to the subject.

In the performance of our task, we have endeavoured to notice, and believe that we have considered, every topic of interest, described the general features of the country, its glorious antiquities and literature, and illustrated the character and habits of its mixed population.

As a book of reference, we have essayed to render these pages useful, by the classification of chapters, each devoted to a particular subject.

The ancient history of Lanka-diva has been glanced at, and its modern, or that portion thereof which is connected with European rule, has been fully entered into, and, being brought down to the present period, it includes A COMPLETE ACCOUNT OF THE LATE KANDIAN REBELLION, ITS ORIGIN, AND CONSEQUENCES, *together with an exposé of the supposed grievances of our fellow-subjects, and the critical position of the colonial government.*

We have also ventured, from personal observation and facts, to show the inefficiency of death, as a punishment, or example, amongst a population professing the tenets of Buddhism.

April, 1850.

1, *New Square, Lincoln's Inn.*

CONTENTS

OF THE FIRST VOLUME.

CHAPTER I.

CHAPTER II.

CHAPTER III.

CHAPTER IV.

CHAPTER V.

CHAPTER VI.

CHAPTER IX.

CHAPTER X.

CHAPTER XI.

CHAPTER XII.

ILLUSTRATIONS.

VOLUME I.

VOLUME II.

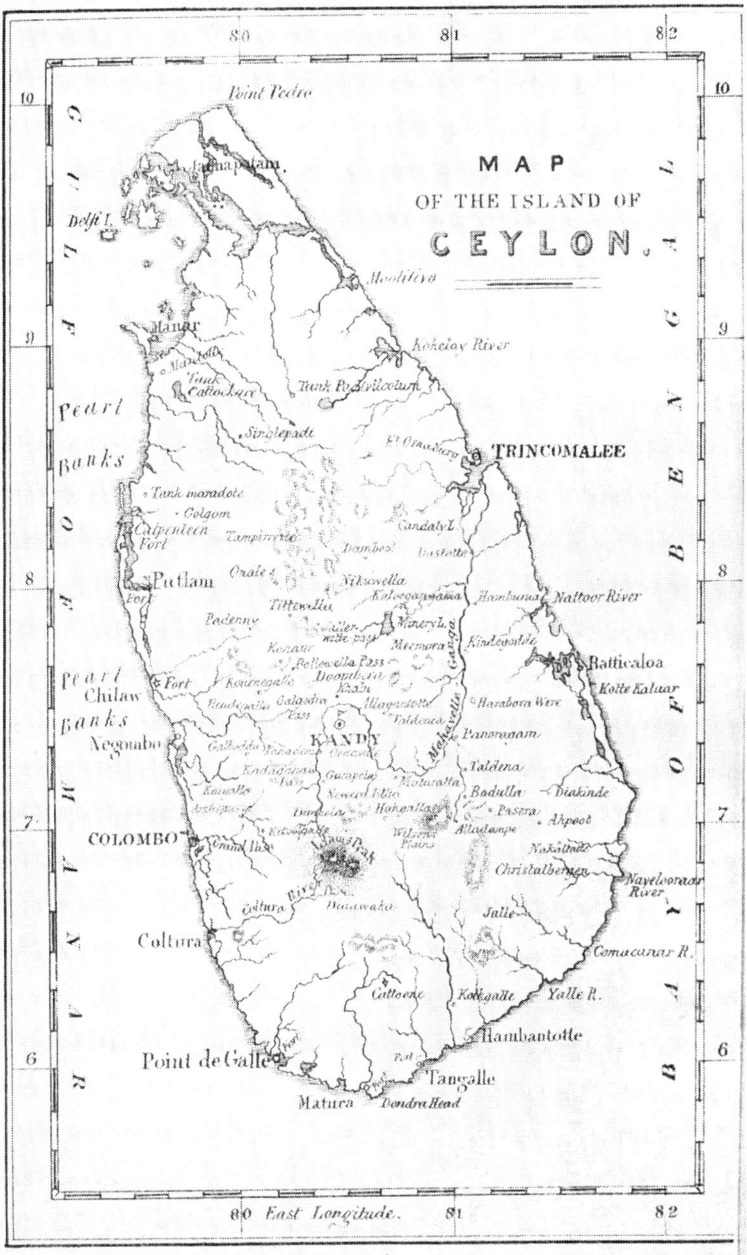

Published by W. Shoberl, 20, Gt. Marlborough Street.

CEYLON AND THE CINGALESE.

CHAPTER I.

Point de Galle—Beauty of the scenery and harbour—Canoes—Arrival of steamer—Scene on board—Native traders—Touters to the lodging-houses—Custom House—Grotesque appearance of Chitty Man—Description of the fort—Guard-house—Queen's house—Dwellings—Moormen—Pettah—Paying for your complexion.

PROSAIC language is inadequate to convey a faithful portraiture of the exquisite scenery, truly oriental in its character, that abounds in the Cinnamon Isle, the poet's plume, and painter's pencil, being alone calculated for the purpose. The extreme fertility of the soil, and the magnificence of the vegetable kingdom, in no part of Ceylon are more perceptible than in the neighbourhood of Point de Galle, the traveller's eye dwelling with delight upon the varied, and verdant foliage which encircles the sea shore. The pellucid azure of the cloudless skies, the sun's glittering beams reflected in millions of sparkling rays on the bosom of the blue ocean, the waves rolling and dashing in volumes of snowy surf over the dark yellow rocks, present a picture of all that is sublime and lovely in Nature.

The harbour of Point de Galle lies at the southern extremity of the Island of Ceylon, being an inland bay of a semicircular or horse-shoe form, constructed by the all-bounteous hand of Nature, and is situate in lat. 6° O 59° north, and long. 80° 17′ 2″ lat. Skirting the harbour, are masses of rock, riven by the dashing of the surge, and worn by the hand of time into many fantastic and picturesque forms. In the back ground are cocoa-nut palms (Cocos nucifera) with their stately but slender trunks o'er-topping all the other trees, and outvieing the rest of the vegetable world in majestic graceful loveliness. Nothing can be more elegant than the elongated green leaves, with their feathery fringe, which wave in a canopied form from the summit of the tree, droop around the slender stem, moving gently to and fro as the sea-breeze wantons among them. Clusters of nuts (or fruit) of an oval shape, measuring from seventeen to twenty inches in diameter, grow amongst the leaves close to the trunk of the tree; and these being of a green less vivid than their brilliant colouring, contrast exquisitely with the subdued hue of the dark brown bark of the trunk. Mingled with these stately trees is the majestic bread-fruit tree (Artocarpus incisa) with its umbrageous foliage, and enormous emerald-green leaves; from the branches are suspended the large round fruit, covered with a rough rind, gladdening alike eye and heart, with the magnificent majestic beauty of luxuriant vegetation. Near to this tree will be seen the slender papaw tree, (Carica papaya,) the stem gradually tapering to the top, where the leaves spread forth in a parachute form, the fruit, bright yellow and melon shaped, hanging beneath them.

Interspersed amongst these monarchs of vegetation are various other trees, clothed in rich foliage, but of smaller dimensions, contrasting well with those of larger growth. Imagine the waves foaming and frothing, dashing against and over the yellow rocks, then a billow gracefully rolling appearing to gain increased strength as it reaches the shingly beach, on which it is precipitately driven in a shower of white spray, the froth remaining for a few moments on the glistening strand, and even as you gaze, becoming absorbed. On the undulating bosom of the swelling blue ocean sparkling with the bright rays of Sol, in all the varied prismatic tints, a few European vessels are riding at anchor, their furled sails hanging in graceful festoons from the yards. Intermingling with these craft are the canoes of the natives, rudely constructed barks hollowed out of the trunk of a tree, with some transverse sticks for benches; to one side of the canoe is fastened an *outrigger*, formed of a slender spar nearly of equal length with the vessel to which it is attached by two curved arms; this outrigger floating upon the water, prevents the possibility of the canoe being capsized.

These primitive craft vary in length from twelve to twenty feet, and in width from two to three, being propelled by paddles three feet and a half long, roughly wrought into a battledore shape, the three or more men using them being seated at either extremity, and in the centre of the canoe. These fragile barks are usually laden with luscious fruits, vegetables, fish, or other articles of an edible nature, for the use of our ships; and the native occupants of the canoes, are men and youths of bright bronze complexion, with well-formed features, and soft black almond-shaped eyes, the luxuriant long black hair of the former being twisted into a thick knot at the back of the head; of the latter, allowed to flow "o'er their shoulders bare," a small handkerchief, scarf, or piece of cotton, tied around their loins forming their sole clothing. Place all these inanimate and animated adjuncts under cloudless skies, and a tropical sun, with the thermometer standing at ninety-six, and a faint conception may be formed of the scenery around, and harbour of Point de Galle.

As soon as the steamer from England arrives, equal excitement prevails on board the vessel and on the shore, and as we wish to edify our indulgent readers "Delectando pariterque momendo," we will imagine the vessel to have arrived during the night, and the captain as anxious to take in his supply of coal, and pursue his voyage, as the passengers are to touch terra firma again, after passing days or weeks without enjoying that luxury, although it may only be for a few hours. The day has dawned, the morning gun has boomed over the waters, wakening all slumberers, and those amongst the passengers who are about to make Lankadivas * verdant shores their home for a time, are soon busily employed in packing up their travelling appurtenances, anxious to avail themselves of the first boat that pushes off, to take them to the shore. Many, buoyant with hope, and in the full strength and vigour of manhood, looking forward with eager anticipation to the completion of schemes and projects, whereby they hope to make a fortune, resolving to devote the whole energy of their nature to ensure the accomplishment of their plans. Could some of the dreamers but raise the veil of futurity, numbers would shrink back appalled; for, in lieu of wealth and renown, they would see the phantoms of disease and untimely death throwing around their gloomy shadows, and hovering in their path. But, as the orient sun rises in unclouded splendour, casting the red blush of his morning beams around on land and sea, so man revels in bright visions of what is to be, until the dull realities of life, like clouds obscuring the brilliant beams of the planet, cast their shade over the rays of hope.

* The ancient name used by the natives for Ceylon.

To return to our description of the harbour. As soon as the sun has risen, the waters appear to teem with canoes, hastening to the steamer, some bringing provisions, others to land passengers and their baggage, whilst large boats heavily freighted with coal, force their way between the lesser craft. The scene of confusion on board the steam-vessel soon becomes indescribable. Passengers are seen tossing their various packages into the canoe that is to bear them to the shore, and hurriedly attempt to descend the ladder at the steamer's side, but in so doing, encounter coolees ascending, carrying baskets of coal, and each then jostles and hustles the other, in the attempt made by either party to pursue their respective routes. Then arises and resounds a confusion of tongues and languages, only to be equalled by that of Babel, exclamations in English, Cingalese, French, Tamil, Portugese, Hindostanee, in short in every known, and almost unknown, language in the world assail the ear, with comments neither polite, nor peculiarly complimentary upon the agility of the tawny sons of Adam. A native with a very minute portion of dirty rag, attached to his person through the medium of a piece of coir rope tied around his loins, will step upon the deck, with some trifling article for sale, and possibly encounter a blushing bride, or fair damsel fresh from Albion's shores. The fair lady retreats a pace or two, with a slight scream at sight of the unclothed dusky figure, placing her hand before her eyes to exclude the disagreeable vision.

Then will follow a Moorman with shaven head, a round embroidered cloth cap, thickly padded with cotton, placed on the top of his shorn cranium to protect it from the sun's powerful rays, with at least six yards of cotton, either white or coloured, tied round his loins with a showy silk handkerchief, forming a kind of petticoat reaching to his ankles, (called by the natives Comboy,) but leaving him in a complete state of nudity from the waist upwards. This demi-nude specimen of humanity has in all probability brought some articles of vertu or curiosity to sell, at all events what he considers so, consisting of knife-handles, and snuff-boxes, cut out of the molar tooth of the elephant, some fine samples of various coloured glass which he endeavours to palm off as precious stones and gems of the first water. These are accompanied or succeeded by divers other natives and inhabitants of the island, some of them offering tortoise-shell and silver bodkins for the hair, others calamander work-boxes inlaid with ivory, carved ebony caskets, and baskets made from the porcupine's quills, for sale. Amongst the multitude who regard the steam boat gentlemen, travellers being thus designated by all the native denizens of Ceylon, as their lawful game, are the touters for the *hottels*, for so lodging-houses are called by these copper-coloured gentry. The touter is invariably a half-caste, or burgher, who generally abounds in a very undue appreciation of his own dignity, and position, and this gentleman, in his own estimation, will place a card in the hands of a traveller and descant most fluently in broken English, upon the good cheer, moderate charges, and comforts that are to be found in the particular *hottel* which he has the felicity to represent.

So soon as the eloquence of the touter has induced a passenger, or passengers, to trust himself or themselves to his guidance, he intimates to a coolee that it is his will and pleasure, that such and such baggage should be placed in a particular canoe, not condescending to lower his dignity by touching, lifting, or carrying portmanteau, carpet-bag, hat-box, or dressing-case. When these minor arrangements are completed, he precedes the traveller down the ladder, elbowing his way, vociferating in an authoritative manner, to clear a path as he rudely thrusts the coolees aside. Most ludicrous is the assumption of these half-castes, who are held in supreme contempt by the full-caste natives, their greatest term of reproach being—"he burgher man," (or half-caste,) and many a hearty *guffaw* is indulged in at their expense by Europeans.

The landing-place is a pier, extending some two hundred feet into the water, at the shore end of which is a rude building, bearing a strong resemblance to a dilapidated barn; this is the Custom-house, and to it the baggage is taken, and the inquiry made if it consists solely of personal effects, or if there is any merchandize intermixed. If the reply is satisfactory, the packages are passed unopened, after the owner has signed a declaration that he has no article for sale or barter; for should there be any marketable commodities, the packing-cases are detained to be examined, and duties levied. Never shall we forget our amazement at the grotesque costume and appearance of one of the subordinate Custom-house officers, who was a native of the Malabar coast, of the Chitty caste, or those professing belief in the doctrines of the Romish Church. The man carried on his head a black velvet cap about six inches in height, which

CHITTY MAN.

projected forward in a horn-like manner, on either side of his head, the edges of the head-dress being trimmed with a thin gold cord. His long black hair, redolent of cocoa-nut oil, was combed back from the copper-coloured face, and twisted into a knot, close down to the nape of the neck, protruding beneath the head gear. In each ear were three gold rings, studded with coloured stones, and these ear-rings being fully thirteen inches in diameter, rested upon the shoulders, a square piece having been cut out of the lobe of the ear, to allow the insertion of these ponderous and barbarous decorations. This mortal had on a white cotton jacket, open in front, thus exposing to view his hairy breast, although to one side of the vest were attached innumerable jewelled buttons; round his loins were longitudinally rolled several yards of white calico, (forming the petticoat or comboy,) the end of which being brought round his body, hung down the front of his person. The comboy was confined round his loins by a handkerchief folded crossways, the extremities of which being pendant at his back, formed a novel caudal termination, not hitherto mentioned by naturalists. The comboy reaching to his ankles, which were guiltless of covering, as well as his unshod splay feet, which appeared doubly brown from being contrasted with the white petticoat. This gentleman carried in his hand as a protection against the sun's rays, a Chinese umbrella, made of black varnished paper, with a bamboo stick for the handle; and we do not think that our visual organs ever beheld a more ludicrous spectacle than the tout ensemble of this being presented.

We cannot dwell upon the impression produced on the minds of those fresh from Europe, when they gaze for the *first time* upon a crowd of half or rather unclothed Asiatics, who throng around them when they land, some being stimulated by the desire to induce the "steam-boat gentlemen" to purchase their goods, whilst others, from mere curiosity and indolence, will stand staring, open mouthed; the boys with no other covering save that which nature has bestowed on all, namely that of their long hair streaming down their backs, clamorously asking for *pice*, or halfpence.

The Fort of Galle, as the town is called, is approached by an ancient moss-grown archway, which, with the ramparts and town, were built by the Dutch after they had obtained possession of Galle, A.D. 1640. Tradition affirms that Galle is indebted for its appellation and symbol—a cock—to an error of the Portugese conquerors, who preceded the Dutch in Ceylon. The natives named this spot most appropriately, as it is surrounded by rocks, Galla, which is the Cingalese for rock: but the Portugese confounded this word with Gallus, or cock. Galle is generally garrisoned by a company of the "Ceylon Rifles," composed of Malays and Kaffres, and a detachment of whatever regiment of the line is on service in Ceylon. The uniform of the Ceylon Rifles is dark green, and the Malays make tolerably efficient soldiers, (being far more intrepid and active than the Kaffres,) when commanded by judicious officers. Under the gateway, a sentinel is stationed; and opposite to the archway, as you enter, is the guard-house, tenanted either by our own soldiers or by the Asiatics, as the duty alternates between the regiment of the line and the Ceylon Rifles. In the verandah of this building, the soldiers lounge when off guard, and if our men are there, they may be frequently seen enjoying the luxury of a cheroot with extreme gusto; but, if the Rifles are on duty, the Malays and Kaffres are *invariably* to be seen masticating a compound of the leaves and nuts of the areka palm and chunam, bespattering the whole verandah and ground with the disgusting red saliva, produced by chewing their favourite combination called betel.

Situate upon an ascent, a short distance from the guard-house, is the Queen's house, a governor's residence, when he visits Galle. This building was erected in 1687, and over the doorway the date is inscribed, above which appears the local symbol—the cock. A verandah extends the whole length of this residence, which is shaded by some magnificent trees introduced from Java by one of the early Dutch governors, the botanical name of these splendid exotics is Mimusops Elengi. The ramparts extend about a mile and a quarter, enclosing the town, which consists of three principal streets, these being intersected by several minor ones. The houses built on either sides of the streets, are but one story in height—or to speak more correctly, consist merely of ground floors, and, to the best of our remembrance, there were but three residences at Galle that had an upper story—these were called an up-stairs. The roofs are tiled, projecting beyond the outer walls, being supported by wooden pillars, thus forming a covered balcony, or verandah, in front of which are suspended *tats,* to subdue the intense glare of the sun's beams, and exclude the gaze of the inquisitive passers by. These tats, or blinds, are composed of split reeds, held together by the interlacing of thin coir or string, and are attached to the roof of the verandah by rope. The roofs of all domiciles in Ceylon, whether tenanted by Europeans or Asiatics, slope outwards from the centre walls, which are considerably higher than the external ones; the timbers resting upon the walls, leave a space between the wall-plate and the tiles, for the admission of air—thus allowing a thorough current to pass through the residence—and this arrangement of roof is met with in all tropica countries. The rooms are usually lofty and large and, instead of glazed windows, Venetian blinds are used, doors and windows being alike left wide open, a white screen being placed before the former, to prevent the persons and actions of the inmates being observed by all who choose to look, and a thin blind of open cane-work is occasionally affixed to the windows. In short, all privacy and retirement are sacrificed to that great desideratum in a hot climate—namely, obtaining and being in as much cool air as possible.

One street in Galle is inhabited principally by Moormen, some of whom are extremely wealthy, although the external appearance of their dwellings frequently indicates abject poverty, combined with uncleanliness. These men traffic in precious stones, rice, paddy, grain of all descriptions, cottons, prints, hardware, groceries, fruits, salt, poultry, saltpetre; in short, in every imaginable commodity whereby money is to be made. In fact, they even trade in that valuable article itself, as they lend cash where they believe repayment is certain, and where they can obtain exorbitant interest—for there are not more avaricious usurers in the world than the Moormen of Ceylon.

The town of Galle, although a clean picturesque little spot, has one serious drawback, namely, the want of pure water; and neither Europeans nor natives will use the water that is procured in the fort for drinking or culinary purposes, as it is peculiarly unwholesome. The prejudice of the natives is carried to so great an extent, that very few, if any, will lave their persons with the water that is obtained from the wells in the fort, as they declare that a disease is produced by it resembling elephantiasis, which they call a Galla leg. Water of the best and purest description is procured in the vicinity of the fort, and the water-carriers gain a good livelihood by furnishing the inhabitants of the town with this essential requisite to health and comfort.

Within the fort is the Dutch church, which is used also for the service of the Established Church, and a Wesleyan chapel, the Catholic places of worship, and the Mahomedans being situated outside the fort. The pettah or bazaar —market in our phraseology—is well supplied with fish, fruits, and vegetables, which are alike plentiful and cheap, the prices of all edibles being materially lower than at Colombo, or Kondy. The trade at Galle is confined principally to the exports—consisting of native produce, details of which will be given in a chapter devoted to the purpose.

Having been informed it was necessary to secure places in the mail, if we intended proceeding to Colombo, we walked to the coach-office to take them, and our astonishment was extreme when we read the following announcement, which was printed in large type—" Fares from Galle to Colombo, European gentlemen, £2 10*s.*; Moodleors, native noblemen, and their descendants, £1 10*s.*; proctors* and natives, £1. Upon inquiring, we were informed, there was no outside or inferior places in the coach, and that the same

* Attorneys are called proctors in the island, and, during our residence in Ceylon, mostly all belonging to the fraternity were burghers, or half castes.

scale of charges was enforced to whatever part of the island the coach went. In vain we expostulated at this absurdity, trying to convince the good-humoured proprietor, that our rank certainly *was* lower than a nobleman, and our dimensions *might* be less than those of a proctor, or native, but, despite our rhetoric, we were obliged to pay the fare ; for said Mr. Christoffaletz smiling, and disclosing a set of well-shaped white teeth, which would be envied by many une belle dame, "You cannot say you are not a European gentleman,—can you?" This argument was conclusive, the money was forthwith placed in his hands.

CHAPTER II.

Going to call the coach, instead of the coach calling for you—Preparations for Departure—Description of the Royal Mails in Ceylon—The Colombo road—Wild Peacock—Guano—Monkeys—Toddy drawers—Bentotte—Restive horses—Anecdote—Caltura—Beauty of scenery—Cinnamon plantations—Pagoda tree—The fashionable quarter of Colombo—Colpetty—The Galle Face—Curious gazers at new-comers—Arrival of the Royal Mail, gives rise to conjectures as to who the new-comers are, and wherefore they have come to Ceylon.

THE journey from Galle to Colombo occupies eleven hours, or eleven hours and a half, the coach usually, or rather nominally, starting at gun-fire, five o'clock in the morning. It not unfrequently happens, that the passengers have to go and call the coach, instead of the coach calling for them, and this has occurred to ourselves more than once whilst resident at Galle; for the natives of Ceylon, like most Asiatics, place little value either on time or punctuality. The gun has fired,—we have walked about, working ourselves nearly into a state of fusion, and quite into a very ill-humour, by anathematizing the want of punctuality of the Cingalese, and at length resolve to sally forth, and ascertain why the coach has not come for us and our baggage. We reach the office, the door of which is closed, the dim light of a cocoa-nut oil lamp is seen glimmering through the crevices of the portal.

Not a sound is heard from within the dwelling; all are, or appear to be, buried in sleep, and the coach also is in a state of tranquillity, snugly ensconced in the verandah, and under the vehicle are comfortably reposing two natives. These sacrifices to the drowsy god are regarded by us as personal insults, especially as we have abridged our matinal slumbers, for the sake of not keeping the coach waiting for us. Exasperated beyond endurance, we batter the house-door lustily for two or three minutes, which at last is opened by a yawning Cingalese, with hair streaming over his shoulders, who inquires in a sleepy tone, "what master want?" "Want, eh? that's too good. Why is not the coach ready that was to have called for us at gun-fire?" The coach master, being aroused by these noises, comes forth from his sleeping apartment, and with many apologies, orders the coach to be prepared forthwith, calling loudly for the horsekeepers. These gentlemen are still revelling in the arms of Morpheus *under* the coach, and, despite the reiterated shouts of their master, continue to dose. Finding words useless, and patience exhausted, physical forçe is restored to, and, by dint of sundry manipulations in the region of the ribs, the dormant faculties of the horsekeepers are aroused, and orders being given in some unintelligible jargon (to us), away they start in quest of the horses; the master assisting the remaining awakened domestics to pull the coach out of the verandah.

So soon as the horses are harnessed to the vehicle, the baggage is attempted to be collected, and although the quantity is *short* that is allowed to be carried by each passenger, being but twenty pounds, the time is *long* before it can be either arranged, or placed upon the conveyance, as each coolee will maintain that he cannot lift a carpet-bag without assistance, and that a portmanteau requires the united strength of four of his brothers in colour and calling. This feat accomplished, then ensues the turmoil attendant upon placing the baggage, as the sole receptacle for it is a board about three and a-half feet long, and a moiety of the width, placed at the back of the mail coach. On this the luggage rests, one package being piled upon another, and attached by pieces of coir passed over and under, crossed and re-crossed, until all is fairly secured.

As we can well remember the astonishment with which we gazed upon the primitive machine, dignified by the name of the "ROYAL MAIL," we will attempt a description of the same for the edification, and we trust amusement, of our perusers. The royal mails in Ceylon are placed upon four wheels, and look like—what?—nothing to be seen in Europe now, but the vehicles have a slight affinity with, and bear a faint resemblance to, the lower half of an antiquated English stage coach, cutting off the upper half, and detaching the doors. The seat for the driver is attached to the coach, so that his back, and those of the passengers on the front seat, touch. The roof is made of leather, painted white and varnished, lined with cotton, and supported by four slender iron rods, which shake with every jolt of the coach. To this roof, leathern curtains are hung, which can be either drawn to protect the passengers from the sun or rain, or rolled up to admit a free passage to the air. The roof of this antediluvian production projects over the driving seat, thus covering seven persons, namely, the passengers in the body of the conveyance, the driver, and whoever may be seated at his side, and the horsekeeper, who indiscriminately perches himself on the top of the luggage, stands on the fixed protruding iron step, or clings to any part of the vehicle most convenient to seize hold of. Picture this machine badly painted, lined with leather filthily dirty, and worn into holes, from which the stuffing, made from cocoa-nut fibre, starts forth. Put this on a carriage, with four wheels of various colours, with two horses badly fed, and worse groomed, caparisoned with worn harness, the buckles and straps of which are replaced with fragments of coir rope, and you will have some remote idea of the royal mails in the Island of Ceylon.

Let us now suppose all minor obstacles surmounted, such as dilatory drivers, and refractory horses, and we fairly clear of Galle, en route for Colombo, the seat of government. The morning breeze is cool, the grey light soothing and pleasant, and our good-humour restored, we are prepared to gaze around, and note all worthy of observation.

We were particularly struck in the tropics

by the non-existence of twilight, for almost immediately the sun sets it is dark, and in the absence of the moon continues so, until he re-appears. The coach proceeds leisurely on its way, and soon our eyes are gladdened by the glorious spectacle of the sun's rising—as gradually Phœbus appears above the bed of waters, on which he casts the effulgence of his beams. Now his rays are thrown upon a grove of waving palms, anon they rest upon the roof of a hut, like a coquettish beauty bestowing bright glances on all around. Soon we encounter a strange-looking vehicle, somewhat like a two-wheeled tilted cart, with a thatched semicircular hood, a white cloth being hung up at either end, to prevent inquisitive eyes from prying into the interior.

This machine is drawn by one or two oxen, and in answer to our inquiries we learn that it is called a bullock-bandy, and contains Moorwomen, who have been, or are going to the bathing-place.

The rumbling of the coach will occasionally rouse a family, (as many of the natives sleep in the verandah, instead of their dwellings, for the benefit of the cool air,) and, as they indolently lift their heads, will gaze upwards, and finding that day has positively set in, will slowly rise from the ground on which their sleeping mats have been spread. Along the coast, almost close to the sea, the screw-pine (Pandænus) flourishes in extreme luxuriance ; and, as the whole shore is planted with cocoa-nut trees, which droop over the road, the lover of nature pursues his way with feelings of intense gratification, especially when he gazes upon the waving palms above his head, then upon the blue ocean, upon whose surface the sun's young beams are reflected. The prospect is so exquisitely lovely, that it appears more like enchantment, or a dream of fairy land, than sober reality. Upon reaching Gindura, the coach is placed in a boat, and ferried across the river, and this spot is also a scene of surpassing beauty. On the bosom of the tranquil stream, floats the pink lotus, the tulip-shaped flower, being enshrined amongst the broad green leaves ; Areca palms (Areca catechu) waving over, and drooping into the river, and here and there a flowering shrub of gorgeous hue, intermixed among the stately trees clothed in their vesture of brilliant green.

Within a short distance of the opposite side of the ferry, the constantly-varying panorama of nature, becomes, if possible, still more enchanting: the boundless ocean, with its ever-changing hues on one side, its white spray dashing over the rocks, with the dense groves of noble trees on the other, are alike sublimely beautiful. Cocoa-nut trees planted on either side of the road, bend towards each other, forming a shady avenue through which the coach passes.

Occasionally young plantations of palms, the leaves spreading out thickly in an irregular fan-like form from the root, will greet the eye, contrasting finely with the older trees, whose slender naked tall trunks are surmounted by a crown-like diadem of leaves.

Startled by the sound of the coach-wheels, a peacock, with a shrill scream, will take flight, his gorgeous plumage glittering in the sun, as he wings his flight upwards, or he may wend his way to a noble ebony tree, and alighting there, will proudly raise his crested head, the feathers of his drooping tail intermingling with the luxuriant foliage of the splendid tree. Sometimes a guano (a species of lizard,) will cross the road in pursuit of his prey, whose short clumsy legs, and slothful ungainly movements, seem ill calculated to enable him to pursue, or entrap a more agile creature. But see—he has marked that beautiful little squirrel as his victim: how nimbly the reptile is ascending the tree after the poor little animal, his clumsy legs move quickly enough now—luckily the agile fellow has seen him, and with a bound to another tree, gets clear of his pursuer. These hideous reptiles are amphibious, and we have seen several that measured more than five feet from the snout to the tip of the tail, and it is affirmed they possess such strength in that part, that with one blow of their tail a man's leg will be broken. They are likewise omnivorous, for they will alike steal and devour your fowls and your fruit.

Indulging in gambols on the boughs of the trees that skirt the road-side, are to be seen monkeys, of every size, and of numerous species, which in the very wantonness of sport, will pluck a young cocoa-nut, and dash it on the earth; then run along the ropes that attach one tree to the other, performing again the same mischievous antic, despite the threatening gestures of the toddy-drawers, who have, for their convenience, thus linked the trees together. It would be impossible to travel seven miles in Ceylon, much less seventy, the distance from Galle to Colombo, without seeing toddy-drawers pursuing their calling, and the first time we saw the operation was during the journey now alluded to. The liquor is obtained from the flower of the cocoa-nut palm, (Cocos nucifera,) in its fresh state being called toddy, which is a sweet refreshing beverage; when fermented, it becomes arrack, the intoxicating qualities of which are well known. The ascent of the tree is thus accomplished: the toddy-drawer knots a piece of rope into a circle, passing his ankles through it, and the resistance offered by the ligature enables him to press the soles of his feet against the naked trunk of the tree, precluding the possibility of slipping down whilst in the act of climbing, the toddy-chatty, or jar, being slung at his back. When the summit of the tree is reached where the flower is, the man cuts off the end, suspending the chatty to the orifice from whence the liquid flows, binding the blossom tightly above the incision. Some of the full-grown trees will yield from one to two hundred pints per diem; but the trees that are tapped never bear fruit.

To the tops of the toddy-trees, the drawers attach ropes, to enable them to move from one to the other, without the trouble of descending and ascending; and, although it is most unpleasant to see these men clinging with hands and feet, whilst pursuing their aerial way, comparatively but few accidents occur. When one does happen, it is usually fatal, as the height of the palms to which these ropes are attached, varies from sixty to one hundred feet. The appearance of a fresh-drawn chatty of toddy is exceedingly agreeable, as the form of the red clay jar approaches the classical; the foaming frothing liquid overflowing the brim, and hanging in creamy drops around the vessel; moreover, the toddy-drawers twine scarves about their brows, to protect them from the sun's rays, carrying their burthen upon their turbaned heads, thus completing their resemblance to the figures of antiquity.

To speak technically, the coach breakfasts at Bentotte at ten o'clock; but, as drivers and horses in Ceylon are equally erratic and self-willed in their movements, the hour varies according to their tempers and inclinations. All the inns, or rest-houses, as they are called in Ceylon, are Government property, and the men placed in them are only legally permitted to charge twenty-five per cent. above the market prices, for the provisions supplied by them, but we never found in our peregrinations, these gentry content with this ample per centage, but, like all other innkeepers, be they in Europe, Asia, or Africa, (for we cannot speak from personal knowledge of America) took every advantage, making travellers pay as much as possible for the slightest refreshment, or smallest accommodation. Bentotte is a lovely spot, and the rest-house for

Ceylon, is tolerably good, that is to say, the roof does not admit the pitiless storm, or the sun's rays; neither are there holes in the doors to admit when closed, pariah dogs, reptiles and rats, and there are a table, a chair, and a bedstead, guiltless of Mosquito curtains, however, in one of the sleeping-rooms. This we can vouch was the case when we left Ceylon, but deponent cannot adduce farther evidence as to the furniture in the other apartments of the building. Oysters are obtained here from the river, and, although their appearance, size, and colour, which is of a purplish tint, differ materially from our own, the flavour is good. It is rather remarkable that in no other part, through which this river flows, nor from whence it has its source, are oysters to be met with, Bentotte being the sole place.

Again, the coach has to be placed in a boat to be ferried over the stream, and, upon reaching the shore, we were highly diverted at witnessing the attempts made by several horse-keepers, to harness two restive horses, and attach them to the Mail, the driver warning them, speaking or rather shouting at the highest pitch of his voice, to hold "Peter Layard's head and keep clear of Dr. Prin's heels," and requesting us to take our seats as quickly as possible. The scene that ensued is beyond our powers of description, consequently we think it better to narrate verbatim the adjurations the driver bestowed upon the horses, endeavouring, by defective spelling, to imitate the half-caste's broken English.

"Now, *genel-men*, *is* you seated in the *coch*, *cos* if you is, the *osses* shall be put to." An affirmative being returned, some orders being given by the driver in Cingalese to the horse-keepers, adding in English, "We shall be soon off now, as you *is* ready." But the horses were not as ready to go as we were, and after some difficulty one was harnessed to the coach, the other creature's head being held securely by two horse-keepers, whilst two others dragged, more than led, the animal towards the vehicle and attached the traces, the horse rearing and plunging, as much as it was possible, with two men holding his head. During the hazardous performance of putting the horses to the coach, the driver placed his feet firmly against the splash-board, grasping his whip, with a most determined expression of countenance, whilst we watched the whole proceedings in a state of delightful expectation. At length the operation was achieved, and no sooner was the last trace buckled, than the horse-keepers let go the animal's head, rushing on either side of his path, with the celerity of an arrow sent from a well-strung bow. *This* horse plunged violently forwards, whilst *the other* planted his four feet firmly in the loose ground, evincing a resolute determination not to move one inch either for entreaty or castigation.

Now commenced a resolute battle for mastery between the horses and the driver, who thus alternately addressed each. "Peter Layard *yer* brute, *kim* up *yer* ill-tempered lazy thing—yer *vont, vont yer?*" Thump, bump on the creature's back went the butt end of the whip, the driver standing up to give greater force to the blows. "Dr. Prins, *yer willin,* do *yer vant* to *brek* the *coch* to bits? *is eels vill* be in my *mout* in *minit.*" (They were battering away at the splash-board.) "Peter Layard, yer *hugly* beast, kim up, if yer *doesn't*—" Another heavy blow, which combined with the implied threat had the desired effect, for off started both horses at full gallop, rushing close to a hut, the wheels grazing the dwelling, and catching the screen made of platted cocoa-nut leaves, and dragging it away. "Now, *genel*-men," said the driver, "*we* shall *go* along *boo*-tiful, its *honly* at *fust* starting that we *ave* a bit of bother, I *dunt* mind these *osses* when we *hant* got lady passengers, for they do squeal so; when Dr. Prins begins *is* tricks, that it's puts me *hout*. You see *ere* we *hal*-vays call the *osses* hafter the *genel*-men we buys 'em on, for whoever *as* a bad *oss* he sells *he* to us; we *giv* £15 for Dr. Prins, and £18 for Peter Layard, but he is a good *un* to go though he is hugly, and fights shy of his work at *fust;* but *as* for Dr. Prins, he is not worth *alf* the money, for he is a *arty* feeder, *werry* lazy, *werry wicious*, and *werry* often kicks over the traces." Although we cannot vouch for the gastronomic capabilities of the quadruped Dr. Prins, we can bear testimony to the driver's veracity, as regards the three latter propensities of the animal.

The noble stream, the Kalloo Ganga, has yet to be crossed, and again the ferry boat is freighted with the Royal Mail and its cargo. The river divides Caltura from Pantura, the former place being celebrated for its pure water, and salubrity, and, before the discovery of Newera Ellia, was regarded as the Sanitorium of Ceylon. The scenery about Caltura is lovely in the extreme, (almost equalling that around Galle, though of a less bold and imposing character,) the banks of the river being wooded down to the water's edge with stately palms, noble bread-fruit, tamarind, and jack trees. Scattered be tween these majestic specimens of vegetation, is the pomegranate-tree with its bright scarlet flowers, the cinamon-laurel with its delicate white blossom, and the tube-rose shrub, loading the atmosphere with the fragrant aroma of their flowers. On the pellucid rippling waters float luxuriant aquatic plants, the numerous white water-lilies, and pink lotuses being entwined with a small creeper, the elegant blossom of which resembles our own "forget-me-not" in size and colour.

From Caltura to Colombo, the hand of nature and of art appear to combine to make the vista as glorious as it is possible to conceive; the distant view of lofty mountains, and rich groves of trees, and palm-shaded bungalows, situate in the midst of cultivated gardens, radiant with the gorgeous hues of the tropical flowers. Combine this with the heaving ocean, on the bosom of which float numberless fishing canoes; the yellow sandy beach, glittering with the bright scales of the newly-caught members of the finny tribe; and all must admit the scene to be one of surpassing sublimity and loveliness. For some miles, as you approach Colombo, the road runs between cinnamon-plantations, the dark shining leaves of the laurel contrasting exquisitely with the pearly hue of the blossom; but the shrub is clad in its greatest beauty when it first puts forth its pristine vesture, the young leaves then being of a pale delicate yellowish green, streaked with bright red.

On the right-hand side of the road, (near to the tamarind-tree, where the élite of the colony go about six o'clock in the morning, to drink fresh toddy,) grows one of the most magnificent pagoda, or banian trees (Ficus indica) imaginable.* The foliage of this tree is splendid, and it bears a minute fig-shaped, scarlet-coloured fruit; nevertheless the principal beauty consists in the innumerable fibres sent forth by the branches, which enlarge as they reach the earth, and there take root, forming a complete grove, or series of trees; these fibres in their turn producing shoots, which will again multiply and take root; and it is asserted, that in the province of Guzerat, one of these trees measures more than two thousand feet in circumference, near the bottom of the stems, the branches of which naturally cover a much larger space. Although the tree we allude

* This tree is considered sacred by *all Brahmins*, who affirm the God Vishnu was born under it, and that the characteristics of the deity are *emblemized* in the tree. The Bo-tree (Ficus religioso) is held sacred by all Buddhists, Buddhism being the national religion of Ceylon.

to, on the Colombo Road, does not cover near the same extent of ground, we can speak as to its beauty, more especially after dusk, when its numberless dark leaves are illuminated by myriads of fire-flies, (Elater noctilicus,) whose quick flitting movements dazzle and delight the beholder.

In Colpetty, (the fashionable quarter of Colombo,) large bungalows, (dwellings on the ground floor,) surrounded by highly-cultivated compounds or gardens, become more frequent, and occasionally a palanqueen carriage will be met, in which recline one or two European ladies, hastening to make some purchases in the fort before the shops close, which they invariably do by half-past five or six at the latest. Then the Galle Face, the Hyde Park of the colony, is attained; the fresh sea-breeze, as it blows over the greensward, cooling the heated traveller's brow, vehicles of all descriptions are met, from the haccary of the native, drawn by a bullock, to the carriage of one of England's merchant-princes, to which a high-bred Arab horse is attached, the inmates of all these conveyances alike bestowing inquisitive looks upon the passengers in the Royal Mail; and, when a strange face is discovered, every attitude and gesture of the starers evince the utmost curiosity; for, believe us, no new arrival in a country village, or town in England, no presentation at a drawing-room, of beauty or bride, causes so great a sensation, as a new arrival in a colony. For in a colony everybody troubles his or her head with every one else's business, most philanthropically at times neglecting his or her own affairs to attend to other people's. The Mail is now at the end of the Galle Face, now it rattles over the drawbridge of the fortifications; now it is under the archway; now it has entered the Fort; and now it jingles and rattles down the principal street of the "Fort of Colombo," many of the inhabitants, of all shades of colour and denominations, being on the qui vive to see "who is in the Mail."

So soon as the last passenger and his small quantum of luggage have been disposed of, the Royal Mail jolts and jumbles to its own halting-place, the driver retailing every look and observation of the passengers, with, at times, sundry additions and embellishments, spreading the news also, that one or more "*strange Englis' genelmen*" were come to the colony, and where they have been domiciled. Every eager listener then gives an opinion concerning the new-comer's profession, or avocation, surmising how much each individual may gain by, or be interfered with, in his peculiar calling by this, or those "strange English gentlemen."

CHAPTER III.

Colombo — Harbour — Custom-house — Animated scene — Derivation of the name of the Port—Fortifications—Troops -Queen's House—Public offices in the Fort—Pettah — Native traders—Churches, chapels, religious and chari table institutions—Public offices in the Pettah—Native police—Slave Island—Galle Face—Colonial manners—The effect of climate upon the female character — The fashionable drive — Beauty of the spot—Sunset—Sea-breezes — Evening — Fire-flies — Cinnamon—Tribute demanded by the Portuguese—Cultivation introduced by the Dutch—Value of the monopoly to the Dutch and English governments—Description of the shrub—Uses of every portion of the cinnamon-laurel—Peeling knives — Number of crops in the year—Preparing the spice—Challias, or cinnamon peelers—Punkahs—The result of an unex pected downfall — Dessert — Crows, their boldness and audacity.

COLOMBO is alike the seat of the colonial government, and the capital of the maritime provinces, being situate in lat. 6^0 57″ north, and long. 79^0 50″ east. The harbour is semicircular, but only boats and very small craft can find refuge within it, vessels of any size being compelled to anchor in the roads, from one to two miles distant from the shore. Extreme caution is requisite in piloting a ship into Colombo roads, as there are sunken rocks, sand banks, and a coral reef, and the waves break heavily on the bar during the prevalence of certain winds.

The principal part of the export and import trade is carried on at this port, consequently, the scene at the Custom-house, during the hours of business, is one of great activity and excitement. Coolees, carrying bags of coffee, bales of goods, casks of cocoa-nut oil, bundles of the fibre, baskets of the nuts, packages of cinnamon, and sacks of grain,—hustle each other, whilst the shrill cry of the bullock-driver, as he attempts to clear a passage for his heavily-laden waggon, or bandy, serves only to make "confusion *more* confounded."

During the time this is being enacted at one part of the quay, boats loaded with various commodities, either endeavouring to land the articles, or take them to the outward-bound ships, are trying to leave or approach the small landing-pier; and, as the tawny boatmen pursue their task, sing at the top of their voices a monotonous song. Occasionally a wave will break over the boat; then ensue shouts and exclamations not intended for ears polite, from the *canicople*, or man in charge of the merchandize, as he urges the rowers to perform their task with greater caution and celerity.

Colombo is mentioned in Cingalese historical annals, about A.D. 496, where it is recorded that one of their kings, Moongaallonoo, there erected "warlike defences." Tradition declares that *Calamba* derived its name from a grove of mangoe trees, called also *Calamba* in Cingalese; but, in one of the most ancient native works extant, we read that *Calamba* signifies a sea-port, and a fortified place. What the origin of the cognomen may have been, can be a matter of little import, but it is quite certain that the Portuguese conquerors corrupted or changed the name of the spot from *Calamba* to Colombo, in honour of their celebrated navigator, Columbus. In 1505, the Portuguese visited this port, and obtained permission to traffic with the natives; disputes ensued, and we find that in 1518 the Portuguese had taken possession of Colombo, and commenced erecting the fortifications. The Fort is built on a small promontory, which is washed by the sea for more than half its extent, and was completed by the Dutch after they had expelled the Portuguese, and could contain, on an emergency, nine or ten thousand souls. The extent of the fortifications exceeds one mile and a half, the ramparts being well constructed, having eight chief bastions and several minor ones, with banquets, parapets, &c., &c., communicating one with the other, mounting 125 guns and six mortars. The Fort is garrisoned by European troops, the number of which vary, the Ceylon Rifles and gun-lascars being stationed outside the Fort, in a spot called Slave Island. When the governor is a military man, he has the command of the troops; but, when his Excellency is a civilian, like the present Governor, Viscount Torrington, the commander of the forces is usually a major-general.

The principal street in the Fort is called Queen Street, and in this street, which is remarkably wide, and kept scrupulously clean, stands the Queen's or Government House, the gardens of which are laid out with great care; for a specimen of almost every flowering shrub or plant indigenous to the island, is to be found in them. In the rear of Government House stands the Lighthouse, the height of which is ninety-six feet above the level of the ocean, and sailors affirm that in clear weather this building can be discerned from an almost incredible distance at sea. Near to the Queen's House are situated the various military and civil offices, one of the English churches, that of the Scotch Presbyterians, the Banks, General Post Office, Normal School, and the principal Library. From Queen Street, several side streets branch off, the minor ones crossing at right angles, and in these are situated the Military Hospital, the Medical Museum and Library, with warehouses and shops. All the European commercial houses carry on their business within the Fort, be their trade wholesale or retail, but all the merchants and nearly every one of the shopkeepers reside elsewhere.

Without the Fort, an extensive trade is carried on in every saleable article, both of native and foreign origin, by the Moormen, whose shops and stores are situated in the Pettah, the main street of which is one continuous line of shops and warehouses. Every imaginable commodity is here to be procured, from a lady's bonnet to a ship's anchor, from a paper of pins to a marlin-spike, from a bottle of pickles to a saddle, from a web of fine muslin to strong canvass for sails; in short, it would be impossible to enumerate what these men have for sale, and equally impracticable to say what they have not. Moreover, we can positively affirm, these traders vend their goods at one half the price, that is demanded at the principal European shop in the Fort. In the Pettah is situated the chief bazaar for edibles of every description; and here also reside the greater number of the burghers, or half-castes; in the streets that break off from the main street, and in the abodes of these people, is frequently to be seen some of the most exquisitely-carved ebony furniture conceivable, the designs, usually of fruit and flowers, being chiselled out with the utmost accuracy, depth, and sharpness.

Adjoining the Pettah are places of worship for the English, Portuguese, and Dutch protestants, belonging to the established church, and in the church of the last are deposited the remains of all the Dutch governors who have died in the island. The Wesleyans, Baptists, and Roman Catholics, have also their chapels, the Mahomedans their mosque, and the Brahmins their temple, the walls of which are decorated with carvings of elephants, lions, and tigers. In this district is situated the buildings that belong to the Society for the Propagation of the Gospel,

Promoting Christian Knowledge, Bible Association, Church Missionaries, Colombo Friend in Need, Government Schools, the Leper and Pauper Hospitals, the Dispensary, and other charitable institutions. The Supreme Court House, the District Court of Colombo, the Court of Requests, Police Office, Cutcherry, and Fiscals' Office, are all outside the Fort.

Public order is maintained (to a very limited extent, however,) by a body of native police, who are similarly organized to those of our Metropolitan force, and are under the superintendence—or were so when we left Colombo—of two most efficient superintendants. But zealous as Messrs. Thomson and Colpepper were in the discharge of their duties, they were not ubiquitous, and, as soon as they had left a street or district to visit another, the greater number of the policemen would sit down in some shady nook, commence chewing betel, and eventually indulge in a siesta, until roused by the visit of their superior officer, or relieved from their active occupation by a brother dozer. This efficient (?) force are clothed in the same dress as the London police, with the exception of the hat, a peaked cap being substituted, and the effect produced by the latter is most ludicrous, as their long hair is twisted into a knot above the nape of the neck, and on this the cap rests. Their European attire also is ill calculated either for the climate or for their comfort, the stiff collar, tight coat and trousers, being most distasteful to those who have been habituated, from infancy, to the loose garments of the Asiatics, and their clothing is as little conducive to their health as it is to their ease.

The artificial lake of Colombo runs at the back of the Fort, and Sir Edward Barnes, during his Governorship, caused a lock to be constructed, whereby the inland navigation is carried to the sea. A small slip of land lies in the centre of the lake, named Slave Island, so called by the Portuguese and Dutch, who used here to lock up the government slaves after their day's labour. A certain space was enclosed, around which huts were built, these dwellings being surrounded by a lofty wall, the gates of which were fastened at sunset, and unclosed at sunrise. Since the abolition of slavery, all these buildings have been demolished, barracks for the Ceylon Rifles, and tasteful bungalows for Europeans, having been erected in their stead.

One portion of Slave Island has the advantage of the sea-breezes, being only separated from the ocean by an isthmus, called the Galle Face, and this is the fashionable drive or resort in the evening, from the hours of five until seven. When we first arrived in Colombo, we felt much astonished at finding but few external marks of respect paid to the governor. For instance, his Excellency's carriage would drive round the Galle Face, and scarcely a hat would be raised as he passed, although some of the heads on which the hats rested belonged to civilians, some of them high in the government service; or to merchants, who, from their birth, education, and position, as members of the legislative council, ought to have felt it their bounden duty to have rendered "honour to whom honour was due." Surely it cannot be derogatory to any man, however high his station or birth, to evince, by a courteous demeanour, proper respect for the individual who is deemed a fit and proper person by his sovereign, to hold the reins of government. It has been previously remarked, by those who have resided in colonies, that generally the tone of conduct of most colonists is one of assumption; and, as far as our own experience permits us to form an opinion, we coincide heartily in this observation, as too many endeavour to assume a position that can only belong to the Governor, and act as if they believed that undue familiarity and disrespectful demeanour to superiors, would ensure the social position they were endeavouring to usurp. Although we thus contemn the manners of men, we regret to say that numbers of our fair countrywomen lose many attractive attributes from a residence in a colony, or presidency. We believe a lengthened sojourn in the East to be as prejudicial to the mental as it is to the physical powers of the female sex, the climate alike enervating body and mind, rendering the one incapable of taking sufficient exercise to preserve health, and the other of pursuing those studies that enlarge its own capabilities. Thus, after a comparatively short residence in India, China, or Ceylon, a woman loses her vivacity, the principal part of her beauty, the whole of her energy, becoming equally disinclined to corporeal or mental exertion. The routine of a lady's existence has but little variety under a tropical sun; the greater part of the morning is passed reclining on a couch, en dishabille, being fanned by an Ayah, who tries to amuse her mistress by relating the occurrences that take place in the abodes of her acquaintance, this gossip being duly embellished with scandal. After tiffin,* the fair dame will either receive or pay morning

* The mid-day meal, denominated luncheon in England, in the East is called tiffin.

visits, when more gossip and scandal are indulged in; or she will read some silly tale of excitement to beguile the time, or soothe her to sleep. For seldom, we grieve to say, is any intellectual occupation pursued that tends to strengthen the mind.

About four o'clock the fair one retires to make an elaborate toilette for the evening drive, or to "don equestrian gear;" in either case, the attire of every friend that she meets is severely criticised, and wonder expressed as to how their husbands can afford to supply them with this expensive finery, feeling *quite sure* they must be over head and ears in debt, strangely forgetting that, in all probability, she, the censurer of extravagance, has assisted in, if not insisted upon, incurring debts, which may preclude the possibility of her own spouse returning to his native land for many long years. Add to this flirtation which, if practised in England, would not be tolerated, and a slight idea may be formed of female occupations in a presidency, or eastern colony. Let it, however, be distinctly understood that we do not thus condemn the conduct of *all* ladies who sojourn in presidencies, or colonies; far be it from our intention so to do, for we have known women who were as good wives and mothers, and as valuable members of society in every respect, bestowing attention alike on their domestic duties, and the cultivation of their minds, with the same assiduity they did, or would have done in Europe. Nevertheless, truth compels us, although we feel a pang of regret whilst penning the line, to say, such estimable women as these cannot be regarded as specimens of the female character when removed from the wholesome restraints of English society, and enervated, if not demoralized, by the luxuries and customs of the East.

About half-past five o'clock, the Galle Face, or Hyde Park of Colombo, begins to wear an animated appearance, there being many vehicles and horses in motion, although the majority of the fair occupants of carriages and saddles, are alike listless in demeanour, and the eye of the stranger seeks, and seeks in vain, for the clear complexion, roseate hue of cheek and lip, vivacious expressive countenance, and sparkling eyes, which are so pleasingly characteristic of Albion's daughters. Every description of conveyance is to be seen driving round the Galle Face, from the Long Acre built carriage of the governor, the dashing phaeton of the wealthy merchant, the unassuming gig, the country-built palanqueen, and the humble bandy. The horses that draw these vehicles are invariably attended by their keepers, (grooms being called horse-keepers in Ceylon,) who run by the side of the conveyance, when a gentleman, or coachman drives; at other times, they lead the animal, accommodating their pace to that of the horse.

These men wear a sort of livery, their turbans and loose clothing being composed of bright tinted, or white calico, the colours varying according to the taste or fancy of their employer, and many of their costumes are both pleasing and picturesque, adding materially to the *strangeness* of the scene. The view from, and of the Galle Face, is absolutely entrancing to the lover of nature, for cast the eyes where you will, the gaze is involuntarily arrested by the extreme beauty of the surrounding scenery. There lies the boundless ocean, with a ship in full sail gliding over its undulating surface, the canoes of the natives lightly floating on, and skimming over its waters, whilst the waves curvetting and rolling, dash in a shower of white foam on to the shore. Bordering the beach is the carriage-drive, which encompasses greensward, whereon high-bred Arab horses are bounding and prancing, in the full enjoyment of exuberant health and existence. On the opposite side is the race-course,

D 2

over whose variegated turf the steeds are caricoling in high glee, whilst the carriage-drive that divides the race-course from the greensward is thronged with carriages of every shape and description, principally, if not entirely, occupied by Europeans, whilst the fantastically-clad Eastern attendants run at the horses' head, or at the side of the vehicle.

At the back of the race-course flows the lake of Colombo, the banks being studded with drooping palms, whose branches overshadow the clear waters, on which float the pink lotus, and white lily—whilst a bungalow, the verandah of which is overgrown with graceful creepers, the grounds belonging to it being filled with gorgeous-coloured flowering shrubs, complete the vista of loveliness on that side. Looking from the bungalow, with nought to impede the view, save the stand on the race-course, you can distinctly see the grey time-mossed ramparts of the Fort of Colombo.

In due time, sunset arrives,—then how gloriously the planet sinks into the bosom of the sea, in majestic tranquillity, as his parting beams illumine the green waters, on which they glitter in thousands of sparkling rays, whilst over the azure vault of heaven float violet, crimson, and golden-tinted clouds, which, as you gaze, fade away, in ever-varying tints. No language can describe the gorgeous, glorious, magnificent beauty of the sun's rising and setting in the tropics; the constantly-changing and numberless hues which tinge the clouds in constant succession, are beyond the powers of language of the orator, the pen of the scribe, or the pencil of the painter, to delineate. See Sol is now dipping; he almost appears to be toying with the waters, into whose bosom he is sinking, and on which he throws his lurid beams. How gloriously refulgent is the sun's hue, how noble and clearly defined is the arch! Gradually he sinks lower—lower—lower—and now he has gone to illumine another quarter of the globe, and cast around his life-imparting beams.

After sunset, the sea breezes become most refreshing, and, as they are wafted across the waters, their delicious coolness invigorates the wearied frame, exhausted by the depressing heat of the atmosphere during the day. The equestrians now seem to be more at their ease, the gentlemen indulging in occasional vigorous gallops, the ladies putting their steeds into a gentle canter, the inmates of the carriages appear to be somewhat less listless, and will gaze around, or enter into conversation with some degree of animation; possibly a cavalier will arrest the horse's progress to salaam his fair owner, and retail, or inquire the last on-dits, as he leans on the carriage-door.

In the same ratio as Europeans enjoy the cool breezes, so do the Asiatics dislike them, and frequently the horse-keepers will cast an imploring look into the vehicle, giving a slight shiver, their countenances clearly implying "this may be sport to you, but 'tis death to us." As the shades of evening advance, gradually the Galle Face becomes deserted, and, long before nightfall, the neighing of the horses and the rumbling of wheels are no more heard, the only sounds greeting the ear being the soughing of the night-breeze and the breaking of the waves on the shingly beach. When night has thrown her sable mantle o'er the earth, the aspect of the scene changes, for over the lake hover myriads of fire-flies, clouds of them flitting about in the air, then alighting on the waving leaves of the palms, causing the foliage to appear illuminated. Some few will settle on the floating leaves of the lotus, two or three will creep into the flower, sparkling like brilliants, then more of these luminous insects will alight on other aquatic plants, and the waters will glisten with a million minute specks of light. Then, innumerable numbers will wing their flight upwards until the air appears replete with a shower of the moon's beams. Many will then settle, possibly on a tall banana; the outline of the gigantic graceful leaves being distinctly defined by the dazzling specks of fire upon them. Nought can be imagined more exquisitely lovely than this varied natural panorama; and although in the mountainous parts of the island, the face of nature may assume a sublimer aspect, never does she wear a more pleasing, characteristic, and truly oriental one, than in the vicinity of the Galle Face of Colombo.

The cinnamon-gardens in the neighbourhood of Colombo are the most extensive in the island; and, although the beauty and fragrance of the shrub are much exaggerated, still the plantations present a most pleasing spectacle. It has been asserted by many, and still is by some, that the aroma of the spice is perceptible at sea, even when a vessel is some miles distant from the "Cinnamon isle:" this statement is as complete a delusion as can well be imagined, for, *if* the effluvia of cinnamon *is* apparent at sea, it is when the captain or some one else on board the vessel has rubbed a portion of the fragrant oil upon the sails, to mystify travellers. We admit that an aromatic effluvia is diffused, whilst the operation of peeling is being carried on, but this odour is only apparent close to the spot where the cinnamon-peeler is performing his task; and were every bush in the island to be barked simultaneously, we are perfectly convinced the smell would not be felt a mile on land from where the work was being effected, and that it would be a perfect impossibility, for the scent of the shrub so to mingle with the atmosphere as to be perceived at sea.

Cavilists have recently endeavoured to prove the Laurus cinnamomum not to be indigenous, but that it was introduced into Ceylon by some of the early traders, assigning as their most cogent reason, that the early Roman and Greek writers, when speaking of the products of Trapabane (Ceylon) do not enumerate cinnamon among them; strangely, in our opinion, overlooking, that although not mentioned individually, this spice may have been included among the numberless fragrant productions, for which this island was celebrated. To pursue this subject farther, or to attempt to prove by quoting authorities, and using arguments that we are borne out in asserting the Laurus cinnamomum to be indigenous to Ceylon, would be alike uninteresting to the general reader, and unnecessary for our present purpose; as we treat principally of Ceylon, after it became known to the Portuguese.

This shrub attracted the notice of D'Almeida, who, with the shrewdness and observation usually, if not invariably apparent in the mental organization of discoverers, instantly perceived the valuable article of commerce this spice would eventually become. In 1505, Ceylon was first discovered by D'Almeida, (then governor of Goa,) and permission was granted by the monarch of Colombo to the Portuguese to traffic with the natives; and, in the succeeding year, we find the crown of Portugal demanded for the protection promised to be afforded the Cingalese sovereign against his enemies, that a certain quantity of cinnamon should be annually given. This demand was complied with, and, although no care was bestowed upon the cultivation of the shrub, either by the natives or Portuguese, the revenue derived by the sale of the spicy tribute proved a considerable and welcome addition to the finances of the king of Portugal. Although the Dutch gained a footing in Ceylon in 1640, we find no attempt was made by them, to improve the staple commodity of the island by cultivation until 1765, and no strenuous exertions were made for the furtherance of the plan until 1770, and in this year the Governor Falck resolved to adopt energetic measures for the culture of the cinnamon-laurel. In this he was opposed by the native nobles and chiefs, who unanimously stated the quality of the spice would be deteriorated by cultivation. Despite these gratuitous assurances, the governor caused several plantations to be formed, and tended with the greatest care. The young shrubs throve, and promised to repay, by a superabundant crop, the capital bestowed upon their cultivation, when suddenly every plant was found to be withered up.

Falck instituted a rigid investigation into the cause of this phenomena, and discovered that the chiefs had employed men to pour boiling water over the roots of the laurels. Many of the offenders were severely punished, and no ulterior attempt at the destruction of the shrubs ensued. The reason why the cultivation of cinnamon was discouraged by the chiefs, was, in the first place, that when it grew only in a wild state, they were paid a certain per centage for allowing their slaves to collect a stipulated quantity of the bark; as no European could be found sufficiently courageous to risk his health, or life, in the forests and jungles of the Kandian provinces, where the best cinnamon was produced. In the second, it had become bruited that it was the intention of the Dutch government, if it should be found that cinnamon could be improved by cultivation, to forbid any natives or Europeans trafficking in or having plantations of the laurel, save those appertaining to, and for the benefit of the executive powers. Dispassionately regarding this affair, we cannot feel surprised that the Cingalese should discourage, and throw unlawful impediments in the path of the cultivation of a shrub from which they had hitherto derived emolument, and which was the spontaneous production of their native soil.

So unjustly rigid was the monopoly of cinnamon maintained by the Dutch government, that neither the European nor native proprietor of the land was allowed to destroy, cut a stick, touch the bark, or pluck the leaves of a shrub, (the seed of which might have been dropped by birds) that grew on their property; and they were also compelled to give notice to the superintendent of cinnamon-plantations when a cinnamon-laurel sprouted from the earth's bosom, or severe penalties were imposed.

Every cinnamon-shrub was declared to be the sole property of the Dutch government, and the superintendent was authorized to send the peelers into a man's grounds to search for the shrubs, and, if any were found, they were immediately stripped of their bark, which was transported to the public warehouses, and the owner of the land either fined or imprisoned for having infringed the Dutch laws by not giving information that a cinnamon-plant grew on his land.

The Portuguese were hard task-masters in Ceylon, but the yoke imposed by them, was not so oppressive as the iron fetters which shackled the Cingalese during the period that the Dutch had possession of the island. The spirit of avarice so completely reigned lord paramount in the breasts of the Dutch rulers, that history affirms, when the bushes yielded a superabundant crop, bales of cinnamon were burned, or otherwise destroyed, both in Ceylon and Holland, to keep up the exorbitant price then demanded and obtained for the spice. From old Dutch records we learn that for more than one hundred years, the revenue derived annually from the sale of cinnamon was seldom less than four hundred thousand pounds. When the island came into our possession, the cinnamon monopoly was granted to the East

India Company for the yearly payment of the sum of sixty-thousand pounds: this was ultimately increased to one hundred thousand, which sum was received by our government until 1823, when the right of cultivation and sale reverted to the Crown, and the amount realized by the sale of cinnamon varied to an almost incredible extent, the annual receipts fluctuating between fifty thousand, to one hundred and seventy thousand pounds. In 1832, a commission of inquiry into the effects of this monopoly was instituted, and in the following year, by the judicious policy of Lord Goderich this obnoxious measure was abandoned, and the cultivation of the shrub has been thrown open since that period. Many improvements have been introduced by private individuals.

A cinnamon plantation somewhat resembles a luxuriant laurel copse, as the bushes are, by constant pruning, not allowed to exceed twelve or fifteen feet in height, except those that may be required for seed; and these will occasionally attain the height of thirty or forty feet, the trunk of the shrub measuring from eighteen to twenty-three inches in circumference. The propagation of the Laurus cinnamomum is conducted with facility, seeds, plants, and roots, (if transplanted with caution,) alike thriving in an appropriate soil, that consists of a pure quartz sand, which to the depth of many inches is as fine as moist sugar, and perfectly white; it then assumes a grey tint, and in some of the mountainous districts, layers of black moss are found immediately under this species of sterile sandy soil. It is remarkable that although white ants infest and abound in all cinnamon plantations in the island, these destructive insects do not injure the bushes in the slightest degree. And it is a proverb with many of the Cingalese, that to have a thriving plantation of cinnamon bushes four *plenties* are requisite, namely—"plenty of sand, plenty of sun, plenty of white ants, and plenty of water."

The foliage of the laurel is thick and of a dark shining green when arrived at maturity, but when young, the leaves are exquisitely beautiful, as their colour then is a pale yellowish green, striped with bright red: from the old leaves a fragrant oil is distilled, which the natives use for medicinal purposes, and which is applied by us to many uses. The cinnamon blossom is pure white, and scentless, the fruit or berry, acorn-shaped and small, the hue of which as it ripens gradually changing from green to purple, and from this is obtained, by boiling, a substance like wax, which is frequently made into candles, and these emit an agreeable perfume whilst burning. Some enormously large tapers made from this wax were found by our troops in the king of Kandy's palace. The spice is the inner bark of the shrub, and, in order to ascertain if this is in a fit state, the peeler makes a diagonal incision in a shoot, and, should the inner bark readily separate, the shrub is in a fit state for peeling. The knives used by the cinnamon-peelers are of a peculiar form, being heavy, long, convex on one side, concave on the other, and the point of the instrument is remarkably fine.

The bushes are generally peeled twice in the year, the first crop being the most abundant, and producing cinnamon of the finest quality. The first is obtained between the months of April and August, the second between November and January. The mode of obtaining the cinnamon is the following: the cinnamon-peeler cuts off the shoots of a year old, which are of the thickness of a man's finger, varying in length from one to four feet. The leaves are then carefully stripped off and placed in heaps, the peeler makes an incision with his knife the entire length of the shoot, separating the bark from the wood; he then carefully scrapes off the grey exterior skin, and the green inner epidermis, leaving the bark free from all fleshy substance, about the thickness of vellum, and of a greenish white colour. The man then places the small portions of the bark on the larger pieces, spreading the cinnamon out in a warm and shady spot, so as to enable the spice to dry gradually but thoroughly. The sun's rays and atmospheric influence cause the bark to assume a brown hue, and pipe-like form; and, when all moisture is evaporated, the cinnamon is tied up into sheaves, or bundles, weighing from fifty to seventy pounds, and is sent to the market for sale. From the refuse of the bark, a golden-coloured fine-flavoured aqueous fluid is distilled; from the root camphor is procured, and the peeled twigs are converted into walking canes; in short, there is no part of the Laurus cinnamomum that cannot be applied to the use of man.

The men who peel the cinnamon belong exclusively to a very low caste, called *Challias*, or cinnamon-peelers; and no native woman or man of a higher caste will associate with, or partake of food that has been prepared by these people—the poor Challia being despised in the maritime districts, as the unfortunate Rhodia is in the Kandian provinces.

The abodes of all Europeans in Ceylon bear a striking similitude to each other, the houses being constructed upon the same plan; every door and window alike open, and the portals of distinct apartments having moveable blinds placed mid-way in the frame-work. The dining-room usually extends the whole length of the dwelling, consequently the width of this apartment is generally disproportionate to the length; and in this hot climate, to enable the residents to partake of their meals in some *degree of coolness*, a punkah, nearly the length of the apartment, is suspended from the ceiling over the dining-table.

As we have a vivid recollection of the astonishment with which we gazed, the first time we saw one of these singular machines, we will describe what a punkah is like, believing there are many in this country who have not the most remote idea what this essential requisite to comfort, in an Eastern dwelling resembles. In the first place, a frame of wood, considerably longer than wide, is covered with white calico, to the bottom of which is attached a deep frill—flounce we believe to be the correct feminine term for this sort of garnishing. The frame-work is suspended from the ceiling by strong cords, while to the centre of the punkah is attached a very long rope, passing through a pulley which is pulled by a man stationed outside the dining-room, and by this means the machine is kept in constant motion. The use of the flounce is to catch the air as the punkah waves to and fro over your head, and very necessary and pleasant are the artificial breezes thus created by the waving of a certain quantum of wood-work and calico, where the thermometer ranges from eighty-six to ninety-eight.

There is one slight drawback to the delight of owning a punkah, even in the tropics, for it is almost certain that your careless servants will never inspect the ropes by which the punkah is suspended, to see if they are worn by the friction, caused by the constant pulling of the punkah. It is very, very, very hot indeed, the mosquitoes are tormenting you beyond endurance; you slap your own face *fifty* times, in the vain endeavour to annihilate *one* of these tormenting insects; at last, in a fit of angry despair, you call out to the punkah-puller, "Can't you pull STRONG, you lazy mortal?"—The biped, stimulated to exertion by your angry tone, gives an energetic PULL—one in right good earnest, as much as to say, "Does that please you now, master?" You hear a sort of rustling above your head, look up—crash—smash—down comes the punkah on the dinner-table, making a most awful uproar, shivering all the glass and crockery, and, worse than all, utterly destroying your meal. This disaster assuredly does not please you, although your orders were obeyed, "to pull strong," but even the downfall of a punkah, under different circumstances, excites dissimilar passions in the human breast.

If this contretemps happen in your own domicile, you rave at your appoo (or head servant) about his neglect of duty, carelessness, laziness, stupidity, &c., &c., &c.; vow that you will make him replace all that is broken, stamping, fuming, fretting, working yourself into both fever and fury. But let this disaster occur at a friend's house, you view it with the indifference of a stoic and the tranquillity of a philosopher, the equanimity of your temper not being in the most remote degree affected, or ruffled:—quietly rising from the table, you employ your *serviette* in wiping from your waistcoat a portion of the contents of the curry-dish, which delicious combination of vegetables and fish, with some chicken cotelettes, and a claret jug, may have been deposited by the fall of the aforesaid punkah in your lap, not to the improvement of your white clothing. Your tone of voice is mild, your speech deliberate, your manner calm, as you beg your host to moderate his vexation, consoling him by remarking—"That it is a horrid bore, to have a dinner spoiled and the breakables demolished, but it is just like these fellows, so insufferably indolent in every way, neglecting their business to chew betel, and gossip about master's business." The host thanks you again and again for your consideration, becoming at last insanely profuse and prolix in his apologies for the mishap. You beg of him to say no more on the subject, but order his appoo to clear away the débris, and see if some edibles cannot be found either on the table or in the cook-house, that will serve as a substitute for the sumptuous and varied repast that WAS spread before you, in numberless dishes, but which the perverse punkah has converted into an unpalatable pôt-pourri, or hodge-podge.

It is the invariable custom to place dessert upon the table after dinner, and, although this consists of every variety of tropical fruit in season, none save *recent arrivals*, ever venture to eat fresh fruit in the after part of the day: the older residents occasionally venture upon a little dried ginger, or try an *English biscuit*, the crispness and flavour of which have not been improved by its travels. We have noticed the flush of delightful anticipation pass over a new-comer's face, as he gazed with evident satisfaction upon the cool-looking tempting fruits, garnished with gorgeous flowers, that were spread in trim array before him; what delicious-looking pine-apples and mangoes, what magnificent bananas and custard-apples, what luscious pumbelows and guavas, what inviting water-melons and green-figs! The custard-apples are near "the new man," he takes one on his plate, and carefully bisects the mellow, melting fruit, preparing to devour the same with great gusto. His neighbour, if charitably disposed, and an old resident, in which case he is almost certain to possess a yellow skin and diseased liver, may whisper with an air of compassion for such ignorance, "I would advise you not to eat fruit after dinner, as it is very likely to produce cholera;" (the plate is pushed away with extreme avidity;) "eat as much as you like at breakfast, or tiffin, that won't harm you in the least." The *green* thanks the *yellow* man, resolving to indulge his gourmandise and affection for fruit the following morning.

We cannot dismiss Colombo without noticing the immense flocks of carrion crows that infest Cólpetty; these birds abound in every port of Ceylon, but we think their number and audacity are more manifest in this part of the island than elsewhere. These creatures are much larger than their European brethren, the plumage is thicker, and more glossy, and assuredly there is much speculation in their eyes; in short, we think them very handsome-looking, intelligent birds. No sooner did the first glimmer of daybreak appear, than their loud and incessant guttural, kha—haa, kha—haa, kha—haa, used to break our matinal slumbers. The boldness, thievish propensities, and perseverance of these creatures, are almost incredible.

We have known a crow to fly into the breakfast-room, hover over the toast-rack, seize a slice of bread, and fly off with it, although there were people seated at table: we have witnessed other marauders hop on to the sill of the cook-house-window, and there remain watching, with the utmost inquisitiveness, the movements of the cook, and no sooner was the man's back turned, or a favourable opportunity occurred, than the *bare-faced* feathered thieves would pounce on some article of food, and make for the nearest tree, or roof of the building, there to devour it at their leisure. We have heard, but did not see the act perpetrated, that a crow appropriated a piece of cake, that a child of six years old was eating, despite the efforts of the little unfeathered biped to drive the feathered one away; but we can positively affirm that we have seen the crows flying off with substances from our dwelling in Colpetty, that were nearly as heavy and bulky as their own bodies. There was one fellow whom we had christened the old soldier, (from his bravery, and because he had lost the lower half of one leg in the field of battle possibly, as a piece of red rag was tied around the stump; for aught we know to the contrary, this might have been a novel order of the garter,) whose daring and audacity were beyond credence. This bird used absolutely to attempt to take food from a dog whilst eating, and very frequently succeeded; the animal would naturally open its mouth, to snap or bark at the creature who was pecking or pulling at the food—the crow would then avail itself of this opportunity to fix the beak in the coveted morsel. Constantly we have seen these daring exploits rewarded with success, the bird flying off in triumph with the spoil, and perch on the branch of a neighbouring tree, under which the dog would stand angrily barking, as he looked up at the robber leisurely eating the food in security, that had heen purloined absolutely from between his teeth.

CHAPTER IV.

Situation of Kandy—Route—Bridge of boats—Paddy terraces—Aspect of the people—Ambepusse—Mountain zone—Kadaganawa pass—Mountain scenery—Talapat, or great fan palm—Animal life—Draught elephants—Peredenia — Bridge and Botanical gardens—Curious specimens of the vegetable kingdom—Travellers' friend—City of Kandy—Artificial lake—Bathing house of the Queen's—Palace—Native shops—Customs—Buildings—Artillery-barracks—Deficiency of water—The governor's residence—Beauty of the architecture and site—Views of the valley of Doombera—Major Davie's tree—Grounds of the Pavilion—Lady Horton's road—Grandeur of scenery—Altitude of the mountains—Military station on One-tree hill—Legend—Kurunaigalla tunnel—Compulsory labour—Animals, birds, and reptiles, in the surrounding country.

KANDY, the former capital of the interior, called by the natives Maha-neura, or the great city, is situated in lat 7°—21′ N. and in long., 80° 48′ E., at the summit of an extensive fertile valley, which lies more than 1500 feet above the level of the sea. The distance from Colombo to Kandy is seventy-two miles, the route crossing the bridge of boats, which was constructed during the government of Sir Edward Barnes, to obviate the unavoidable delay attendant upon the use of ferry-boats, to cross the Mutwal-Oya; which delay more than once led to serious results, when the assistance of our troops was required on the opposite side of the river. For the first eighteen miles of the road, the scenery is of the same character as that on the coast, with this exception, that rice is cultivated in a different manner to that adopted in the southern provinces.

Instead of planting the grain on a level surface, in this district it is more general to sow it in terraces of irregular dimensions and construction, the usual mode being to make an elevation in the centre of the paddy field, round which a terrace of less height extends, below which is a smaller one, each one decreasing towards the bottom of the artificial mound. Every level space is kept well supplied with water, and is separated from the terrace underneath, by mud walls, in which are perforations, to allow it to descend and irrigate the lower terraces. And although the Cingalese agriculturist is far surpassed in the construction of the paddy terraces, by the ingenuity and regularity evinced in the formation of the same by the Chinese, still the beautiful appearance of the young rice is everywhere alike, and nothing can be imagined more pleasing than the exquisite brilliant tender green of the growing paddy.

Soon the aspect of nature changes, the cocoanut palm plantations become less frequent, groves of areka and suriya trees, (Habiscus zeilanicus,) gradually taking their place; the latter is a majestic tree, bearing a strong similitude to an elm, and, when it is covered with its yellow blossoms, the lovely appearance is indescribable.

The air of the people also varies considerably, as the maritime districts are left in the rear—the high comb and long comboy are no longer visible, a handkerchief taking the place of the first, and a very short cloth or petticoat being used as a substitute for the last. The black paper umbrella is scarcely seen, a leaf of the talapat palm being used as a protection against the sun's rays in its stead; priests of Buddha, with shaven heads, and flowing yellow robes, wending their way to some temple, are much more numerous than in the southern province; in short, all around tends to impress upon the traveller's mind, that he is in a country and among a people totally dissimilar in all essential characteristics, to the lowland Cingalese.

The road to Kandy is planned, and the skill of the engineer has been displayed in the most masterly manner; as the hilly and mountainous districts are ascended, the views become sublime in the extreme; and the contrast presented by the huge masses of black gneiss rock, to the delicate and luxuriant flowering creepers that cling to some part of them, is alike wonderful and delightful. The prospect from the Rest-house at Ambepusse, situated thirty-five miles from Colombo, is surpassingly fine. This building lies in a valley that is formed by a semicircle of hills, which are wooded from base to summit, the luxuriance and gigantic character of the vegetation of Ceylon, in the mountainous districts, alone distinguishing it from that of Switzerland, Scotland, and North Wales. Although the country around Ambepusse is beautiful, and its soil fertile, the district is exceedingly unhealthy, the residents, both native and European, being liable to debilitating fever and ague. From Ambepusse to Attoomakandy, the whole route, for eighteen miles, is enlivened by the spectacle of land in the highest state of cultivation; coffee, sugar, and indigo crops alternately greeting the traveller's eye; and two miles from the latter place, the mountain-zone commences in all its sublimity and stern grandeur. At the first view of these stupendous and lofty mountains, which stretch in an enormous chain, (and which, during successive native dynasties, had formed the boundaries of the Kandian monarchs' territories, and which also enabled them, for more than three centuries, to set at defiance all the arts of war practised by the Portuguese, Dutch, and English conquerors of the maritime districts,) all farther progress seems to be debarred. We believe the road that winds round Kadaganawa Pass can be compared to nothing of the same construction in modern times, save the Simplon; and the officer who planned the first had innumerable difficulties to contend with, in the shape of inefficient assistants, unskilful and unwilling labourers, a tropical sun and unhealthy atmosphere, whilst those who executed the latter task, were aided by willing hands, ready hearts, and a genial atmosphere. We know that the sacrifice of human life, whilst clearing the dense jungle for the formation of the road was immense, and we regret to say that numbers of our officers were claimed by death, whilst superintending the tardy labours of the natives, in the discharge of their duties.

A series of views of the most magnificent and varied character open forth as the mountain is ascended; on either side of which appear cultivated lands, bounded by dense forests, and rocks, whilst the clearness of the atmosphere enables the traveller to see the undulating lowlands stretching far into the distance. As the steep sides of the mountain are climbed, ravines and fissures are wound round, and often a perpendicular mountain rears its lofty crest on one side, and descends in the same manner on the opposite. Sometimes a brawling waterfall appears over the traveller's head, as if threatening instant annihilation, by hurling him into the deep abyss below; then the road will become so narrow that there appears to be scarcely room sufficient for the vehicle to stand on, and the strongest nerves may be shaken, as the eye glances below at the steep precipice, down which some crumbling earth is rolling, loosened by the coach-wheels. To this circumscribed path, upon turning the next angle, succeeds a wide road and view of the surrounding country—terminated by the Blue mountains in the distance, whose towering heads blend with the azure heavens, Adam's Peak rearing his lofty crest above his fellows. The combination of sublime and beautiful scenery, brought under notice during the ascent of the Kadaganawa Pass is nearly incredible; roaring torrents dashing down frightful abysses, from whose sides spring enormous trees, and at whose base are lands teeming with grain. Terrific chasms, and overhanging masses of rock, where bright coloured flowering shrubs have taken root, rapidly succeed each other; and, when the summit of the mountain is attained, and the boundless extent and beauty of the prospect fully perceptible, many beholders of this magnificent scene cannot find utterance to express their sense of the might, majesty, and glory of the Almighty's works, and the humiliating feeling of their own littleness.

The freshness of the atmosphere, and the splendour of the scenery, are admitted by all, and extolled by numberless Europeans who have ascended the Kadaganawa Pass; and amongst those who are keenly alive to the beauties of nature, and consequently possessing acute sensibilities, we never knew one, whose feelings were not alienated from HOME, or blunted by a prolonged residence in the East, who did not declare they felt saddened, as the distant mountains and cooler air recalled scenes and persons in their native land, they might possibly never behold again,—while they compared the mountains they were then gazing upon to those in England, Ireland, Scotland, or Wales. A column of noble design and just proportions is placed on the summit of the mountain, erected in honour of him who planned the Kadaganawa Pass.

The remaining portion of the route to Kandy is diversified by many beautiful specimens of the animal and vegetable kingdoms, as numbers of monkeys belonging to different species will sport among the branches, whilst flocks of parrots and birds with gaudy plumage will wing their way from, or settle upon, the boughs of the trees adjacent to the road-side. Every tint of verdure is to be seen upon the trees, from the bright green of the young leaf, to the sombre tint of maturity, which will gradually subside into a rich brown, assuming a brilliant orange colour, before it drops from its parent stem; and as the eye wanders farther into the jungle, the trees appear to form one vast natural bower.

Attracted by the warmth, occasionally a speckled serpent may be seen gliding from his retreat in the underwood, to enjoy the full power of the sun's beams, or the reptile may entwine itself round the trunk of a tree in pursuit of some lovely bird, (not sufficiently strong on the wing to elude by flight the creature's deadly fangs,) or to rob the nests of the eggs, or unfledged young.

It would be impossible to enumerate a tithe of the trees appertaining to different species that are to be met with in this vast garden; but what principally attracts the stranger's attention, is the large talapat palm that grows a short distance from the right-hand side of the road, a few miles from Kandy. This magnificent tree towers above all the other gigantic monarchs of the vegetable world, and it is utterly impossible to find words adequate to describe its splendid beauty. The talapat, or great fan palm, is designated by most authors as Corypha umbraculifera, but some few call it Licuala spinosa. Leaving those botanists to settle the disputed name that have a penchant for disputation, we will give a cursory description of this celebrated palm—which varies in height from seventy to one hundred feet. The leaves frequently measure, from the extremity of the stalk to the point, more than twenty-four feet, and the width varies from twelve to seventeen, and these are used by the natives for fans and umbrellas. Under the native kings, none save these belonging to the highest caste were allowed to use these leaves, and the number was fixed that each chief, according to his rank, was to have borne before him. The flowers spring from the diadem of graceful verdure that crowns the palm, the blossoms being of a most exquisite pale yellow, and continuing in bloom for the space of three months, when they gradually disappear as the fruit forms.* Near this gigantic tree, are to be seen the banian tree, the myrtle (Myrtus), the bay tree (Laurus,) and the tick seed sunflower, which bears an immense number of golden-coloured blossoms, and is a species of Coreopsis; whilst on the opposite side fragments of yellow rock are clothed with luxuriant balsams, (Impaticus coccinea,) whose delicate white, and brilliant red blossoms, stand out in bold relief from the shining foliage. Ever and anon, some sportive green lizard will dart from out the long grass, and run across the road, or large carpenter bees, or beetles, whose wings are resplendant with the rainbow's hues, will in their airy flight poise on the wing, preparatory to settling upon some sweet-scented flower, thus giving the traveller an oppor-

* For a detailed account of this palm, see a future chapter

tunity of noting their several characteristic beauties. Possibly the eye may rest upon a small lizard, whose delicate brown skin is spotted like the tiger's, or striped like the leopard's, or on a tree frog, whose peculiar formation and movements delight as well as astonish; the former may be resting tranquilly on the trunk of the tree, with extended tongue, to catch the mosquitoes, or other small insects, and the latter may be creeping into the cup of the beautiful blossom, also in search of food.

It not unfrequently happens, the next strange object that arrests the traveller's attention, may be a tame elephant harnessed to a roughly-made cart, (as these creatures are used by the government in this district,) the driver walking quietly by the animal's side, unprovided with any means of enforcing his commands by severity, the ponderous brute obeying his keeper's voice with the docility of a well-trained little child. In fact, earth and air in this fertile island teem with such infinite variety of natural productions, that the man devoted to scientific pursuits, and he whose sole aim is the acquirement of wealth, find alike a wide field for their respective occupations.

Three miles from the town of Kandy is Peradenia, celebrated alike for its bridge and botanical gardens; the bridge being built entirely of satin wood, one noble arch of two hundred and seven feet, spanning the swelling waters of the Mahavelle-ganga. The Botanical gardens, whilst under the superintendence of the celebrated oriental botanist, Dr. Gardner, were maintained in admirable condition, and every facility was afforded by that talented and courteous man, for the student or enquirer to obtain information.

We believe these extensive gardens contained a specimen of every plant, shrub, or tree, indigenous to the island, (with the exception of the talapat tree,) as Dr. Gardner was indefatigable in the performance of his duty, and many rare specimens from the mountainous district, whose existence was previously unknown, were obtained by the energetic exertions of this gentleman. Among the curious foreign plants in these gardens, is a species of banana (Musa sapientum), native of Madagascar, called by many the "Traveller's friend," owing to the sweet aqueous fluid that flows from the sheath of the leaf when punctured. Every member of this tribe is exceedingly graceful, but the beauty of the one now alluded to far outvies its compeers, as the leaves sprout with extreme regularity from either side of the stem, in regular gradations, each leaf elegantly drooping over a lesser one, from the base to the summit of the stem. The trunk also is the same beautiful green as the leaves, and its formation is most peculiar, as it is flat, and has a platted appearance, looking exactly as if three stems had been regularly entwined. The height of this extraordinary specimen is nearly eighteen feet, and, although we have given an exact description of this beautiful tree, we feel that we have not been able to impart an adequate idea of its excessive loveliness and singularity. The lei-chee trees, natives of China (Dimacarpus), usually attract much attention, but as we had seen them in this parent land growing to an enormous size, we did not feel the peculiar interest that we otherwise might have done. The fruit, the shape of which is oval, is considered extremely delicious, varying in size from a damson to a small plum; the portion that is eaten, is a semi-transparent jelly-like substance, that is contained in a tough, thin, rough, red rind: when dried these fruits are very palatable, and can now be obtained in England, but in our estimation the lei-chee to be eaten in perfection, should be preserved; the jelly prepared from them by the Chinese, is as delicious a compound as can well be imagined. The trees belonging to this species in the botanic gardens have not attained their full growth, nevertheless they are universally admired; the foliage resembles that of the laurel in size and colour, and the fruit grows in bunches suspended from stalks six or eight inches long; the bark is a rich shade of bright brown, and in China, these trees, when arrived at maturity, are as large and lofty as a full-grown oak; those now alluded to at Peradenia are only of a moderate size.

Although not in these gardens, we cannot refrain from noticing one of the most noble specimens of vegetation in the world, that is to be found in the Mahomedan burial-ground at Putlam, in this island. This is a tamarind tree, (Tamarindus indicus,) and called from its enormous size the giant's tree; the height is ninety-eight feet, and seven feet from the root, the solid stem is thirty-nine feet in diameter: just above, the tree divides into two branches, one of which is twenty-one feet, and the other twenty-seven feet in circumference. The natives affirm that it increases in size annually, and that it is not more than a hundred-and-thirty years old. At one time tamarind trees, but of a smaller size, used to abound in the jungles, but immense numbers have been destroyed in the formation of coffee estates, and many have been felled to obtain their exquisitely variegated timber, which is often manufactured into furniture.

The position of the former capital of Lanka diva, is as beautiful and romantic as can be well depicted by the most vivid imagination; being situated in a valley, partially surrounded by lofty mountains, which are clothed in the perpetual verdure of trees, whose enormous girth betoken these were saplings in ages past, The mountains (varying from 300 to 2000 feet in height) are nearly in the form of an amphitheatre, and, when their shadows are reflected in the lake's clear waters, the scene is more like enchantment than reality. This artificial lake was formed by the last tyrant monarch of Kandy, out of paddy-fields, which he forced the owners to yield up to him; and many thousands of men were compelled to labour without the slightest compensation, at the embankments, and numbers of wives were made widows, as score after score of the labourers fell victims to the unwholesome exhalations of the disturbed stagnant waters. Notwithstanding all the atrocious associations connected with the construction of this lake, it is a most refreshing sight, as the silver stream extends nearly a mile and three quarters in length, the breadth at the widest part exceeding five hundred and ten feet.

A winding road encircles the lake, which being at the base of the surrounding hills, is sheltered in some measure by them from the scorching rays of the sun; consequently, Europeans can indulge in pedestrian and equestrian exercise at a later hour in the morning, and an earlier one in the afternoon, than they can either at Galle, or Colombo. A small artificial island stands in the centre of the lake, on which is an octagonal building that was used by the Queens of Kandy as a bathing-house; since we have had possession of the capital, it has been converted into a powder-magazine. Near the lake is the palace, and, although the building has suffered fearfully from the wanton destruction of our troops, still much remains to show what its magnificent decorations must have been in its hour of pride. The massive walls bear impress of the sculptor's art, and they are equally remarkable for their solidity. From the palace to the side of the lake, runs a beautiful low trellised wall, in which are perforations of every shape and size, for the purpose of illumination upon occasions of public rejoicing and festivity; and nothing can be conceived more picturesque than the view of this low wall from the opposite hill. Alas! we grieve to say, this elegant structure was fast crumbling away, and, as it is not repaired, in a comparatively short time not a vestige of it will remain. The great objects of interest in Kandy are the temples and tombs of the kings, and as a full account of them will be given in a future chapter, we omit especial mention of them here.

The town of Kandy is insalubrious, as it lies in a basin, open drains running at either side of the principal streets, and the effluvia from these receptacles of filth, especially after rain, is absolutely pestiferous. Improvements were commenced, by covered drains being constructed, and stagnant waters drained off, but as all labour proceeds in Ceylon in an inverse ratio to the growth of vegetation, it will be years before (if ever) these sanitary measures are effected. The present town consists of two main streets called Colombo and Trincomalee Streets, the former running east and west, the latter north and south; and the principal market for edibles is situated in the middle of the intersecting roads. On either side of the streets are small open shops, where the indolent owners sit chewing betel, being almost too lazy to serve a customer with their wares, presenting a correct type of oriental customs and productions. Spread upon small wicker trays, are all sorts of spices, from the small round black peppercorn to the oval nutmeg and long pipe of brown cinnamon; intermixed with these, are heaps of brilliant red chillies, white rice, and golden turmerick, whilst from the roof are suspended bunches of the green and yellow plantains, and mat bags containing curry stuffs, coffee, and sugar. In one corner may be a pile of oranges and citrons, whilst the others are occupied with cocoa-nuts divested and undivested of their exterior green covering. Occasionally these articles are so arranged, and the colours blend so harmoniously, that one is almost tempted to believe an artist's hand alone could thus have placed them.

When a buyer approaches one of these receptacles, and the proprietor is sufficiently roused from his favourite employment of betel-chewing, to state the price of the required commodity, a wordy war immediately ensues, for the native purveyor, let him traffick in the cheapest fruit, or the costliest jewel, invariably asks double the value of the article he has for sale. The native buyer in all probability requires a fanam's-worth of curry stuff or spice, double the amount is asked, until fraction by fraction is abated, and the just price agreed to be taken; each party chaffering with as much vehemence, energy, and gesticulation, as if three thousand rix-dollars were at stake, instead of three-halfpence.

During the Kandian monarchy, the relatives and connexions of the royal family resided in a particular district, situated in a south-easterly direction from the principal temple and palace, and which is now called Malabar Street. The ruling despot invariably deeming it essential to be prepared for rebellion, naturally placed reliance upon his relatives.

The Kandian laws forbade all save the nobles and chiefs to construct their dwellings with bricks, or kabook, or to roof them with tiles, or to elevate them from the ground; the domiciles of all of inferior rank being composed of a compound of mud and sticks, called waretchie, and roofed with platted cocoa-nut leaves, or paddy straw. A Kandian chief informed us the following was the original plan of the city; all the streets, including the principal, being five in number, ran in straight lines, inclining from west and east to the north, forming a triangle based by the artificial lakes.

There are a few good shops where European

articles can be obtained in Kandy, but on account of the expense attendant upon inland transit, the prices are exorbitant. The religious edifices and public buildings are of the same description as those at Colombo, but their number is materially less. A very handsome church was built by subscription, and consecrated by the pious prelate, Dr. Chapman, the present and first Bishop of Colombo. Previously to the erection of this edifice, divine service was performed in the Hall of Audience, formerly used by the kings of Kandy for the reception of ambassadors, which was, and is, used also as the Court-house.

The town is garrisoned by a detachment of our troops, and of the Ceylon Rifles, the barracks for both affording ample accommodation for a large number of soldiers. Near the tombs of the kings are the artillery barracks, situated in a most picturesque spot, the grounds of which are stocked with flowering shrubs, and many European vegetables, that are reared and tended by the soldiers with the greatest care; the men taking pride in, and bestowing extreme attention upon, the well-kept garden. Scattered over the lower hills are some houses of a better description, that have been erected within the last few years, and are inhabited by the government employés and Europeans. Although these dwellings are commodious, and built in comparatively salubrious spots, they have one most essential drawback, namely, want of a plentiful supply of good water; for as gneiss forms the bed of Kandy, water is difficult to obtain in certain situations, being particularly scarce on the hill sides.

His Excellency's residence, called the Pavilion, is the only structure in Ceylon that is calculated for the abode of one who is entrusted with the government of Asiatics, and, moreover, is the representative of the Sovereign of Great Britain. It is a fact of which most are cognisant, that Eastern nations place extreme value upon all the appliances of state, although this is admitted theoretically, it is too frequently disregarded practically, and we have heard the remark made many times, both by highland and lowland nobles, that the Queen's House of Colombo "was plenty small for great man, all same Rajah." Surely it is unwise to practise niggardly parsimony in such matters, giving a people, (whom we have conquered, and wish to impress with an idea of our notions of wealth and power,) the conviction that we either cannot, or will not provide suitable residences for the Governors who are sent to rule over them.

The Queen's House at Kandy was planned by Lieut.-Colonel Brown, R.E., and built while Sir Edward Barnes was Governor. This building is composed of a centre and two wings, which form in the rear three sides of a square, is elegant and commodious, combining every requisite for a dwelling in a tropical climate, and beautiful architectural proportions. The house is surrounded by regular collonades, and, as the entire surface of this handsome edifice is encrusted with a preparation that bears a high polish, the whole of the building has the appearance of being constructed of white marble. The pavilion commands a view of the principal part of the town, as well as an extensive prospect of the adjacent country; and it would have been impossible to have selected a more advantageous site in every way. The house stands in the centre of a large lawn, about which are planted at regular intervals groups of magnolia and palm trees: the park-like grounds cover a large space, and are well stocked with flowering exotics, and kept in excellent order. The park extends to the sides of the hills, and beautiful views of the mountain landscape valley of Doombera, and the meandering river are obtained. But in the centre of this lovely valley stands a gentle elevation, on which is a large and solitary tree, that recalls mournful recollections, for it is called Davie's tree; and it was in this vicinity in 1803 the fearful massacre of our poor soldiers took place, occasioned by the cowardice of the officer who commanded them, Major Davie; a man who alike disgraced his country and humanity.

The beautiful grounds were planned and laid out during the government of Sir Wilmot Horton, who succeeded Sir Edward Barnes, and the road that winds round the hills in the rear of the Pavilion is still called, and known only by the name of Lady Horton's road. The rapid succession of magnificent views that meet the eye from this mountain path are most glorious, as the rapid waters of the Mahavelle ganga flow below, the forest-clothed mountains, and hills, on which every tint and variety of foliage are to be discerned. From the main road, a minor path leads to the one that encircles the lake of Kandy, (whose level is sixteen hundred and fifty feet above the ocean,) the height of the mountain immediately over it, being three thousand feet. A mile beyond is the rocky ridge of Hantanna, which is four thousand three hundred feet high; the Peak of Hoonasgiri again towers above this, and the summit of the Knuckles, then proudly rears its lofty crest towards the heavens above all, the height of this mountain exceeding six thousand one hundred feet. From other parts of Lady Horton's road, various mountains are perceptible, besides those already enumerated, whose altitude varies from three to five thousand feet; but although we can give the heights of the eminences, we cannot impart an idea of the transcendant sublimity and grandeur of the scenery that surrounds Kandy.

The Citadel, or stronghold of our troops at Kandy, is situated upon one-tree hill, communicating by signals with Atgallee, which is distant seven and a half miles on the Trincomalee road, and is a military station of great importance, as it stands upon rising ground that commands a vast extent of country, and this part proved of the utmost service during the late rebellion. On every side Kandy is approached by mountain passes; and through one of these ran the celebrated Kurunaigalla tunnel, which was five hundred and thirty-seven feet in length. The road through the tunnel united at the base of the mountain, with the principal route to Colombo, thus enabling troops advancing on Kandy, to turn the heights near the Kadaganawa Pass. This tunnel was constructed by order of Sir

Edward Barnes, to consolidate, so to speak, the British power after Kandy came into our possession; for a legend has been extant, from time immemorial, THAT NO FOREIGN POWER COULD retain the Kandian dominions, UNTIL A PATH WAS BORED THROUGH THE MOUNTAIN. And a chief told us, that when his countrymen beheld this task commenced, their hearts failed them, but, when they saw it completed, and men walking through the bowels of the earth, they then knew it was their destiny to be ruled by a nation who could pierce rocks, and undermine mountains.

The tunnel was completed on the 8th of December, 1823, but we regret to say this has now collapsed, and the road is impassable. This tunnel, the principal carriage roads, and bridges, never could have been constructed, had not the system of compulsory labour been adopted by our government, as it had been carried on under the native dynasty. By order of the King in Council, in 1832, all compulsory services, and forced labour of every description was declared illegal and abolished. Whilst making the excavations for the tunnel, some rare and valuable gems were discovered, and the only ruby we have ever seen without flaw or defect in colour, was found at that period.

Wild animals and game abound in the neighbourhood of Kandy, as the jungles and forests afford them safe retreat. For as the surrounding country consists alike of mountains and valleys, hills and dales, woods and plains, rivers and streamlets, every animal from the elephant to the cheetah, every bird from the peacock to the snipe, every reptile from the python to the centipede, or amphibious guano, can find secure shelter in one or other of their respective haunts. We have known discredit cast upon an officer's assertion, who stated that during Sir Edward Barnes' government, he had heard continually after nightfall, the shrill cry of the elephant, and bellowing of the elk, in the jungle behind, and close to the Governor's temporary residence. We feel certain that every syllable of this statement was strictly correct; as we have heard Kandians affirm, that formerly beasts of prey would constantly come into the city during the night, when pressed by hunger, and that leopards have often been found drowned in the wells. Much of the dense jungle that surrounded the town is now cleared away, but we can positively declare that very recently a cheetah was seen close to a dwelling-house, in the early part of the day, and, despite the shouts of the servants, pounced upon a large turkey, deliberately *walking off* with his prize, not bounding, into the neighbouring plantation. Neither can we forget that during our residence in Kandy, a cobra capello was seen within a hundred yards of our abode, nor that we killed a black scorpion, (the most venomous of this tribe,) fully nine inches in length, in the verandah, narrowly escaping treading upon the reptile, which we mistook for a piece of stick, nor that we were roused from our slumbers by the efforts of a favourite dog, who was endeavouring to kill an enormous centipede, that was crawling up the bed-post under the mosquito curtains.

CHAPTER V.

Route to Trincomalee—Native suspension bridge—Caves of Dambool—Remains of tanks—Difficulty of constructing a portion of the road—Hot wells—Temperature of the waters—Beneficial application in certain diseases—Legend attached to the waters—Coast and harbour of Trincomalee—Situation, latitude, longitude—Size of harbour — Fort of Trincomalee — Town — Buildings — Troops—Insalubrity of the climate—Trincomalee named in ancient records—Colony of Malabars established there before 125 A.D.—Interesting religious ceremony on the promontory in honour of Siva—Pillar to the memory of Francina van Rhede—Melancholy history—Fantastic appearance of the Quartz Rocks—Principal roads.

THE route from Kandy to Trincomalee abounds in objects of novelty and interest; the first one is situated six miles from Kandy, and consists of a cane suspension bridge, thrown over the De-

deroo-oya. The construction of this fragile medium of communication to the opposite sides of a rapid stream, evinces alike the ingenuity and readiness of the natives to avail themselves of those means most easily obtained, and calculated for their purpose.

This structure is composed of cable-rattan, which frequently grows to the length of two hundred yards; and varies but little in thickness from one end to the other, is extremely light, flexible, and tough. The bridge is commenced by entwining canes a few feet apart round the trunks of two large trees that grow on the opposite banks of the stream, and whose branches bend over the river; when the required number of canes are securely fastened in this manner, portions of the same material are laid across to form the path, which is the same breadth as the circumference of the stems of the trees. Rattans are then placed at a sufficient height to form hand-rails, these being attached to the bridge by thin bamboos, or sticks, which alike support and retain the rails in their proper place.

From the overhanging boughs are suspended cane or coir ropes, which are attached to the bridge, thus strengthening the structure, and lessening the vibration. The means of ascent are by a ladder composed of the same materials, which rests against the trunks of the opposite trees; and it is perfectly astonishing to see the fearlessness with which women, children, or men carrying heavy burthens, will cross one of these aerial structures.

Thirty-five miles from Kandy is Dambool, near which place are the celebrated Buddhist rock cave temples, which may almost be classed among the wonders of the world, as they are complete specimens of man's skill, perseverance, and ingenuity.* The remains of tanks, that once fertilized by their waters whole districts, now suffered to fall into decay, becoming choked up with dense underwood and rank vegetation are continually passed; causing sensations of surprise and pain, that our government should suffer such sources of wealth to become the focus of disease, instead of having them repaired, and applying them to the purpose for which they were constructed.

The last thirty miles of the road are peculiarly interesting to the antiquarian, as they lie through a forest, in which are scattered remains of temples, tanks, and villages. The officer who

* For the detailed account of these extraordinary excavations, see the chapter devoted to the antiquities.

traced this portion of the road, had to overcome innumerable difficulties, and endure both toil and privation in the performance of his task, as nearly the whole of this portion of the road was traced from the summit of the trees, and great difficulty was experienced in obtaining sufficient water for the large number of men necessarily employed. Captain Atchison was indefatigable in his exertions, and the road was completed in an incredibly short time; and we cannot do better than quote his own words, showing the obstacles he had to surmount, and the remains of civilization that were brought to light.

"The ruins of Wihares (temples), remains of deserted villages, tanks, and other remnants of antiquity, prove that the vast wilderness of beautiful and valuable forest-trees through which the new line of road passes, heretofore supposed a trackless desert, obnoxious to the existence of man, and destitute of water and inhabitants, once contained a considerable population, by whose labours an extensive tract of irrigated lands was regularly cultivated."

Seven miles from Trincomalee, near a ridge of wooded hills, are the hot springs of Kanya: there are seven wells of various sizes, containing pure water, the temperature of which is unequal, the thermometer ranging in different wells from 100^0 to 112^0. The enclosure in which the springs are, is about forty feet long, and eighteen wide, being surrounded by a wall of kabook, each well likewise having a low embankment. The taste of the waters is not unpleasant, although they are not drank, the natives believing only in their restorative qualities, when applied externally.

These waters are considered efficacious in cutaneous and rheumatic diseases, and some of our medical men recommend their application. The mode of using these waters is by affusion, the invalid standing upon a square stone tablet, whilst chatties of water are poured over his person. The springs are deemed sacred by the natives, and under the especial protection of Ganeesa, (the Hindoo god of wisdom,) to whom there is erected a temple near the spot, and in which is a stone statue of the god; and the following legend is extant among the natives regarding the origin of the springs, which they view with awe and reverence.

The god, Vishnu, being resolved to prevent the hero King, Rawana, going to war, with one of his devotees, assumed the form of a venerable man, and appeared before the monarch, just as he was setting forth to battle, and with loud lamentations informed him that his mother, Kanya, was dead. The king, deeply afflicted, immediately ordered his soldiers to their homes, stating that he could not go forth to war until the solemnities and ablutions were gone through that were enjoined to be performed for deceased relatives. Vishnu disappeared, but, fearing his favourite might be accidentally encountered by the monarch, if he went to the bath, caused the hot springs to burst forth on the spot, and as the king laved his person, the waters miraculously appeased his wrath, and from that time have never ceased to flow; being called Kanya, after the mother of the monarch.

The beauty of the coast and harbour of Trincomalee has been expatiated upon by many, and the eulogies bestowed upon the immense tracts of inland forests, groves of palmyra palms, adjacent country, and bold shores, are fully merited. Trincomalee is the capital of the eastern province, and is situated in lat. 8^{0} 33′ 5″ north, and in long. 81^{0} 13′ 2″ east, possessing a harbour which is invaluable for its safety, position, and size; naval men have declared in our presence, the greater portion of our men-of-war could find room, and ride in it with the utmost security. The inner harbour or bay is land-locked, and being nearly unfathomable, vessels of every class can there find shelter from, and in the most violent storms.

The entrance to the harbour is nearly five miles wide, and lies between Foul Point on the south-east, and Fort Frederick on the north-west, the width gradually decreasing to three miles between Norway Point to the south-west, and Chapel Island on the north-west, when it expands suddenly, and forms Great Bay to the southward, and Trincomalee harbour to the northward. During war, this is the principal depôt for the Indian navy, as there is an excellent dockyard and arsenal, capable of holding and refitting the largest man-of-war.

The fort of Trincomalee extends over a space exceeding three and a half miles, and commands the entrance to the inner bay; within the walls are buildings, erected for the defence of the low ground by the landing-place. Three miles west of Trincomalee is a cliff which projects into the sea, and on this is the citadel called Fort Osnaburgh, which is built exclusively for the defence of the harbour, and which cannot be taken, until the lower fort has been captured.

The town of Trincomalee extends in a north-easterly direction, along the outer bay, being situated in a well-wooded, hilly country, and is separated from the fort by a wide esplanade. Although the population is extremely limited when compared with that of Colombo, the houses are scattered over a much greater extent than they are at the seat of government, but few Europeans have settled at Trincomalee, consequently the society is restricted to the families of the military and civil officers who are stationed there.

The native population is composed chiefly of Malabars and Moors, who pay comparatively little attention to agricultural pursuits, consequently large tracts of valuable land remain uncultivated. The government offices are comparatively few; the religious edifices are calculated for the accommodation of much larger congregations than are likely ever to fill their walls, as, from the insalubrity of the climate, few Europeans would reside at Trincomalee unless necessity compels them to do so. The Wesleyans and Roman Catholics have each appropriate places of worship, and the nàtives likewise have their temples and mosques.

The fort is garrisoned by a detachment of our

soldiers, and the Ceylon Rifles, and our troops evince great dislike to being sent to this station, as the enervating nature and excessive heat of the climate, the thermometer ranging from 74^0, to 91^0 throughout the year, almost incapacitate Europeans from exerting themselves, especially when encumbered with a soldier's uniform and accoutrements. Occasionally spasmodic cholera will break out suddenly in a most virulent form, attacking and destroying alike in a few hours the European and the native, the drunken and the sober, the brave man and the coward, the happy and the wretched, and after committing fearful ravages will as suddenly cease. Nevertheless, cholera is always more prevalent in Trincomalee and Jaffnapatam, than in other parts of Ceylon.

If we are to credit traditions, Trincomalee appears to have been well known in the earliest ages, as it is stated there was a temple erected on this spot, that was celebrated all over the continent of India. Brahminical records declare that in the earliest wars of the gods, three of the peaks of the Maha-meru, or abode of celestial beings, were thrown down, and driven into various parts of the earth, and that one of these is Trincomalee, and that it immediately became the abode of Siva, or Eiswara.

The heir apparent of Manoo Salen, sovereign of the Coromandel coast, hearing of the sanctity of Trincomalee, left his father's dominions, erected a temple to the god, on the summit of the rock, built a town, constituted a Malabar chief the governor of the city and adjacent country, inviting his father's subjects and other emigrants to settle there. This is stated to have occurred 1589 B.C., and, although this early date cannot be authenticated by the testimony of contemporary writers, the Malabars possess several works in the Tamil tongue that profess to describe the beauty of this temple and other sacred buildings.

Cingalese historical records to some extent corroborate the Tamil, as they say their King, Gaja Bahoo, who reigned between 113 A.D., and 125, gave rice-fields and lands as endowments to the temple for *entertaining the intention* of destroying the fane of Siva, and building a new one to Buddha in its place. The Cingalese account also states that Gaja Bahoo took the natives of the Coromandel coast prisoners, and sent them to Trincomalee; whilst the Tamil writers declare that at a much earlier period, their forefathers had voluntarily emigrated to this spot.

Without attempting to reconcile these conflicting statements, it is an indisputable fact, that in the second century of our era, and during the reign of the Cingalese monarch, Gaja Bahoo, a colony was established at Trincomalee, and it is rather remarkable that many of the Malabars at Trincomalee can distinctly trace back their pedigree to the period above named.

The promontory on which the fort is built is dedicated to Siva, and this rock is regarded with peculiar veneration by the god's worshippers, as they believe that on this spot the first temple dedicated to his service, by the Prince Kalakootu (the king's son before alluded to) was erected. Some oriental scholars maintain that Siva means destroyer, whilst Wilson, who is no mean authority, states in his Sanscrit dictionary, that Eiswara, the ancient designation for Siva, is "an universal spirit."

Although every vestige of the temple has long since been obliterated, at stated periods oblations are offered to the god on the presumed site of his original temple. Shortly before sunset, the Brahmin priest ascends the rock, wearing a peculiar costume for the occasion, which consists of a yellow cloth twisted round his loins, and a chaplet of large and many-coloured beads bound around his brow. The officiating priest climbs to a lofty part of the rock that overhangs the sea; the subordinate priests standing upon the adjacent crags, some of the worshippers ranging themselves by their side, whilst others stand or kneel in more secure situations.

The priest first performs various ablutions, then makes several low salaams towards a deep chasm in the rock, (in which the deluded beings suppose the god they worship dwells,) casting rice and betel leaves into the fathomless ocean that rolls below; then again bows lowly to the chasm, and stands in a devotional attitude gazing upon the sun. So soon as the sun touches the waters, a subordinate priest hands a species of censer to his superior, who holds the vessel above his head with one hand, waving it to and fro in the air; he then ignites the incense, which being composed of inflammable and fragrant preparation, bursts instantaneously into lurid flames, diffusing a powerful perfume around. When the flame has subsided, the priest casts two young cocoa-nuts into the ocean, and receives the oblations and offerings of the congregation, for the god. When these have been collected, both priests and people make low reverences, in the direction of the chasm, and the service concludes with a few muttered words from the officiating Brahmin.

The offerings made by the devotees are of little value, as they consist of small quantities of rice, betel leaves, flowers, and cocoa-nuts, and, when money is presented, the coins are generally copper. This ceremony is remarkably interesting, as it undoubtedly is one of great antiquity; and, from being performed upon a lofty precipice, whose steep sides beetle o'er the deep, and at the hour of sunset, has a character of mystery and wildness about it, that bears a stronger affinity to romance, than to the realities of life.

As recently as 1622, an extensive range of temples dedicated to Siva, were levelled by the Portuguese, when Trincomalee was in their possession, and they applied the materials, to the construction of a portion of the fortifications.

Above the part of the promontory where the officiating priest worships the god, is a monumental pillar, erected to the memory of Francina van Rhede, who in 1687 committed suicide by leaping from a projecting crag. A lengthy inscription was originally carved upon the pillar, but time and exposure to the elements have nearly obliterated the whole, leaving merely the name, date, and a few words visible. Tradition has handed down the cause of the sinful act, and some descendants of the lady's family are still in Ceylon.

Francina van Rhede was the daughter of a Dutch gentleman in the government service; and had formed an attachment to an officer in the army, which was sanctioned by her father, and the day was fixed for the celebration of the nuptials. Misunderstandings arose as to the amount of the bride's dowry, and other matters being disputed, the intended bridegroom broke off the match, and shortly after obtained leave to return to Europe. The unfortunate and misguided girl, rendered desperate by the desertion of her lover, resolved that he should not leave the island during her lifetime; and, having obtained information as to the time of the ship's sailing, watched from her chamber-window the sails spread that were to waft him from the cinnamon isle.

Before clearing the coast, the vessel was compelled to tack, and pass close to the precipices that bound the southern part of the Fort. For this moment she had watched; she rushed from her dwelling, darted along the edge of the cliffs, under which the swift vessel was gliding, for an instant balanced on an overhanging crag, then, with a wild exclamation of revengeful despair, leaped from the giddy height, and was dashed against the rocks below. With some difficulty, her mangled remains were collected, by the order of her heart-broken father, to receive christian burial; and, although we can only hope the act of self-murder was perpetrated during temporary insanity, as that alone can extenuate the commission of so fearful a crime, we have often felt surprise that the family should have commemorated so awful an occurrence by the erection of a pillar in this conspicuous situation.

Some of the quartz rocks at Trincomalee have a most picturesque appearance from the sea, and a low hill, (that extends a distance of nearly two miles,) from Chapel Point to the opposite one of Fort Ostenburgh, has a fantastic and singular aspect. The sides of the rock are precipitous, being perfectly bare, standing out like denuded veins, exhibiting a strong similitude to the ruins and columns of ancient monastic edifices. The principal route through the island ends at Trincomalee; for though roads diverge at various points both at Galle, Colombo, and Kandy, the main road commences at the former town and terminates at the latter.

CHAPTER VI.

Newera Ellia—The sanatorium of the island—The road—Mountain conflagration—Convalescent station for the military, established 1829—Cascades of Rambodde—Newera Ellia a royal residence in 1628—Scenery—European aspect of the dwellings—Vegetation—The town—Public buildings—Salubrity of the climate—Farming experiments—Great capabilities and fertile soil of Newera Ellia—Proposed plan of emigration—Price of stock and produce—Iron found on the plain—Carriage roads—Footpath to the summit of Pedro-talla galla—Horton Plains, the highest table-land in Ceylon—Luxuriant specimens of the Nepenthes distillatoria, or pitcher plant—Nelu, or honey plant.

THE road to Newara Ellia, the sanitorium and convalescent military station of Ceylon, (called by the natives the City of the Plain,) commences at the Peredenia bridge, three miles from Kandy, whence it runs through the mountainous parts of the island, which are celebrated in Cingalese records from being connected with the names of the heroes, Rama, Rawana, and the lovely Seeta. The route winds round precipitous slopes, the recesses of which, from their peculiar formation, are called the Devil's Punchbowls, and, during the whole of the journey, wide-spread valleys, gently undulating ground, flowing rivers, towering mountains, gushing cascades, and a well-wooded country, are passed in quick succession by the delighted traveller. Moreover, the invigorating coolness of the atmosphere, as the higher ground is reached, enables an European to enjoy the exquisite scenery in comfort. Some will commence the journey in the after part of the day, remaining at Gampola, twelve miles from Kandy, (where there is the best Rest-house in the island,) for the express purpose of witnessing the sublime spectacle of a mountain conflagration, which frequently occurs during the hot and dry season.

The mountain of Ambulawe overhangs Gampala, and the coarse vegetation which clothes it frequently ignites spontaneously: much of the grass grows to a height of seven or eight feet, being distributed over the hill in patches; this peculiar herbage being one of the characteristic productions of Ceylon, called lemon-grass, or Andrapogon Schænanthus, and in this part of the island generally covers the hills that are not overgrown with underwood and jungle.

The appearance of this burning grass is most magnificent: a lurid flame suddenly bursts forth in distinct spots over the mountain, and the conflagration goes on rapidly against the wind, the breeze causing the long grass to bend towards the flames, which drying it instantaneously, immediately ignites, casting around a lurid light. When the blaze has subsided, myriads of sparks, borne aloft with the volume of dense smoke, illumine the atmosphere; or, falling upon other tufts of grass, set fire to them also. By these means the conflagration extends, a loud crackling sound being perceptible in the immediate neighbourhood, and in the distance a roaring hollow sound, until the advancing flames are arrested by the dense woods that clothe each ravine. What appears extraordinary is, that the roots of the Andrapogon Schænanthus are neither injured nor destroyed by the conflagration, for, after a two-days' rain, from the midst of the calcined and blackened masses the young shoots will burst forth; and in a week the whole mountain will be again dotted over with patches of waving grass of the most brilliant green.

Newera Ellia was first visited by Dr. Davy in 1819, and, although he at once saw and stated the immense advantages to be derived from its salubrious and temperate atmosphere, it was not until ten years had elapsed that a military convalescent station was established on this spot, and this desirable measure was adopted in 1829 by Sir Edward Barnes. Many serious difficulties had to be contended with in the formation of the latter part of the road, as from Rambodde to the plains the route through the pass is on an inclined plane, which ascends one foot in every fourteen. Even now much difficulty is experienced in keeping the road in repair, for continually masses of soil and stones roll from the mountain's sides and block up the path. It is rather singular that it should have been during the government of Sir Edward Barnes that nearly every important road in Ceylon was either commenced or completed, and these vast undertakings were carried into execution before the abolition of compulsory labour.

The cascades of Rambodde are superb, and during the rainy season the vast volume of the torrents that dash down is incredible, the noise of the waterfalls being heard distinctly at a considerable distance. Near Rambodde is the lovely valley of Kotmaale, through which meanders a flowing stream, whose waters possess peculiar efficacy, according to the superstitious belief of the natives; as they assert that whatever woman bathes in the river within three months after she becomes a wife, will be blessed with a beautiful, numerous, and fortunate family.

From the summit of Rambodde Pass the first clear view of Newera Ellia is obtained, which lies about six thousand three hundred feet above the sea; and, although it is called a plain, it is not such in reality, as a chain of hills, running from south-west to north-east, divide it unequally. When we took possession of this place, in 1829, the only vestiges found of former occupants were the remains of a temple, and one or two buildings, although it is an historical fact, that the Queen of Kandy, in 1628, here took up a temporary abode after her second marriage, when she was compelled to leave the capital by the Portuguese.

Game abounds in this district, and it was in the pursuit of elk that a party of our officers discovered the plains, some natives having volunteered to conduct them to a spot where the animals abounded. The boldness of the scenery around Newera Ellia can only be equalled by that of Snowdon, as it is encircled on every side by craggy mountains, amongst which is the loftiest mountain in Ceylon, Pedro-talla-galla, whose towering peak rises eight thousand three hundred feet above the ocean's level.

The plain is dotted over with white-washed residences, recalling many home recollections, for on the roof of every dwelling are to be seen chimneys; the cool and bracing atmosphere not only rendering fires pleasant morning and evening, but causing them to be absolutely necessary. To those who have not visited the tropics this remark may appear puerile, but will be fully appreciated by those who have sojourned in the east, for none can tell, save the latter, the feeling of *strangeness* that pervades the mind when the beholder first looks upon dwellings unmarked by this sign of the household hearth.

Nothing about Newera Ellia Plain tells of the tropics, the bracing air enabling Europeans to walk out at any hour of the day, the mental and bodily faculties soon regain their lost vigour, the frame is invigorated, the palled appetite recovers its tone, and speedily the hollow sallow cheek becomes rounded, and assumes health's roseate hue; many a desponding invalid, whose large family and slender means forbade return to his native land, has reason to bless the day the sanitorium of Lanka-diva was discovered.

The beauties of vegetation also wear a familiar aspect as the eye is gladdened with floral gifts that appertain especially to the temperate zone, such as rhododendrons, the white guelder, damask, and pink rose-trees, violets, sweet-peas, acacia, peach, apple and pear-trees, with nearly every fruit and vegetable that are produced or consumed by us, can be met with in the immediate neighbourhood. And all this is found upon the summit of a mountain seven degrees from the equator, where occasionally the thermometer has fallen below 28°, and where ice half an inch in thickness is sometimes found in the morning.

The town of Newera Ellia stands upon a plain, 6,300 feet above the level of the sea, and from this table-land mountains rise in various directions, diversified with gentle slopes and undulations, over which are scattered various residences. Perpetual cascades burst from the sides of the neighbouring mountains, and pure rapid streams of wholesome water wind through the valleys, whilst much valuable timber clothes the hills; and for an extent of several miles well watered, and alternate plains, hills and dales, give the surrounding scenery the appearance of a natural park. A church has been built near the Governor's house, and there are also residences belonging to the Bishop, Commander, Colonial Secretary, and other government servants.

A detachment of our troops is always at Newera Ellia, and their barracks, hospital, &c., are excellent. Throughout the district, from November to the end of April, the thermometer seldom rises above 65° Fahr., and, although frosts are not unfrequent during the night, snow is unheard of: the temperature of the winter months resembles the bracing atmosphere of a fine October in England, and the summer months combine the genial warmth of August with the beneficial showers of April; in short, the oppressive atmosphere of the tropics is unknown at Newera Ellia.

The soil varies as in Great Britain from the rich brown to the black loam, and all English produce succeeds in a most luxuriant manner, although hitherto the farming has been almost entirely in the hands of the natives, who, notwithstanding their ignorance of the subject, have amassed large sums from the cultivation of potatoes, carrots, turnips, and other vegetables; their farming experiments not extending beyond these simple endeavours. Many gentlemen for their amusement have planted English grass, clover, wheat, oats, barley, beans, peas, and have found green crops of every description thrive and yield in the most extraordinary manner.

It has afforded us great pleasure to peruse the circular of Mr. Baker, an energetic and enterprising gentleman, who has located himself at Newera Ellia, wherein he sets forth in most glowing language, the agricultural advantages which this district possesses, and where an arrangement has lately been made for opening a new field for agricultural enterprise; suggesting also a system of emigration, which offers both peculiar advantages to the colonist, and ensures him, on his arrival in Ceylon, a comfortable farm with a dwelling-house and requisite buildings, ready for his immediate occupation. This forethought for the emigrant's comfort, the writer very justly remarks, obviates his exposure to the usual hardships experienced by those, who under ordinary circumstances seek to improve their fast-decaying prospects in their fatherland, by migrating to unknown shores; and the fact undeniably bespeaks a most favourable impression for the honesty, integrity, and sincerity of the promoter of the scheme. Mr. Baker is said to have engaged the services of seventeen English farm-servants of both sexes, who, with a large supply of farming implements, have ere this, in all probability, reached their destination, where that gentleman is stationed exerting himself in the development of his laudable plan, which, if successful, must be alike beneficial to the colony, and the new settlers.

Although we are not prepared to agree with Mr. Baker in *all* his sanguine expectations of the results likely to accrue from Newera Ellian emigration, still, making due allowances, we think his plan is most deserving of the serious consideration of those amongst our own Irish farmers, who contemplate a change, and we wish him, and those British subjects who may follow him, the success which his energy, honesty, and forethought so eminently deserve. The circular before us draws most forcibly the contrast between the settler proceeding to Australia, or America, and the emigrant to Ceylon, the former landing in a wild and barren country, *houseless* and *friendless*, with nothing but the certainty of the greatest privations before him ; while the latter is landed free of expense in Ceylon, and without delay takes possession of his farm, and, settled in his house, is ready to commence his operations immediately.

We can bear witness to the advantages offered in this mountain district for a European settlement, and the only matter of astonishment is, that so many years of British rule should have elapsed before the attempt was made. Newera Ellia is a district blessed with a peculiarly salubrious climate, and in every way adapted for the production of those necessaries of life, which at this moment are imported into the colony at an enormous expense, and capable of raising supplies considerably beyond the wants of the inhabitants, for which ready markets may be obtained. The natives, says Mr. Baker, now produce five successive crops of potatoes from the same land: thus, even from their ignorant farming, they adduce a proof of the peculiar quality of the soil.

Stock of all kinds is remarkably cheap, and the draught buffalo is an animal which entirely supersedes the horse for all heavy work, not only on account of his great strength, but from the fact of his requiring no other food than pasture.

Cows and buffaloes may be purchased from 25*s*. to 40*s*. per head; sheep, from 3*s*. to 7*s*.; pigs from 3*s*. to 7*s*.; fowls, from 7*s*. per dozen; ducks, from 12*s*. ditto. Mr. Baker proceeds to show that, notwithstanding the very low price of stock, fine meat is unknown in Ceylon, the beasts being unfattened, and slaughtered without discretion. Although in many parts of the island the calf is permitted to take the whole supply from the mother, yet not a cheese has ever been manufactured in Ceylon, and butter sells for 2*s*. 6*d*. per pound. Notwithstanding the abundance and cheapness of pigs, hams and bacon have never been cured; and yet all these articles are consumed in large quantities, and imported from England at an enormous price, cheese, hams, and bacon being generally sold at 2*s*. per pound.

All these articles may be prepared at Newera Ellia, with the same facility, and at one-fourth of the cost, of those produced in England, and would therefore sell at a large profit both for home consumption and for exportation. The island is chiefly supplied by Bombay with potatoes, but those of a superior quality now produced at Newera Ellia sell at 28*s*. per cwt. In three months from the planting of the sets, they are fit to dig, and one set has frequently been known to yield fifty potatoes. Wheat has been experimented upon, and the quality produced proved infinitely superior to the seed imported, and yet Ceylon is entirely dependant upon America for the supply of flour. Oats and beans thrive well, but have been neglected, consequently the horses in the island are fed expensively upon paddy and gram, the principal portion of which is imported from India: thus a most extensive market is open to supply the home market, as well as that of the Mauritius.

Mr. Baker offers to the enterprising farmer of small capital, a comfortable and most profitable farm, free from those heavy taxes which burthen his industry at home, where he may not only amass a considerable fortune, but may live a happy, luxurious life, with the advantages of residing in a comparatively civilized society, with a school for the education of his children, and the house of God within his reach.

We feel bound to correct an error of Mr. Baker's, who states that cheese and hams were never produced in Ceylon, as the former have been made, and we believe are still, at the island of Delft, near Jaffna, and also at Manear; the latter have been cured at Newera Ellia by British soldiers—however this has nothing to do with the fact, which must be apparent to the meanest capacity, that were those articles produced at Newera Ellia equal to the English, they would bring remunerative prices to the farmer. We should also observe another mistake, namely, that the Colony is not entirely dependant upon America for flour, large quantities being annually imported from the Bombay Presidency. In respect also to the successive crops of potatoes, we fear the promoter has overlooked the necessity of manure, and his circular makes no mention of whence he proposes to derive his supply, as well as the fact, that in all probability the market would be limited to the European population of the island. We have been informed that recently potatoes grown at Newera Ellia were offered in the Colombo market at 24*s.* per cwt. being four shillings less than stated by Mr. Baker.

We repeat that the scheme of Mr. Baker is highly deserving of consideration; what he states of the climate, circumstances, and position of the settlement is perfectly correct, and there can be little doubt that the fattening and improving of the breeds, both of cattle and poultry, would be remunerative, as well as the growing of seed and green crops—luxuries and enormous fortunes are out of the question—some comfort and an honest livelihood are to be found; and we should think that there is a good opening for some able-bodied industrious Irish labourers, and their wives and families, who are more inured to hardships than their English neighbours; the men could be constantly employed in this delightful climate in the cultivation of the soil, while their women might find profitable employment in dairies and poultry-yards.

The difficulties are great which encompass the agriculturist in Ceylon, for want of a sure supply of labourers. The local press is full of constant complaints and communications on the subject such as these,—"Some estates are hard up for coolees, and very few are appearing from the coast. Indeed if it be true, as it is said, that in their own country fine rains have fallen after long drought, filling their tanks and fertilizing their lands, we cannot expect men, for it is only in their exigency, having no work in their own country, that the Malabars come here."

"Accounts of the most deplorable nature continue to reach us on the difficulty of obtaining coolees. There is every reason to apprehend that a large portion of the crops will be lost for want of hands." "A friend has just been here on his way to the Four Korles in search of coolees.

He gives a most melancholy account of the scarcity of labour which prevails everywhere. Nearly all his coolees have bolted, and there is little hope of being able to replace them. Happy is the man who can muster thirty coolees on an estate of three hundred acres in bearing. Nearly all the superintendents have gone to look for coolees, with but faint hopes of success, and the comfortable conviction, that if they do not succeed, the crop must be entirely lost. On some large estates the coolees have fled to a man."

By the foregoing, our readers will perceive that the agriculturist in Ceylon is entirely dependant for labour upon the periodical visits of the coolees from the Malabar coast, who require but little for their support, which consists for the most part of rice, and when they have acquired a small sum in wages, immediately return to their families, regardless of acquiring more money, and leaving their employers without notice, or redress.

Taking this fact, therefore, into consideration, as well as the utter hopelessness of being able to induce the Cingalese to work, if they have sufficient food to eat, and which they can procure with very slight exertion, it would appear to us to be indispensably requisite, as an element of success in Mr. Baker's undertaking, to secure the assistance of a sufficient number of Irish, English, or Scotch labourers, who, being accompanied by their families, would not have the same inducement to make a speedy retreat after the Malabar fashion. The Irish, we know from experience, have many good qualities, and that of attaching themselves to those who give them food and raiment, and treat them with consideration, is not the least; and Paddy is a right good fellow at heart, when beyond the reach of political agitation. For all further particulars on the subject of the settlement at Newera Ellia, we refer our reader to the promoter, S. W. Baker, Esq., whose circular is dated from No. 4, Wolseley Terrace, Cheltenham.

Iron of good quality is found on the plain, and the natives say that formerly precious stones were also occasionally met with in the swamps about Newera Ellia. This statement is disbelieved by many, although excavations are still to be seen that were made by the gem-seekers; and we, who know the inert disposition of the Asiatics, can hardly imagine they would have exerted themselves, had they not anticipated and found profit arise from their toil. Dr. Davy alludes to these jewel-hunters, for he writes, in 1819, "There is good reason to believe that the individuals engaged in this pursuit, who are not very numerous, and chiefly Moormen, would be better employed in cultivating the ground that they ransack." Carriage-roads and paths have been constructed around and through the plain, which branch off into the surrounding valleys and wind round the mountain's base; and a foot-way has been constructed that leads to the cloud-capped crest of Pedro-talla-Galla.

The ascent of the mountain is remarkably steep and fatiguing; nevertheless, we have known ladies attempt and accomplish this hazardous journey, and have been well rewarded for their exertion by the sublime scenery that surrounds "Mat wove rock," the altitude of which, as we have previously remarked, is eight thousand three hundred feet above the sea. The richest and most luxuriant parts of Ceylon, namely, Upper and Lower Ouva, are seen in the distance, and in the background towers Samenella, or Adam's Peak, clothed in perpetual verdure; whilst the projecting mass of the nearer mountains are distinctly visible, whose bold sides are clad with impervious forest and dense underwood.

The highest table-land in the island is situated some few miles from Newera Ellia, and is called the Horton Plains, as it was discovered during the time Sir Wilmot Horton governed Ceylon. This district is celebrated for the rich botanical specimens that it affords, the most curious of which is the pitcher plant, (Nepenthes distillatoria,) that thrives and grows in great luxuriance, as the extraordinary blossom, or vessel from which the plant derives its name, is frequently ten or eleven inches long, and the graceful effect of these beautiful productions, as the breeze plays among them, is indescribable.

In this neighbourhood a plant flourishes that is called by the natives nelu, or honey-plant, as the flowers emit a powerful effluvia resembling new honey. This is a jointed plant that flowers but once in eight years, and, as the blossoms decay, large numbers of bees appear to be attracted by the peculiar effluvia; and so delighted are the insects, that clusters of them will hang suspended from the branches for hours. Around the nelu-plant a leafless parasite often entwines, whose beautiful blossoms are bell-shaped, having amber hearts and scarlet edges; and as these appear to be united with the nelu at the root, the natives declare that this plant bears two kinds of flowers, which are totally distinct in form and colour.

CHAPTER VII.

Geological character of the island—Minerals—Salt lakes —Revenue arising from them—Tanks—Agriculture—Native plough—Mystic rite when the paddy is trodden out —Cultivation—Lemon grass—Value and uses of cocoanut trees—Cinnamon—Coffee—Sugar—Cotton—Tobacco —Areka nuts—Ambuprasudana, or water nut—Jack and bread-fruit trees—Indigo—Mulberry trees—Talapat palm —Mee tree—Ebony tree—Calamander tree—Red sandal and satin-wood trees—The kabook tree—Variety of the vegetable world—The bo, or sacred tree—Capabilities of cultivation and extraordinary fertility of the soil—Expense of housekeeping—Prices of provisions at Galle and Colombo—Meat—Poultry—Fish and fisheries—Fruit—Vegetables — Servants' wages — House-rent — Same at Kandy and Newera Ellia.

The simile of a pearl, to which Lanka is likened, is most peculiarly appropriate, not only in reference to the form of the island, but from the natural beauty of its scenery, the productiveness of its soil, and the richness of its mineral kingdom. We have previously referred to the beauty of the scenery, which we have witnessed with such deepfelt gratification, and we purpose devoting this chapter to the mineral construction, produce, revenue, and capabilities of Ceylon.

The geological character of the country is distinguishable for uniformity; primitive rock, with little exception, constituting the whole island. The exceptions consist of recent formations, and are only to be found in the neighbourhood of Jaffnapatam, and at a few places along the shore. The varieties of primitive rock are innumerable, but the species are ill defined and few. Granite is the most dominant species, whilst domolite, quartz, and hornblend, are less frequently to be met with. Gneiss and granite exist in countless varieties, and offer considerable difficulty to the mineralogist, who attempts to name them. Fine-grained grey coloured granite is occasionally to be met with, and the best we have seen was at Point de Galle, but graphic granite is still less common. We have seen, however, very beautiful specimens from the sea shore in the vicinity of Trincomalee, in which the quartz is of a grey or blackish-coloured rock crystal, and the felspar of a vivid fleshy hue.

Gneiss and sienite are found in the Kandian provinces; the former is very abundant and beautiful, and is composed of quartz and white felspar, with black mica and innumerable garnets of a pale colour. Hornblend, dolomite, and quartz are rarely to be seen in massive forms. Hornblend and greenstone are plentiful, forming portions of hills in the Kandian provinces, but it is not believed that they constitute the whole formation of any hill, or mountain. Dolomite is found in as large varieties as granite, generally crystaline and of a pure white colour, and very frequently it is formed of rhombs, which a blow of a hammer separates with facility. It is met with imbedded, and in veins, and in this form it abounds in Kandy; while small hills are composed of it in other parts of the island. In ancient days, dolomite was exclusively appropriated for the use of the king. Quartz is very abundant, and a very remarkable hill is completely formed of this rock in the neighbourhood of Trincomalee; on the side towards the sea the hill is laid bare, and presents to the spectator the appearance of a mass of ruinous buildings, and possibly owing to this, the name of Chapel Point was given to one end of this hill.

In the north of the island, at Jaffnapatam, which is at once the most populous and productive portion of Ceylon, we find two instances of recent formation, namely sandstone and limestone. Sandstone however cannot be said to be confined to this district, as it is found in a variety of places, extending round the coast, in general between high and low water-mark, where it is seen in horizontal stratified beds. In some instances, the sandstone is very dark coloured, approaching to black, and in others it is of a greyish yellow colour.

Limestone however has been considered, and is believed, to be confined to the north; it is very compact, of a fine grain, containing innumerable shells, of a pale brown or grey colour, and its fracture is conchoidal.

Iron and manganese are the only metallic ores of any consequence which have been discovered in Ceylon: the former is plentiful, and may be found all over the island, either as magnetic iron, bog iron, red hematite, iron pyrites, specular iron, or blue phosphate of iron. But we do not know of any vein, or large bed, of iron ore having as yet been discovered in Ceylon. Black oxide of manganese occurs scattered and imbedded in gigantic rocks in small quantities, but at so great a distance inland, that the carriage would be too expensive to admit of a profitable export trade. It is very remarkable, that no other metals have as yet been discovered, in a country, where the nature of the rock would indicate their existence. However, although some authors have asserted, that gold and mercury are found native in Ceylon, such we believe to be most incorrect, and we have never heard, that either lead, copper, or tin, has as yet been discovered.

Lanka-diva abounds in every variety of the quartz family; hyalite, chalcedony, iron flint, and rock-crystal, which latter is found crystallized and massive, in great quantities, and of a variety of colours. This is made use of by the Cingalese, who form lenses for spectacles from it, and employ it for statuary and ornamental purposes. Rose quartz, phrase, amethyst, and cat's eye, are also abundant. The Ceylon cat's eye is the most valuable in existence, and is much more prized there, than in Europe.

Topaz and schorl are also found in Ceylon; the former is commonly of a yellowish, or bluish-white colour, but perfect crystals of it are very rarely to be met with. Common schorl occurs very plentifully in granitic rocks, and in some places, it is mixed with felspar and quartz; tourmalin is occasionally to be met with, but of a very inferior description, and these are either of red, green, or honey colour.

In the granitic rock, garnet, cinnamon-stone and pyrope abound, and the common garnet is found diffused in gneiss through the whole island, the crystals however are diminutive and ill-defined. The precious garnet occurs in hornblend rock in the neighbourhood of Trincomalee, but of an inferior description. Cinnamon-stone has heretofore been exclusively found in Ceylon, where it is very abundant, although confined to particular districts, and is principally met with in Matura. It is found in very large masses of many pounds in weight, and small pieces of irregular form in the granitic alluvial. The zircon, called by the Cingalese "Matura diamond," which is found in the island, is considered to be the best in the world; besides zircon and hyacinth, there is another species in Ceylon, which is opaque, uncrystallized, and massive. Zircon is found both of yellow, green, red, and light grey colours, which the native merchants dispose of respectively for topaz, tourmalin, rubies, and diamonds.

Ceylon has for a considerable period been renowned for its rubies, of which there are four species, namely sapphire, spinell, chrysoberyl, and corundum, which are found in granitic rock. The principal varieties of sapphire, such as red, purple, yellow, blue, white, and star stone, are met with, sometimes of large size, and in perfection at Matura, Saffragam, and other places. The purple, or oriental amethyst, is rare, and the green still more so. Spinell is very rare, and is occasionally met with in the clay-iron ore in the Kandian provinces, where gneiss is abundant. Chrysoberyl is peculiarly rare, and is said generally to come from Saffragam. Corundum is very plentiful at a place called Battagammana, where it is found on the banks of a small river, called Agiri Kandura; it is of a brownish colour, and is in the form of large six-sided prisms.

In the family of felspar, Ceylon produces tablespar, Labrador stone, adularia, glassy felspar, compact felspar, and common felspar. The Labrador stone is found at Trincomalee, and adularia is plentiful in Kandy. Common hornblend is abundant, and glassy tremolite and pitch-stone occur in the neighbourhood of Trincomalee.

Mica, forming a component part of granite and gneiss, is very plentiful, and frequently is found enclosed in these rocks, where it occurs in very extensive flakes, which the Cingalese employ for ornamental purposes. Green earth is rather uncommon; but is found in Lower Ouva of a green and pea-green colour. At Galle and Trincomalee common chlorite is found scattered through quartz. Talc, dolomite, carbonate of magnesia, and native carbonate of magnesia, are occasionally discovered. Sulphur and graphite also occur, the former rarely, but the latter is abundant in Saffragam.

Nitrate of lime and nitre are very common, and the nitre caves appear to be formed of carbonate of lime and felspar.

Salt lakes exist to a large extent in the district called Megam-pattoo, on the sea shore, and which in all probability are supplied from the sea, as the saline contents of both prove to be of a similar nature. The salt monopoly produces the government a yearly revenue of £42,000, and, were this portion of government property superintended and conducted upon scientific principles, there can be little doubt that the revenue would be twice, if not three times the amount. It appears to us rather extraordinary, that the attention of the home and colonial government has not been directed to such a legitimate source of revenue, in preference to the tax upon dogs, and such like, which has created so much discontent amongst the followers of Buddha.

All the soils of the island appear to have originated from decomposed granite rock, gneiss, or clay-iron stone, and in the majority of cases quartz is the largest, and frequently nearly the sole ingredient. It is very remarkable that the natural soils of Lanka-diva do not contain more than between one and three per cent. of vegetable substance, which may be attributed to the rapid decomposition, occasioned by a high degree of temperature, and heavy falls of rain.

The most abundant crops are produced in the dark brown loam, which is formed from decomposed granite and gneiss, or in reddish loam, which is formed from Kabook stone, or clay-iron stone. The soils, which have been found to produce inferior crops, are those in which a large proportion of quartz is contained. The soil derived from clay-iron stone is of a reddish brown colour, and has the property of retaining water for a very long time, to which may be attributed its productive quality. To the practical and scientific agriculturists, Lanka-diva affords abundant opportunity for experiment and investigation, where the soil is in a state of nature, and unimproved by the admixture of any description of manure.

Ceylon possesses one great advantage over many other countries, namely, a very abundant supply both of spring and river water, which, in most instances, is of a pure description. The ancient inhabitants of the island seem to have been fully cognisant of the advantages of irrigation, and they availed themselves of the best means to secure a constant supply of water for the purpose. Tanks and lakes were constructed by them, which irrigated the whole island, "and were hardly surpassed by the kindred wonders of Egypt," and the ruins of these stupendous works indicate a degree of prosperity, civilization, and population, which can scarcely be credited by those who visit the country at the present day.

It is much to be regretted that a British Colonial Government, which has now been established for upwards of half a century in Ceylon, should not have learned a lesson from these gigantic remains, and restored them to the useful purposes for which they had originally been constructed. Had such a course been adopted, capital and labour would have been expended to some purpose, occupation and employment would have been given to a population, who are naturally indolent, the country would have produced more abundant crops, and the land would have been rendered doubly valuable.

This important question has been under the consideration of various colonial governments, commencing with Sir Thomas Maitland, in the year 1806, who proposed the restoration of the tanks, and the Colonial Engineer of that period, Captain Schneider, made his report upon the subject, wherein he estimated the expense of restoring the Giant's Tank, Cattoekare, at twenty-five thousand pounds, and considered that it would occupy three years. Tradition attributes the construction of this national work to the giants, which is by no means unreasonable, as the people in those days must have been giants at all events in energy, when compared with the present race.

The tank is situated in a large tract of low land near Mantotte in the northern province, and covers a space of twenty thousand parrahs of sowing land, a parrah being equal to about an English bushel and a third; it is bounded from north-west to south by an earthen dyke, to confine the water in the rainy season; and, when necessary, to irrigate the paddy-fields, which are now broken, and in several places scarcely traceable.

On the south side, the river, during heavy rains, carries the water from the high lands to the sea, and at some seasons rises nine feet above its banks, notwithstanding the bed of the river is twelve feet in depth; about nine miles from the south end of the dam of Cattockare, there is another, six hundred feet long, from forty to sixty broad, and from eight to twelve in height, built of large hewn stones, some measuring seven and eight feet in length, from three to four in breadth, and from two and a half to three in thickness, firmly cemented together, which must have been constructed at enormous labour. Near to this dam there is a canal to lead the river-water to the tank, but it has now the appearance of not having been completed, and is broken at several places. The height of the dam above the level of the sea varies considerably, at some places it is thirty-six feet, while at others it is sixty-seven.

The natives consider that the water of the rivulets running into Cattockare, independently of the river, would be sufficient to supply the tank; if this be the case it would cost a much smaller sum than Captain Schneider's estimate, and would consequently take a much shorter time to accomplish. Villages have been formed *within the tank*, whose inhabitants have constructed smaller tanks for the irrigation of paddy-fields, which are also cultivated within the same limits. A large tract of country in the vicinity of the Giant's Tank, is now unproductive, which might be converted into paddy-fields if the people had the means of artificial irrigation; and it has been calculated that if the tank were repaired, it would be sufficient to irrigate land, capable of producing annually one hundred and fifty thousand bags of rice. This one instance, therefore, we consider sufficient for our purpose, without reference to the other tanks and lakes of Ceylon, as ex uno disces omnia.

After Sir Thomas Maitland, Sir Robert Brownrigg supported this measure, who was followed in the same views by Sir Robert Horton, and Mr. Stewart M'Kenzie, all of whom concurred in the opinion that the undertaking should be made a government one; still no scheme was arranged, the tanks continue unrepaired, and the whole question lay dormant until Sir Emerson Tennent, the present Colonial Secretary resuscitated it from the colonial archives, and it is to be hoped that the same energy which has restored it to light, will ere long devise a scheme whereby the tanks and lakes may be gradually restored to their original purposes of irrigation, an undertaking which according to the report of the Committee of

Finance and Commerce "is so certain to repay the revenue the whole, and more than the whole of the expenditure incurred."

As the inhabitants are now compelled, either to contribute labour or money towards the construction or repairing of roads, this labour, or subsidy, may be very fairly employed in the equally, if not more beneficial work of repairing these ancient fountains of wealth, whereby the colony would become not only self-supporting, but would export rice equal in amount to the quantity for which she now exports specie.

Agriculture has been conducted in Ceylon by the natives on the simplest principles, the cultivation pursued by them being of two descriptions, namely, the dry, and wet. The chenas, or grounds which are overgrown with underwood, are cultivated in the dry manner, which is commenced by cutting down the jungle, by fencing in that portion which is intended for cultivation, and by consuming the timber which has not been employed for the latter purpose; the ground is immediately after turned up and sown. Great care is subsequently required to protect the crops from the wild animals which abound in Ceylon, and accordingly the natives are obliged to keep strict watch during the night.

Those crops which are chiefly grown in dry ground consist of a species of rice, called corrican, and Indian corn; these are occasionally weeded, and no further trouble is taken by the agriculturist until the time of harvest, when the crop is either reaped, or the heads of the corn are cut off, in case the straw is not preserved. The chenas do not grow crops the second year, first owing to the underwood, which soon springs up into a plentiful crop, never having been properly extirpated, and secondly, owing to the want of manure, which is never employed. This dry cultivation, however, is only adopted by the poorest classes, and is very inconsiderable in comparison with the wet, which is entirely used for the growth of paddy. This last description of cultivation requires an abundant supply of water, and is followed by the natives in every part of the island and in every locality, where sufficient water can be commanded for the successive stages of the paddy.

The fields devoted to the cultivation of paddy are surrounded by embankments; each field is flooded with water between two and three inches in depth, and, when sufficiently saturated, is ploughed while under water; this process is again repeated, or the ground is trodden by buffaloes until the whole is worked into mud. The mud thus formed is made perfectly level, the water drawn off, and the paddy-seed, which has already germinated, owing to its having been steeped in water, is thrown over the muddy surface. Immediately after the seed has struck root, the apertures in the embankments, by means of which the water was drawn off, are closed up and the field is re-flooded.

The weeds are carefully eradicated from the paddy when it has attained about three inches in height, and those parts of the field which appear too thin, are supplied from others where the paddy has sprung up too thickly. The field is kept under water until the paddy is nearly ripe, when it is again drained, and when ripe is reaped, and immediately trodden upon the threshing-floor by buffaloes. During the whole period from sowing time until harvest, the farmer is obliged continually to watch the corn-field, day and night, to prevent the destruction of his crop by wild animals. Where a sufficient supply of water can be had, two and three crops are annually grown in the same field, but where the farmer can only get a supply in the rainy season he can only grow one crop. This circumstance alone is sufficient to prove the great advantages which would accrue to the colony, from the repairing of the ancient tanks and lakes.

From the want of water in the lowland districts, as we have said, only one crop can be grown, and the fields are generally of a large size; but, in the mountainous and higher districts, irrigation is more conveniently managed, there being a more abundant and easy supply of water; and here, as in China, cultivation is carried up the sides of hills in the form of terraces, and the paddy may often be seen in its various stages, in adjoining fields, from the newly sown to that which is being reaped, and trodden out by buffaloes, or oxen.

The plough which is used in Ceylon is of a most simple nature, the shear and single upright handle being made out of a curved piece of timber; the single handle is surmounted with a cross-tree, a pole is fastened into a mortice with a wedge, at the curve between the handle and shear, while a yoke is attached by coir ropes to the pole, which is fastened by coir cords to a pair of buffaloes or oxen; one man in general holds the plough, and guides the buffaloes, or oxen, with a goad, occasionally urging them with his voice.

On every occasion where the plough is not, or cannot be used, the mehmotte, or large hoe, of an unwieldy nature, is employed, which in their hands is made a most useful implement. Instead of a harrow after ploughing the ground, they employ an implement which they call anadatpoorooa, which is a board with a pole, to which oxen or buffaloes are yoked, and upon which the driver sits. A lighter implement is used with the hand, like a rake without teeth, for the purpose of preparing the mud for paddy seed. The jungle-hook, axe, and reaping hook, are all too similar to our own implements to need description.

The treading out of the paddy is performed upon a hard floor, prepared for the purpose by beating the clay; before the natives begin the work, however, a mystic rite and incantation are observed by the owner of the paddy, in the expectation of preserving the produce from the evil spirits. The ceremony is performed by describing three circles, one within the other, on the centre of the floor, with the ashes of wood, which the owner scatters from a large leaf; the circles are equally quartered by a cross, the four points of which are terminated by a character resembling a written letter *M;* within the inner circle, the owner lays some paddy straw, upon which he places a few pieces of quartz and a small piece of the kohomba tree, the whole of which he covers over with paddy-straw; he then walks round the cabalistic figure three times, and stops at one of the ends, salaams three times with upraised hands, and finally prostrates himself upon the earth, all the time repeating incantations. When this ceremony has been completed, the paddy is piled upon the concentric circles, and the buffaloes are immediately after urged to the task of treading the corn.

In the vegetable kingdom, sweet potatoes, yams, occus, brinjals, and other Eastern vegetables are cultivated, but the natives do not construct regular gardens for the purpose. In Newera Ellia English potatoes, cabbage, peas, and other European vegetables have been introduced, and they are grown there with great success, which the climate will not admit of in other parts of the island.

We must here introduce the most characteristic production of Lanka-diva, the Andropogon schœnanthus, or lemon-grass, which is a hard grass, growing from two to eight feet in height, emitting when crushed a powerful smell of lemon; very agreeable in the first instance, but after a time the effluvium is most oppressive and sickening; in taste it is an acid of a very refreshing character; this grass is the usual clothing of the Kandian hills, and when young is considered choice pasture for buffaloes. We have seen a very fine essential oil extracted from this grass, which would no doubt be most valuable to perfumers.

The cocoa-nut (Cocos nucifera) is very extensively cultivated in Ceylon; indeed nearly the whole island is encircled with this useful and productive tree, which may be justly designated the *summum bonum* of the native population. The cultivation of it is rapidly increasing, for it is found to be a most valuable and safe investment of property, as it requires a trivial outlay, and little further care than the planting, except protection from cattle during the first two years; thriving as it does most luxuriantly in sandy soil, and bearing fruit in the fifth year. The estimated value of the produce of a single tree is a rix dollar per annum. This tree frequently exceeds one hundred feet in height, and there is no part of it which is unproductive to the owner; from the flower he obtains toddy, from which the finest arrack in the world is distilled, and from which is also prepared a coarse-grained brown sugar, called by the natives jaggery, and an excellent description of vinegar.

The green fruit yields a delicious cooling beverage to the weary traveller, and a vegetable pulp, highly esteemed by the natives; the ripened fruit is also used as food, or oil is extracted from it, which is now manufactured into candles and soap, and the refuse, or oil cake, is used for feeding cattle; while the external husks, after long soaking, are beaten into coir, which is now well known in England, and is used for stuffing mattresses, &c., and from which cordage and matting are manufactured. The leaves, when interwoven, are called cajan, and make excellent thatch, and afford protection from the sun's rays, or, when burned, are converted into an alkali. The young leaves are used by the natives for a variety of useful and ornamental purposes, particularly the latter on joyous and festive occasions, when bamboo arches are decorated with them, and brooms and mats are made from the young pine.

A medicinal oil is extracted from the bark, which the native practitioners use as an efficacious remedy in cutaneous diseases; the root is also used for medicinal purposes, and its elastic fibres are woven into strainers for liquids, while the timber may be used in building, or converted into beautiful articles of furniture. But it would be endless to describe the various additional uses to which every portion of this valuable tree is convertible, which are said to be upwards of one hundred, and have formed the theme of many native poets. There are annually exported from the colony about eight thousand pounds' worth of cocoa-nuts, thirty thousand pounds' worth of cocoa-nut oil, seven thousand pounds' worth of arrack, and ten thousand pounds' worth of coir.

Cinnamon (Laurus cinnamonum) is a staple article of produce in Ceylon, but it is not necessary for us here to enter upon the appearance of the gardens, in which it is cultivated, or the mode of barking the twigs, as we have described both in a former chapter. A very accurate account is given of the shrub by Nicolo De Conte, not only of its appearance, but also of the manner in which the bark was prepared in his day. During the sway of native rulers, as well as that of the Dutch and Portuguese, cinnamon was a government monopoly, and was so continued after the establishment of British authority in the island, until the year 1833, when it was abolished, and many large cinnamon gardens, which had been previously cultivated by government, were disposed of to private individuals, and those that remained in the hands of the crown were farmed to the highest bidder.

The enormous sum of two shillings per pound was levied upon all exported cinnamon until the year 1842, when it was reduced one half. Still it was found incompatible with the existence of the export trade in this article to continue this reduced duty; as from careful investigation it was proved that cinnamon could not be cultivated, prepared for market, and delivered in London, paying a shilling per pound export duty, under two shillings and fourpence per pound; which was of course without allowing profit upon outlay, or interest of any description. Accordingly, in 1848, the whole tariff was considerably altered, the export duty upon cinnamon was again reduced to fourpence per pound, with a duty of threepence per pound on importation into the parent country; and the government confidently expect the trade in this spice, which has fallen off more than one half, will be revived.

But this hope seems to us to be fallacious, and we fear that this tardy legislation will not enable Ceylon to compete with the East India Company's possession on the coast of Malabar, or with the Dutch settlement in Java, where the shrub has rapidly increased in cultivation, since the prohibitive export duty of two shillings was imposed by Ceylon legislation on its own produce. We say this advisedly, particularly with regard to Java, as the cost of the grower there has been calculated at a considerably smaller sum than that of his competitor in Ceylon, and the former can import his cinnamon into this country paying sixpence duty, which gives him in duty alone, the advantage of one penny under the latter, therefore something more remains to be done by our legislators for the cinnamon proprietors of Ceylon. The amount of export duty received upon this article in 1844, was fifty three thousand one hundred and ninety-seven pounds; while, in 1846, it amounted to only twenty thousand and eighty-two pounds.

Coffee (Coffea arabica) we believe to be indigenous to the island, as we have questioned an erudite priest and noble upon the subject, and they both agreed in stating that a decoction from the berry had been used by the natives from time immemorial. Some authors state that coffee was introduced into Ceylon, from Java, by the Dutch, who procured seedlings from Mocha, in 1723, and that under the auspices of the Governor-General of Batavia, Zwaardenkroom, the first plantations were formed in Java.

When and wherefore coffee was introduced and cultivated in other settlements, it is not our purpose to investigate, as we treat solely of Ceylon and its productions; but we feel convinced the coffee shrub has been known in the island in a wild state for ages past. Coffee was first cultivated in 1820, and has become an object of great speculation amongst British residents, who have expended large sums of money in clearing, planting, and cultivating estates. Many individuals have been ruined by coffee plantations, some few have succeeded in improving their financial resources, who were sufficiently prudent or fortunate to purchase land at a fair valuation, and either had experience to guide them in the personal superintendence of their properties, or entrusted the management to those who were worthy of their confidence. The quality of the berry is considerably improved by cultivation; many like Ceylon coffee: for our own part, we candidly confess we prefer Mocha, and we have very rarely tasted coffee in Ceylon, which could bear comparison with it.

The expense of clearing jungle, and forming it into a coffee estate, have been calculated at eight pounds per acre. The first step in this clearance is both curious and imposing to witness; the plantations being formed on the mountain sides, the coolees are set to work on the forest trees at the base of the hill, whose trunks they notch half way through, thus labouring on their way up to the mountain's summit, upon attaining which the uppermost trees are completely felled, and these simultaneously falling on those beneath, carry them, with a terrific crash in their downward course. The falling mass, like the avalanche, increasing at each step in bulk and weight, acquires fresh impetus in its progress, overpowering all obstacles, and thus with the roar of thunder, thousands of noble forest trees are laid low in a few seconds. The prostrated timber is usually fired and reduced to ashes. The seedlings are generally planted out in the rainy season, and require constant care and attention to prevent them from being overgrown with weeds, and jungle grass.

The appearance of a coffee estate in flower is truly beautiful, the bushes being completely covered with a mass of silvery white blossoms, which are thrown out in strong and bold relief by the glossy, deep-green coloured leaves. Then in the advanced stage, when these blossoms are changed into ripened berries of a deep red colour, under whose weight the branches yield, the spectacle is extremely pleasing, and must be witnessed to be appreciated; the reader must take our word for it, that at these periods the sight is one of immense beauty, while the general appearance of the coffee estate is somewhat like an extensive plantation of evergreens, dotted here and there, with enormous forest trees, purposely left in clearing the jungle, for the protection of the young plantation.

The coffee exported in 1846 amounted to one hundred and seventy-three thousand eight hundred and ninety-two cwt., which was increased in 1847 to two hundred and forty-five thousand cwt.; and, during the year 1849, forty millions of pounds have passed over the roads to the coast.

We will not go through the mechanical preparation of the berry for the market, but glance at the difficulties that to a greater or lesser extent every planter must have to contend with. In the first place, it is impossible to ascertain from the soil if a plantation is certain to succeed or not, as we have known contiguous coffee estates, although the same attention has been bestowed and plan pursued upon both, produce totally different crops, the one having thriven, the bushes yielding an abundant harvest, whilst the other has been a total failure, from the rats having gnawed the roots of the plants, or the attacks of insects having entirely ruined the young shoots, or from some inexplicable cause. The coffee-plant also speedily exhausts the productive quality of the soil, and, unless manured, the earth loses the elements of fertility, finally becoming incapable of producing even a scanty crop.

Labour likewise is extremely difficult to be procured at times, as the planter depends in a great measure upon the labourers who arrive from the coast, and possibly they may have amassed a sufficient sum, and choose to return home either when the crop is ready for gathering, or when the berry is fit for peeling. Thus large quantities of coffee are annually spoiled. Many capitalists have suffered severely from this cause, and those especially whose superintendents maltreat the coolees, either by beating them, or by mulcting them of their scanty and hardly-earned wages. We feel convinced that a more certain supply of labour might be depended upon, were the unfortunate coolees treated with the consideration due to human beings—which we regret to say they too frequently are not.

It is many years since the cultivation of the sugar-cane was first commenced, but the plantation at Caltura failed, owing principally to want of experience on the part of the cultivator, in the selection of a congenial soil. The estate of Mr. Hudson, at Peradenia, however, having been more judiciously formed, led to a successful result, and was the cause of many planters following the indefatigable proprietor's spirited example. Several sugar plantations are now actively and successfully managed, producing an article inferior to none grown in the East, either in appearance or for use, and at no distant period, we may fairly conclude, that the sugar of Ceylon will be a most important article in her export trade.

Cotton-cultivation is very much neglected in the island, although there is every just ground to believe, that it is capable of producing as fine a quality as any which has ever been grown; indeed the importance of this branch of produce has not, as yet, arrested either the attention of the local authorities, or of the agriculturist. In this opinion we are fortified by an American planter in the East India Company's service, who thus reports, "I am of opinion, from what I saw of the climate, temperature, and soil, that Ceylon will produce cotton *equal in quality*, and when the comparatively *small amount of capital* required is considered, I doubt not it may even produce the article *cheaper than we can in America*, where a large sum must be laid out for labour, and where the expense of food and clothing is much greater than the cost of importing labour into Ceylon, independently of the risk of a mortality among the labourers after they had been purchased."

The advocates of slave emancipation should be amongst the first to encourage the growth of cotton in Ceylon, and produce an article which can fairly compete with the slave-grown cotton of America. A commencement has been made in the neighbourhood of Batticaloa, where American seed has been sown, and country cotton is grown by some in conjunction with maize, or Indian corn. The quantity of cotton however which has heretofore been grown is insufficient for the consumption of the island.

The tobacco-plant has been for a considerable period grown, and very extensively cultivated at Jaffna, and its quality is held in high estimation amongst the Malabars and Malays, so much so, that some years ago the Rajah of Travancore contracted for an annual supply of it. The quantity of tobacco now exported from the island amounts in value to some thirteen thousand pounds per annum.

The Areka, or Betel-nut tree (Areka-catechu) flourishes in great abundance through the island. It is a slight tall palm, with much smaller leaves than those of the cocoa-nut, and more feathered in their appearance: these are attached to the tree by a tough impervious skin, which is used by the natives to carry their provisions in.

The nuts hang in luxuriant branches, one tree producing several hundreds, which are used by Easterns with chunam, for the filthy purpose of chewing. A large export trade is annually carried on in this article, amounting to about the value of thirty thousand pounds, which is likely to be increased, since a dentifrice has lately become much esteemed in this country, which is prepared from the nut.

The ambuprasudana, or water-nut, is a most valuable provision of nature, for purifying muddy and unwholesome water; the natives use it for this purpose by rubbing it over the internal surface of their water chatties, which has the property of precipitating all impure and earthly particles, thus rendering the water pure and drinkable.

The jack-tree (Artocarpus integrifalia) grows to an enormous size, is a most beautiful object in nature, affords most agreeable shade, and produces an immense quantity of fruit both from its branches and trunk. The fruit are of a somewhat oval form, in size varying from half a foot to five or six in circumference; their external covering is rough and of a greenish hue, and their section of a whitish colour, containing a number of kernels, enveloped in a yellowish coating, which is of a most luscious flavour, but peculiarly disagreeable to the olfactory nerves. The kernels are the size of a pigeon's egg, and when cooked make good food, and excellent curry. The timber is of a yellow colour, but when polished with bees-wax it approaches to a light-coloured mahogany, and all ordinary furniture is manufactured of it.

The bread-fruit-tree (Artrocarpus incisa) is also one of large size, and abundantly productive. Of this, there are two descriptions, the one bearing fruit with seed and which is much larger than the other, which has no seed. The greater and lesser sort are both used in culinary preparations, as well in the green, as in the maturèd state, the natives making a curry of one, whilst Europeans eat the fruit as a vegetable either boiled or fried. The native who has a bread-tree, cocoa-nut-tree, and jack-tree, has nearly all his wants provided for, and it is to this bountiful provision of nature, we may attribute the inactive disposition of the people.

Indigo was formerly exported from Ceylon, during Dutch rule; notwithstanding, however, that the plant is indigenous to the soil, which with the climate offers every inducement for its cultivation, and that the greatest facilities for manufacture are at hand, still no step has yet been taken since Great Britain has had the island, to unfold this source of wealth. A proposition, we believe, was made to government in the year 1817 to embark capital in this cultivation, upon condition that the speculators should be assisted with a grant of land, which, in the event of the abandonment of the design, should revert to government. This does not appear to have been entertained, and it remains for some other enterprising individual to set the example in indigo, as Mr. Hudson did in the culture of the sugar-cane.

The mulberry tree flourishes in the island, and might easily be propagated, for the nourishment of the silk-worm; had the natives a moiety of the industry and perseverance of the Chinese, we see no reason why silk of as fine a quality as any exported from the Celestial Empire, should not be produced in Lanka-diva.

The most glorious vegetable production of the island is the Tala, or Talapat palm, (Carypha umbraculifera,) which varies in height from seventy to one hundred feet. The circumference of the trunk near the ground is about nine feet, and gradually tapers to the summit, where the gigantic leaves droop and spread out in a parachute form; it is a singular fact, that wherever a leaf has sprung from the trunk of the tree, an indelible mark is left after the leaf has fallen. The natives affirm, that the tree never lives more than one hundred years, and that it commences to decay as soon as the blossom has arrived at perfection. The flower is large and of a most exquisite yellow; whilst in blossom this is enclosed in a sheath, which bursts with a loud explosion as soon as the flower has arrived at maturity. The flowers remain in full bloom for nearly three months, when they gradually disappear, and the fruit, which is about the size of a plum, ripens.

The leaves of this magnificent tree frequently measure, from the extremity of the stalk to the tip of the leaf, twenty-five feet, and the width varies from twelve to seventeen feet—these imperishable leaves, when dried, are applied by the natives to various purposes; from the form of the leaf without preparation, it can be folded like a fan, and this is borne before the chiefs and nobles by their retainers. The leaves are also cut into strips and used for *olas* and books, a thatch is also made from them, which serves as a roofing to dwellings. In the trunk is found a species of pith, which when dried yields a fine meal; the natives make this into cakes, and the flour is most delicate and delicious.

We regret that we are unable to give the reader the name of a tree which grows in Ceylon, whose leaves, owing to their roughness, are constantly used by native carpenters instead of sand-paper; they have also the property of extracting stains from furniture, and are known by the name of "carpenter's leaves."

The mee-tree grows to an enormous size, and the branches afford a welcome shelter to the weary traveller from the noonday sun; nevertheless, the effluvia of its blossom, which is a minute white flower, is most unpleasant, and some affirm especially unwholesome. So luxuriant are these buds, that when they fall to the ground the earth appears to be covered with snow for some distance around the parent tree, and the natives say, that when the periodical heavy rains wash down an accumulation of these pestiferous blossoms into the tanks, and they are allowed to remain floating on the waters, the exhalation invariably produces disease. Notwithstanding this conviction, nothing will induce them to fell a mee-tree, because the fruit produces pungent oil, which they apply to many purposes.

The magnificent ebony-tree (Dyospiras ebonum) is most peculiar in its aspect, as the foliage is almost black, the bark of the trunk nearly white, and the branches sprout forth about thirty feet from the root, giving the tree a mournfully grand appearance. The wood is usually jet black, invariably extremely hard and weighty, and is much sought after both by Europeans and the wealthy natives, for articles of decorative furniture, and high prices are readily obtained for fine specimens, that are elaborately carved. The oldest and best trees, are generally found in the forests of the eastern province. The Calamander tree, (Dyospyrus hirsuta,) or variegated ebony, is most majestic, and is also much prized. At one time, this tree was exceedingly common in the forests; but has become scarce, as it is more esteemed for articles of furniture than ebony, from the beauty of the wood, which is striped or mottled with black and shades of brown, is close grained, will bear a high polish, and is worth a large sum. The red sandal and satinwood trees are natives of Ceylon, but these are now as rarely met with as the Calamander tree, and for the same reason.

The Kabook tree, a species of terminalia, attains a large size, the timber being exceedingly durable, and of a brick-dust colour; the peculiarity of this tree consists in its flourishing, alike on the banks of streams, in level districts, and also at an elevation of two thousand three hundred feet, and what is more remarkable still is, that the natives believe, (and with apparent justice,) that wherever this tree is found, water will be met with near its lowermost roots, and those who have caused the experiment to be made, invariably declare that by digging close to the tree water has been always discovered.

Were we to notice a tithe of the trees and vegetable productions worthy of remark, that are met with in this fertile spot, volumes would not suffice; therefore we shall but give a description of one more, and that is the tree sacred to Buddha, the bo-tree, or Ficus religiosa. Under this magnificent tree, Buddhists believe the god to have slumbered, when he became the incarnation of wisdom. The foliage is peculiarly luxuriant and beautiful, the broad leaves being heart-shaped; and so sacred were these considered, that their semblance was only permitted to be carved or painted upon the palace, or articles of furniture intended for the sole use of the reigning monarch. The blossoms are most lovely and fragrant, being bell-shaped, the colour a milk-white, save in the centre of the flower, which is delicately tinged with gold. These trees are carefully guarded from injury, by terraces of earth and stone, and some from their huge cavernous trunks appear to have braved the sun's beams, and the lightning's flashes for centuries.

In the early morning, the perfume of the orange, citron, wild jessamine, and other flowering shrubs, is delicious beyond conception, and exquisite as these floral beauties are at all times, they are rendered still more so by the fragile parasites, and pepper vines, that entwine around their trunks when met with in a wild state. It is impossible to enumerate the luscious fruits of the island, as every one, save the mangostein, that grows in the torrid zone, is produced by the prolific soil of Lanka-diva; from the stately tamarind, Shaddock papaw mangol, and banana trees down to the small delicate chillie, all alike spring spontaneously from the teeming earth.

What especially demands the attention of the European agriculturist is, that in the various parts of the island, the peculiar productions of Europe and Asia will alike thrive, if care is bestowed upon the cultivation of the former; so that while the fragrant nutmeg and clove-tree, with all tropical productions, attain the utmost luxuriance on one portion of the soil; wheat, barley, potatoes, turnips, and other European vegetables, will yield remunerative crops, and flourish upon another. And we believe that no portion of the globe possesses the same capabilities for cultivation as are to be found on this island, whose internal resources are comparatively undeveloped; thus offering a fair opening for the enterprising capitalist and industrious emigrant.

The expense of housekeeping in Ceylon is considerable; for, although the prices of provisions are generally moderate, the multiplicity of articles required, and used, by the servants, combined with the style of living, render the domestic expenditure, frequently, very great. Moreover, it is impossible to keep such a check as to avoid peculation, as the appoo, or head-servant, invariably goes to the bazaar to purchase all articles of daily consumption; thus it is absolutely impracticable for the head of the household to ascertain the correct price of food, as it not only depends upon the supply and demand, but upon the honesty or cupidity of the appoo.

This only applies to native produce, as all European productions, comestibles, and every other import are paid for monthly—and we can conscientiously aver that either the importers, exporters, or consignees, ought to make rapid and immense fortunes, as the price demanded is often trebled, and frequently quadrupled, when there is a scarcity. Thus, good butter will frequently fetch two shillings and half-a-crown the pound, cheese the same, ham, bacon, dried and pickled tongues, preserves and pickles, being sold in the same ratio.

The prices of all viands are now nearly the same at Galle and Colombo, although before the steamers touched at the former place, we have been informed that edibles were materially cheaper at the former place. Mutton, when it can be purchased in the market, which is but seldom, fetches an enormous price, being sold at the rate of a rupee or two shillings per pound,* but a good succulent haunch or joint of mutton cannot be procured in the bazaar at any price. Kids are sold, and used as a substitute for sheep, and, when the creatures are young, and have been well fed, a quarter of one roasted is not a despicable dish; the price per pound varies from sixpence to sevenpence halfpenny.

* From this arises Mutton Clubs, a certain number of gentlemen, generally four, forming the club, purchase sheep, feed them, and divide the expense amongst them. But even then the price is enormous.

Beef is invariably tough, and lean, the best parts being sold at sixpence per pound: pork is the best animal food that can be procured in Ceylon, and the value of good meat is the same as beef. Poultry is plentiful and moderate in price, turkeys and geese selling from four shillings and sixpence to seven shillings and sixpence each; ducks from three to four shillings and sixpence the couple; fowls from ninepence to one shilling and sixpence each; but we must observe that although the price is low, the birds are never fatted, and are generally sold before they are full grown, therefore the expense of feeding them materially adds to their original cost.

The fishes of Ceylon are numerous, and many of their varieties are unsurpassed, if not unequalled in delicacy of flavour and lusciousness, and the prices of the best descriptions are tolerably reasonable. The fish, *par excellence*, of the island is the seir-fish, which is a species of scomber, having much of the appearance and flavour of the finest salmon, which however it infinitely excels; the flesh is of a delicate pink, but becomes colourless when subjected to any culinary process. This delicious fish is caught with hook and line, is solely found in salt water, and we have seen some whose weight exceeded twenty pounds.

The bull's-eye pomfret is likewise much esteemed, and the beauty of this fish is indescribable, as the head, body, and fins are of a brilliant red, the scales being tinged with gold. Soles, whiting, mackarel, and mullet are also plentiful, attain a large size, are cheap and good, and the method adopted by the natives to catch the last mentioned fish is somewhat singular.

The fishermen push off in their canoes after sunset; and, when they have reached a favourable spot, one man waves a torch over the water, and the fish apparently fascinated, speedily rise to the surface, and remain floating near the torch; another man immediately darts a pronged iron instrument, (not unlike a large horse-comb,) attached to a wooden handle, into the creature's back, and hauls it into the canoe.

It would be impossible to enumerate the members of the piscatory tribe that supply the table of Europeans, or the means adopted by the natives to ensnare them. Suffice it to say that for salt-water fish, the hook, pronged instrument, and nets are used, whilst for a particular fresh-water fish, kraals are constructed of so intricate a nature, that it is impossible for the fish to escape; in some places, conical baskets made from thin slips of bamboo in which an aperture is left for the hand are used: this machine is cautiously lowered over the fish, and the prize is seized hold of by the fisherman.

So primitive are some of the means employed to catch the smaller fry, by and for the poor, that we have seen the men attach a grain of boiled rice to a piece of cocoa-nut fibre, hang it over the side of their canoe, and patiently catch, and detach fish after fish, for hours; the market value of which would not exceed three farthings. Crabs, craw-fish, and prawns, are to be procured along the entire coast, but oysters fit for food are only to be met with in the river that flows through Bentotte, and these the divers detach from the rocks with mallets. The most remarkable circumstance connected with the latter edibles is, that although the stream flows for a considerable distance beyond, and has not its source at Bentotte, it is only at that place the oysters are found.

We cannot avoid expressing our conviction, that the importance of the fisheries in Ceylon, both in reference to the consumption of the island, and as a great source of export trade, has not attracted the attention it deserves. There is a considerable demand for salt fish in the interior, and the Roman Catholic population alone amounts to nearly two hundred thousand, who generally observe most strictly the fasts of the church. To meet this demand, there is an import trade of salt or preserved fish, amounting annually to the value of some £15,000. The waters which wash the coast on every side swarm with the finest fish of every description, and a number of boats are employed in fishing, particularly in the vicinity of Colombo, during the prevalence of the south-west monsoon.

A very small quantity of fish, however, is preserved, and the mode of salting adopted by the Cingalese is peculiarly defective. In a tropical climate decomposition commences rapidly after death ; it is obvious, therefore, that a fish should be salted immediately it is caught, whereas the natives rarely salt any except that portion which they have not been fortunate enough to dispose of, and the curing never takes place until after exposure to the powerful rays of the sun on a sandy beach. Sand and salt are thus mixed together, and the result can easily be imagined; namely, that such fish cannot be eaten by Europeans, who, if they could succeed in eradicating the sand, cannot cure the incipient putridity.

The most judicious method for salting that we have heard of is that which has been suggested by Mr. Bennett, namely, to adopt the practice observed by the nutmeg-curers; and construct, beneath a thatched roof, tiers of open platforms, composed of split bamboo, at distances and of dimensions to correspond with the size of the fish. Thus, any quantity might be cured by smoke, proceeding from the ignition of damped paddy-straw, placed beneath the lowest tier, which would thus ascend to the roof, passing through each tier in its progress. It has also been suggested that, as the boats employed in fishing have little room enough to carry their cargo, a dhoney * should accompany a certain number of them laden with salt, whose crew could be occupied in salting the fish, as rapidly as possible after it had been caught. It must be observed that the extravagant price of salt has acted most prejudicially upon the improvement of the fisheries. The attention of the government appears to have been directed to the importance of this branch of industry during the Government of Sir Edward Barnes, when an ordinance was passed imposing a duty of fifteen per cent upon the prime cost of all salt fish imported into the island, and permitting the exportation, free of duty, of all fish cured in the colony.

The vegetable productions indigenous to the

* Or native sailing-vessel.

tropics are both abundant and cheap; and, although the mangols do not equal those of Bengal, nor the pine-apples those of Singapore, nevertheless the delicious fruits of Ceylon are, as a body, unrivalled for their exquisite flavour and variety. Potatoes are at times exceedingly scarce and dear, and we have occasionally paid at Galle sevenpence half-penny per pound for them, and never less at Colombo than threepence. Some years ago, the island was dependant upon Madras and Bombay for the supply of these vegetables, but in 1823 the first potatoes were planted in Kandy, and good crops are now annually procured, but still this article of food remains dear and comparatively scarce, as there has arisen a greater demand from the influx of Europeans.

Servant's wages are not high, but the sum paid monthly in most establishments is large in proportion to the income; as the number of domestics, although not to equal the retinue kept up in India, far exceeds a moderate household in Europe. The appoo, or head servant, receives from fifteen to twenty-five rix dollars * per month, a good cook the same, the table-servant from ten to twelve, the horsekeepers, and there is one to each horse, receive the like sum, the coolee,

* A rix dollar is one shilling and sixpence.

or servant that sweeps the rooms, and performs menial offices, six or seven, the cook's boy five, the grass-cutter for each horse three rix dollars, and the ayah, or native female attendant where there is a lady or children, is remunerated according to her knowledge of needlework, but never receives less than the table-servant; and, if she understands her business thoroughly as ladies'-maid, or nurse, frequently as much as the appoo.

To these must be added the water-carrier, who is paid according to the number of baths and quantity of water required daily. It is not the custom to provide the domestics with food; nevertheless few edibles ever make their appearance a second time upon the table; for, according to your domestics' account, the rats, dogs, or heat, purloin and spoil everything that disappears. Unmarried men, if economically disposed, (but few are in the East,) can make two or three servants suffice; but, although we have known many families have a larger number of domestics than we have enumerated, we cannot recall to our recollection any that had a smaller establishment; and the whole household of men will not perform their duties as efficiently as two women servants would in England.

House-hire is comparatively low, as there are no

taxes, but in particularly healthy or fashionable quarters, the rent demanded for a good dwelling, will be found little lower than that which is paid in England, and in some instances much higher.

The price of provisions at Kandy is one-third more than at Galle, or Colombo, and at times edibles of every description are exceedingly scarce, and difficult to be procured upon any terms. Servants' wages and house-rent are also exceedingly high. Those who reside or sojourn at Newera Ellia, are compelled to pay exorbitantly for every article of food, and at times a residence, or lodging, is not to be procured for money; and, when the whole or portion of a domicile is to be obtained, the sum paid for temporary accommodation, equals if not exceeds, the rent extorted by the lodging-house keepers of a fashionable watering place during the height of the season.

We have been informed by the descendants of the Dutch and Portuguese that wages, house-rent, the price of provisions and furniture, in every part of the island, have become more than trebled since the English obtained possession of Ceylon; and they have pathetically bemoaned to us that each year the value of everything increased: strangely forgetting that, although individuals might have to pay a higher sum than they formerly did, the diffusion of specie must benefit the majority of the inhabitants, as lands become cultivated, and the market-price of the produce materially enhanced by augmented consumption.

CHAPTER VIII.

Natural history—Elephants of Ceylon spoken of by Pliny and Dionysius—Sagacity—Trained to be executioners by the kings of Kandy—Ancient mode of valuing elephants —Anecdote—Catching elephants with the atmaddoo—Ornaments made from the coarse hairs of the tail—King of Kandy's personal inspection of captured elephants—Tyranny—Knox's account—Rogue-elephant—Elephant-shooting—Major Rogers—His miraculous escape—Singular death—Elephants ascend the mountains—Tusks found buried in the jungles—Elks—Deer—Walmeenya—Beauty and docility—Wild buffaloes—Bears—Cheetahs, or leopards—Kandian mode of snaring them—Distinctive peculiarity—Wild hogs—Animals found in jungle—Rats —Shrew—Anecdote of a musk-rat—Ornithological specimens—Land-leeches—Ticks—Snakes—Anaconda—Cobra capello, or the sacred naga of the Cingalese—Warning—Hair-breadth escape—Tic polonga—Legend—Ichneumon attacking a cobra—Crocodiles—Hunting—Crocodile charmers—Native method of catching and destroying crocodiles—Fecundity—Number of eggs—Pugnacity of the young—Insect tribes—White ants—Destructive propensities—Their nests.

In this chapter we do not pretend to classify scientifically the mammalia, or ophidia, of Ceylon; we merely give sketches that we think interesting and amusing to those who desire general information.

From historical records we find that Lanka-diva has been celebrated for the tusks of its elephants from a remote period; and both Pliny and Dionysius dilate largely upon the superior quality of the ivory, which they represent as being whiter, and of a less porous nature, than the tusks of other animals of the same species.

In ancient times also, the monarchs of the peninsula eagerly sought for the Ceylon elephants, on account of their superior docility and courage; and it is believed that the greater number of elephants that were used in battle by Pyrrhus, as well as during the whole of the Punic wars, were obtained from Ceylon, by the Phœnicians, who shipped them to the Persian Gulf, or the ports of the Red Sea. Cingalese annals state, that in the palmy days of their island, the traffic in elephants and spices, formed their principal exports, as all the Eastern potentates, either when at war with their neighbours or for purposes of stately show, eagerly sought, and gave large sums for these ponderous but sagacious creatures.

Some authors have attempted to cast discredit upon the natural intelligence of the elephant, but from our personal observation we can conscientiously say, that we believe them to be the most sagacious of all quadrupeds, and most capable of receiving man's instruction. Although we make this statement, we do not mean to affirm that all elephants exhibit extreme intelligence ; neither do all men, nevertheless few would be sufficiently fool-hardy enough to declare, that the characteristic quality of manhood was stupidity, because some few are especially obtuse. That elephants possess the faculty of memory to an extraordinary extent, has been evinced in numberless instances, and that they also understand the meaning of language has been distinctly proved, and we will adduce the following in corroboration of our assertion.

During the native dynasty it was the practice to train elephants to put criminals to death by trampling upon them, the creatures being taught to prolong the agony of the wretched sufferers by crushing the limbs, avoiding the vital parts. With the last tyrant-king of Kandy this was a favourite mode of execution, and as one of the elephant-executioners was at the former capital, during our sojourn there, we were particularly anxious to test the creature's sagacity and memory. The animal was mottled, and of enormous size, and was quietly standing, with his keeper seated upon his neck; the noble who accompanied us desired the man to dismount, and stand on one side.

The chief then gave the word of command, ordering the creature to "slay the wretch!" The elephant raised his trunk, and twined it, as if around a human being, the creature then made motions as if he were depositing the man on the earth before him, then slowly raised his fore-foot, placing it alternately upon the spots where the limbs of the sufferer would have been. This he continued to do for some minutes, then, as if satisfied the bones must be crushed, the elephant raised his trunk high above his head and stood motionless; the chief then ordered him "to complete his work," and the creature immediately placed one foot, as if upon the man's abdomen, and the other upon his head, apparently using his entire strength to crush, and terminate the wretch's misery.

When we bear in mind the monarch was dethroned in 1815, and the animal had never since that period been called upon to perform the barbarous task to which he had been trained, few we believe will be disposed to cavil, concerning the extraordinary intelligence and memory evinced by the creature. Space will not permit us to bring forward other instances, to demonstrate our assertion, but volumes might be written in proof of the elephant's sagacity and memory, being second only to those of man.

Cuvier, no mean authority, states that a marked difference is manifest in the formation of the African and Asiatic elephant, and writes, "Elephas capensis, fronte convexâ, lamellis malarium rhomboidalibus. Elephas Indicus, fronte plano-concavâ, lamellis malarium arcuatis undatis."

The height of a full-grown Ceylon elephant varies from eight and a half to ten feet, and their colour is also diversified, as some of the tuskers have a portion of their head and ears of a speckled flesh colour, others are mottled all over their bodies, whilst many are of the usual elephantine hue. White elephants have been occasionally but rarely found in the island, and the natives affirm this breed is not indigenous, but was introduced from Siam.

Although all tusk-elephants are males, not more than three or four in a hundred have these valuable protuberances; the remainder being provided with short tusks like the females, which project eight or ten inches beyond the mouth, and invariably incline downwards. The tusks vary in length from three to seven feet, and their weight ranges between thirty to one hundred and twenty pounds, but sixty-five or seventy are the average weight of those appertaining to a full-grown animal.

Formerly the traffic in elephants was principally carried on by the Moormen, and, as their mode of valuing the creature was singular, we subjoin a statement. They measured from the extremity of the fore-foot to the top of the shoulder, and for every cubit they demanded one thousand rupees, and readily obtained that sum for the Ceylon elephants. Numberless extraordinary anecdotes are extant connected with the acknowledged superiority of the island elephants, even by those of their own species; and, although we will not vouch for the accuracy of the statement, as we have never seen an African and Ceylon elephant in juxta-position, we give the following anecdote from Tavernier, who writes, "One I will tell you hardly to be believed, which is, that when any other king or rajah has one of these elephants of Ceylon, if they bring any other breed before them, in any other place whatever, so soon as the other elephants behold the Ceylon elephants, by an instinct of nature, they do them reverence, by laying their trunks upon the ground, and raising them up again."

In their native jungle, the elephant is tormented by a large species of mosquito, or fly, and an insect called the tick, which pierces the hide, causing excessive pain; and, to baffle these tiny but inexorable enemies, the huge creature rolls itself on the earth, and, when a wild elephant emerges from the jungle, the skin is of a dingy brick-dust colour, from the sand and particles of red earth that cover the hide.

The elephants are now only found in the thickly-wooded forests of the interior, although under the Dutch, and during the rule of the first English governor, the Honourable Frederick North (since Lord Guildford), the great elephant-hunts used to take place in the maritime province, and at times one or two thousand men would be employed for many weeks in snaring elephants, or driving them into kraals.

As the mode of snaring and hunting elephants is generally the same and has been often described, we will only allude to one of the former, that we believe to be peculiar to the island, and which is called ATMADDOO, or hand-snaring. The ropes are made either from buffaloes' or bullocks' hide, and have a running noose at one end; the hunters lie in wait in a jungle where they find recent tracks of the elephants; concealed in the trees, they readily perceive the approach of the animal, and allowing it to pass their ambush, stealthily creep in the rear, getting close to the creature, and awaiting the favourable moment slip the noose under a hind-foot, another hunter twining the opposite end of the rope around the trunk of a tree. The elephant in attempting to pursue the route is checked and tripped up, finally stumbling; the other hunters immediately rush forward with additional ropes, and secure the legs by twisting cords from one to the other in a figure of eight; the elephant is then securely fastened to the neighbouring trees, and a shed erected to protect the animal until sufficiently tamed to be removed with safety.

Under the native dynasty, the successful elephant-hunters were highly rewarded by the monarch, and were allowed to pluck out the long coarse hairs that are occasionally found at the extremity of the tail. These are highly valued by the Kandian women, who weave them into bangles and anklets. The Kandian kings only retained the tuskers and speckled elephants, the others being set at liberty. Sometimes, to please the potentate, the herd would be driven into the city and captured in his presence, and Knox, who was a prisoner in Kandy for twenty-one years, says, " If the elephants caught did not please the king he ordered their liberation, but if they did, he selected some spot near the city, and there they were kept until he ordered them to be secured. This might not take place for two or three years, during which interval headsmen and watchers were set over them, and if the beasts did chance to stray beyond the royal bounds, the headsmen summoned their followers to bring them back again immediately, for, were one only lost, they were apprehensive of the king's displeasure, which was little short of death."

It is well known these animals are usually found in herds, and when a solitary elephant is seen, the Cingalese say that it is a rogue-elephant, " *hora alia*," who has been expelled for nefarious and turbulent conduct by the other members of the herd. It is strange, that whenever a solitary elephant is found or heard of, the creature is invariably viciously mischievous, destroying crops, and taking human life, apparently in wantonness and without provocation, and a rogue-elephant in former days used frequently to lie in wait near a road, rush upon the unwary travellers, trample them to death, then quietly return to the jungle. Such an occurrence took place a comparatively short time ago.

In certain parts of the interior, the natives suffer materially at times from the destructive depredations of herds of elephants; and occasionally, paddy-fields, and topes of cocoa-nut trees, will be completely devastated in the course of the night. Elephants have a strong partiality for the leaves of the cocoa-nut; and, when they cannot reach them with their trunks, they throw their whole weight against the tree, and, by continued pressure, succeed in laying low the stately palm.

The sense of smell and hearing, in these animals is extremely acute, but a strong light, or the vivid glare of the sun, is evidently obnoxious to their eyes; and, for this reason, an experienced elephant-shooter will invariably endeavour to place himself in such a position as to allow, if possible, the beams to fall upon the elephant's forehead, as it is near the eyes, at the top of the skull, the vulnerable spot is to be found. Balls will inflict no serious injury, unless the brain of the animal is perforated; when this is the case, in the time of a passing thought, the ponderous creature lies prostrate and motionless at the feet of the comparative, pigmy destroyer.

As elephant-hunters cannot conveniently bag their game, it is customary to cut off their tail, and bear it away as a trophy, and some amusing anecdotes are current in Ceylon connected with new arrivals and young sportsmen, who have commenced docking a live, instead of a dead elephant, the creature having been merely stunned by the shot; and the pain of the incision acting as a counter-irritant, causing the animal to regain its scattered senses and feet, the animal shuffling off in one direction, and the inexperienced hunter running swiftly in the opposite, bawling loudly for assistance.

The most celebrated elephant-hunter in Ceylon was Major Rogers, and it has been stated to us by those who knew this adventurous man well, that he had slain more than fourteen hundred elephants. His hair-breadth escapes were miraculous, and among the many we will cite but one, which, although it savours of the wonderful, is strictly correct.

The Major had shot at an elephant, but the ball glanced off, merely inflicting a flesh-wound; the creature, infuriated with pain, raised its trunk, uttering the terrific trumpet-like squeal, which they always make preparatory to a charge. The elephant seized Rogers with the proboscis, and carried him a short distance, then dashed him on the ground, into a deep hole, and trampled upon him, breaking his right arm intow places, and several of his ribs; and it was only the small size of the hole into which he had been thrown that saved his life, as the elephant had not sufficient room to use his full strength. When his brother sportsmen came up to the Major, they found him lying senseless, and, so soon as he recovered his speech he stated, that he was perfectly conscious when the elephant both seized and trampled upon him, but that he knew attempting to escape, or struggling was worse than futile, and that he was entirely passive upon principle, as he had often reflected upon such an event occurring, and had resolved to remain perfectly motionless. We believe no greater mastery of mind over matter, or resolution, was ever recorded than this.

The death of this courageous man was as melancholy as extraordinary: he was travelling in the interior with a gentleman and his wife, on the 7th of June 1846, and the party were taking refreshment at a Rest-house, preparatory to pursuing their journey. A violent thunder-storm came on which detained the travellers for some time; it had abated, the sun was again shining and preparations were making to resume their tour, when the Major stepped into the verandah, saying that he thought the rain had entirely subsided, and it was time to set out.

Suddenly, a vivid flash of lightning was seen, a loud crash of thunder heard; his companions called to him, saying they had better wait awhile longer; not receiving a reply, the gentleman went out, and there lay poor Rogers a lifeless corpse, who but a few moments previously, was full of life and merriment. Thus died one whilst under shelter and apparently out of danger, who had often braved the heat of the battle, the fury of the elephant, and who had never shrunk from a hazardous undertaking.

We cannot conclude our observations upon elephants, without remarking upon their capability of enduring extreme atmospheric changes, for, in Ceylon, the tracks of these animals are found alike in the valleys of the interior, and on the elevated thickly-wooded mountains, and many of these elevations exceed six thousand feet, above the ocean's level, the thermometer varying in the valleys, and on the mountains forty-five degrees. These clumsy animals appear also to delight in climbing steep hills, and slippery rocks, and ofttimes their mutilated bodies are found in precipices and abysses below.

Frequently tusks of a large size are discovered in the jungles, but whether they have been buried by the natives, and forgotten, or have been forced into the earth by the animals, none can tell; though it is asserted that elephants in flight will fall upon their tusks, their own impetus and weight snapping them off close to the sockets. But, even presuming the latter statement to be correct, it is a problem to us how the tusks can be found beyond their own depth, unless in the course of time the soil has accumulated over them.

In the central province elks abound and afford good sport; these animals approximate closely to the red deer of Scotland, and at a distance might readily be mistaken for them. When they are full-grown their height varies from four to five feet and a half, their colour a dark reddish brown, which gradually shades into black upon the neck and hinder part. There are several species of deer indigenous to the island, that are remarkable for their elegant forms and beautiful coats, and among them Albinoes are occasionally seen, with the red eyes peculiar to the colour, and these animals are highly prized by the Kandians.

We shall only describe the smallest of the deer tribe called by some naturalists the musk-deer, the Linnæan name of which is Moschus meminna, the Cingalese Walmeenya. These diminutive creatures, perfect in their proportions, are the most exquisitely lovely of all quadrupeds; the beauty of their delicate limbs, lustrous eyes, spotted skins, and graceful forms baffling all description. We had a full-grown male, whose height did not exceed ten inches, and length fourteen; the throat, neck, and stomach, were milk white; the remainder of the body was grey, regularly striped with black, over which were equi-distant yellow spots. The head gradually tapered to the snout, whilst from either side of the mouth protruded a small but perfectly-shaped tusk; the eyes and ears large and open, the tail short, and the weight of the Lilliputian was under five pounds.

It was curious to observe how kindness conquered the animal's natural timidity; when we first had him, if an attempt was made to handle or lift him, he immediately snorted and resisted, kicking violently, and small as he was, he could inflict strong kicks with his slender pointed hind-hoofs. Gradually fear subsided, and, as he became domesticated, he was placed upon the table after dinner, and allowed to nibble first one fruit and then another from the dishes; at last, he would boldly walk about, and, when called by name, would fearlessly approach and take food from the hand, allowing caresses to be bestowed upon him. His terror of the dogs also diminished by degrees; at first, when they barked he would crouch down instantaneously, (as this species do in a wild state, among the grass for concealment, as soon as they hear a noise,) and remain motionless, panting with alarm, exhibiting other symptoms of fear, with dilated eyes. At length, he would become calm, finding no injury inflicted, and before we left the island would allow a small terrier to stand close to, and sniff his coat, and, if the larger dogs barked when he was out of his cage, would gaze inquiringly towards the spot where the noise proceeded from, without exhibiting the slightest uneasiness.

With some difficulty, we obtained a female of the same breed, as these animals are rarely taken alive, and succeeded in bringing both to England, but unfortunately our changeable climate did not agree with them, and first our tame petted favourite and then the female sickened, and eventually each died of inflammation of the lungs.

The wild buffalo of Ceylon is a variety of the Malabar, but much larger and fiercer, and abounds in many of the thinly inhabited districts. Hunting these animals is considered perilous, (although adventurous spirits pursue the pastime) for, should the ball not take effect near the shoulder, the brute invariably charges, in a curved line, inclining sideways, and presenting one horn with unerring accuracy, which too frequently enters the body of the sportsman. Their indomitable courage and tenacity of life, are only equalled by the spirit of revenge evinced when they are attacked. This animal is called gaura by the natives, and formerly this breed overran many localities, that still bear the creature's name.

The bears of the island, though small, are remarkably fierce, and will attack man even when unmolested. These animals are much dreaded by the natives as their powerful fore-legs, sharp claws, and fangs, usually inflict mortal injuries, or so disfigure the person as to leave few pleasing marks of humanity.

The leopard, or cheetah, has a most beautiful coat, and occasionally attains the length of seven and a half feet, and, although extremely destructive to cattle, dogs, and all domesticated creatures, never attacks human beings, unless in self-defence. The Ceylon leopard has distinctive peculiarities, the principal one being, its incapacity to draw back the claws within the sheath.

Cheetahs abound in the Kandian districts, and the natives wage a perpetual war of destruction against them, on account of their partiality for their cattle and poultry. They shoot them, with cross bows, furnished with large bladed arrows, and spring guns; they dig pitfalls over which is suspended a newly-killed animal, and make enclosures, with a dropping gate, under which is laid some tempting morsel; in short, no scheme of extermination is left untried, and our only astonishment is, that the whole race has not been extirpated centuries ago.

The wild hog is found in most of the wooded districts, is both ferocious and powerful, and will readily turn to attack man, or beast. The full-grown males are larger than the Westphalia boar, the colour of their hides being a dark brown or black, which shades into grey on the shoulders and throat. Hunting these creatures is a favourite sport, and the flesh of a young hog is well-flavoured and succulent, resembling newly-killed venison.

In the jungles are also to be found jackalls, hares, the ichneumon or mongoose, a peculiar species of weazel, many descriptions of monkeys, some of them rare and curious; sloths, squirrels of every variety, and the hideous creature called the flying-fox, porcupines, (which seriously damage plantations of cocoa-nut trees, as their favourite food is the centre of the root,) and other animals that our prescribed limits preclude noticing. But in no part of Ceylon are lions, tigers, or wolves, to be seen.

Amongst the greatest domestic pests in Ceylon, are the innumerable legions of rats that abound in every part of the island and infest every dwelling, and the audacious boldness of these destructive vermin will hardly be credited. We have frequently seen the creatures perched upon the back of a chair, or top of a screen, and not offer to move until something was thrown at them; and we will give an account of a rat's presence of mind, that will equal that exhibited by Rogers when he was seized by the elephant.

Hearing a great commotion and barking among our dogs, we went into the verandah to ascertain the cause, and found they were disputing about the possession of a recently-caught animal, which our nostrils soon informed us was a shrew, or musk-rat; we made the dogs relinquish their prize, pro tem., as we were desirous to examine the vermin, promising them that as soon as our survey was completed, the rat should be returned. We took up the creature by the tail, (the dogs leaping and barking around us,) carried it into the dining-room, and held it close to the lamp, to observe its distinctive peculiarities.

The creature was without motion; not a muscle moved, and the limbs hung loose as if life had totally quitted the carcase. This examination lasted fully five minutes, and, when our curiosity was satisfied, we threw the rat to the dogs, (which closely surrounded our legs and the table, yelping with the excitement of expectation,) expecting to see it torn to pieces, when to our amazement the brute not only took to its legs with all imaginable celerity, and ran off, but got clear away, baffling every effort of the dogs to retake it. Assuredly, all must admit that the rat not only "stole away," but also stole a cunning march upon us.

The musk-rat will occasionally measure twelve inches from the snout to the tail; the head is slender, the upper jaw projecting considerably beyond the lower, the whiskers bushy, long and white, the colour of the coat grey, but the feet are totally devoid of hair, and the tail is thick at the root. The effluvia of this creature is most powerful; and, if it runs over any edible, the article becomes so impregnated with the peculiar smell as to be totally unfit for use.

The ornithological specimens of Ceylon are as numerous as beautiful, and no study can be conceived that offers a wider field for investigation. From the gorgeous feathers of the wild peacock to the diversified plumage of the Cingalese starling, from the rhinoceros bird to the jungle-crow and blue rock-pigeon, all being met with on the island, and all furnishing alike subjects of profitable thought and observation; we believe Ceylon to be only second to Australia for the number and beauty of, indigenous birds.

In some parts of the island red-legged partridges, quails, and snipes abound, but the sportsman has to contend with two serious drawbacks, let the game he seeks be an elephant, or buffalo, a partridge, or snipe, as every jungle and morass abounds with land-leeches, and an exceedingly disgusting insect called the tick. The land-leech is found wherever there is long grass, and its slender form when ungorged not being thicker then a very fine needle, enables it to penetrate through the clothing. Some sportsmen wear what are called leech-gaiters, others boots, but we never yet knew, or heard of any one, being able to exclude these blood-thirsty creatures.

The dimensions of the land-leech are about an inch in length, and one-tenth in diameter, their colour a dark green approaching to black; but when gorged they are quite two inches long, and three quarters of an inch in circumference. They draw a considerable quantity of blood, their bites causing great irritation; and, if the places are scratched, eventually inflammation. As their motions are peculiarly agile, they are most difficult to kill, or to remove; for, when you have succeeded in taking them off your legs, they almost instantaneously fasten upon your hands, before you have time to destroy them. It is dangerous to pluck them off quickly, as that increases the irritation of the wound, but, if they are touched with brandy, they immediately drop off.

Lime-juice, and other acid applications, will alleviate the itching and staunch the bleeding, and those who are of good habit of body and abstemious, only suffer temporary inconvenience from their bites, whilst others who live freely, and whose constitutions are debilitated, often find the wounds fester, and ultimately ulcerate. Many animals suffer severely from the land-leech, and sheep will not thrive upon any pasture where they are to be found. During the dry season, these noxious creatures multiply to an almost incredible extent, and especially abound upon all wooded hills.

As leeches abound in the grass, so do the ticks upon the trees, where they lie upon the leaves in myriads, and, if the branch is shaken by the wind or touched by the sportsman, they fall upon his person and drive him nearly insane; as their sting resembles the prick of a red-hot needle, and the skin is no sooner punctured than intolerable itching supervenes. These filthy insects are about the size of a very large pin's head, of an oblong form, and flat, and of a mulberry colour; but, when they are distended with their sanguinary meal, we can positively declare that we have seen many that were quite a quarter of an inch wide.

The legs of ticks seem to be provided with small hooks, as they cling to the skin with most obnoxious tenacity, defying every effort to remove them, without pulling the body from the limbs; these insects are as troublesome to animals as they are to man, and without extreme caution will cluster round the fleshy part of a dog's foot and between the toes, eating into the flesh, inflicting agonizing torture upon the poor brute which, maddened by the pain, vainly essays to pull them out with the teeth. We found that ticks would more readily fasten upon an European than upon the country-born dog, and we shall not readily forget the manner in which our terriers used to be bitten by them, despite the daily ablutions and care taken to free the dogs from these ruthless tormentors.

Snakes, venomous reptiles, and insects, abound

in Ceylon, and it is surprising that so few deaths occur annually from their bites. We shall neither attempt to enumerate, nor classify the Ophidia, merely mentioning what we think most likely to interest the general reader.

The largest of the serpent tribe in Ceylon is the anaconda, (belonging to the genus Python,) and is far from being uncommon in the island; a full-grown snake will measure from seventeen to twenty feet, and we have heard it asserted that one twenty-five feet long, and whose body was two and a half in circumference, was killed by our informant. This reptile is handsomely marked in regular patches of a dark rich brown and yellow; the teeth are large and sharp, and the muscular power of the jaws is very great. The creature has two horny excrescences, or spurs, near the tail, and these enable the reptile to cling with greater security to the branches of the trees, from which it will swing, ready to seize upon and entwine around any animal that may come within its reach. They encircle their victims in the same manner as the boa-constrictor, crushing every bone, and lubricating the carcase with saliva before swallowing it; and, although they have been known to seize upon a deer, or young buffalo, their usual prey is believed to be jackalls. The Cingalese do not particularly dread this snake, as it rarely attacks man.

The cobra-capello, or hooded snake, is called naga by the natives, and is considered sacred, as on the western coast before the arrival of Goutama Buddha, it is believed the people worshipped this snake. The reverence with which this reptile is regarded, although its venomous nature is well known, prevents many of the natives destroying it; and the most ingenious reasons are assigned by them to Europeans, to extenuate or account for the deadly bite too often inflicted by the cobra, or naga.

In Kandy, when a cobra is caught, instead of slaying the noxious vermin, and thus preventing farther mischief accruing, the people wishing to be rid of it, will secure it, and convey it during the night to some distant village, or jungle. Those who fear and desire the destruction of the naga, but whose superstition causes them to hesitate before they take life, make a compromise with their conscience, by enclosing the snake in a mat-bag, with some boiled rice for food, and place the receptacle, inmate, and food in a flowing stream, where the snake is certain to meet death either by drowning, or from the hands of some less scrupulous devotee.

Therefore, we warn our readers, if, in the course of their peregrinations, they should wander through the Cinnamon Isle, and see floating upon a river's sparkling surface a mat-bag, the mouth of which is tied with especial care, not to open the same without due caution, or they may be greeted with a loud hiss, and be severely punished for indulging in the so-called *feminine propensity* of curiosity.

This reptile, when full grown, is often found from six to seven feet in length, and varies in colour, those of a light hue being called by the natives, high-caste, and those of a dark, low-caste snakes. The bite of this reptile is poisonous and generally deadly, but if seen by a *human* being there is time to flee from the impending danger; as the creature is compelled to twine the lower extremity, and erect itself upon the coil, before it can dart. The aspect of this creature with its inflated head, just before it makes its unerring deadly spring, is said to be most terrific; and the following occurrence is indelibly imprinted upon our memory.

A legal friend was going on circuit to Jaffna, and to relieve the tedium of the journey had quitted his palanqueen and taken his gun, resolving to walk in the shade, looking for game, and soon bemoaned his fate at not meeting with sport. He observed for some distance the tracks and footmarks of elephants, but neither bird nor beast presented itself; the footfalls became deeper, thicker, and fresher as he penetrated farther into the jungle, bearing evidence that a numerous herd had but recently passed through.

Our friend picked his way carefully between these tracks, and, as he stepped over a very deep hole, he thought he saw a dark glistening substance filling it up: he proceeded a few yards, then turned round intending to retrace his steps and satisfy himself what the shining object was, when, to his dismay, he saw a cobra with inflated head, rising from the hole over which he had just before stepped; he instantly levelled his gun and shot the venomous brute before it had time to coil and erect itself.

The tic-polonga, although somewhat smaller, is more to be dreaded than the cobra, as the bite is almost instantaneously fatal, and the terrible reptile darts forward without the slightest warning, or giving the victim a moment's notice,—in short, it is the most dangerous and vicious snake in the island, despite the assertion of a recent author to the contrary, who has never been in Ceylon. This snake is peculiarly active and spiteful, attacking alike bipeds and quadrupeds, and the effects of its venomous fangs are the same upon all, the muscular powers becoming paralyzed, and the sanguineous fluid speedily coagulating; and we never heard but of two men who recovered after being stung.

The tic-polonga is frequently three or four feet long, and the body is thick in proportion to the length; the head is triangular, and the colour a dark grey, almost approaching to lead. The Cingalese abhor this snake as much as they venerate the cobra-capello, and the following legend connected with these two reptiles illustrates the different sentiments entertained by them.—

"In the isle of Serendib there is a happy valley, that men call the vale of Kotmalé. It is watered by numerous streams, and its fields produce rice in abundance; but at one season great drought prevails, and the mountain torrents then cease their constant roar, and subside into rivulets, or altogether disappear. At this period when the rays of the noontide sun beat fiercely and hotly on the parched earth, a tic-polonga encountered a cobra-capello. The polonga had in vain sought to quench his burning thirst, and gazed with envy on the cobra, who had been more successful in his search for the pure beverage. 'Oh! puissant cobra, I perish with thirst; tell me where I may find the stream wherein thou hast revelled.' 'Accursed polonga,' replied the cobra, 'thou cumberest the earth, wherefore should I add to the span of thy vile existence. Lo, near to this flows a mountain-rill, but an only child is disporting herself therein, while her mother watches the offspring of her heart. Wilt thou then swear not to injure the infant, if I impart to thee where thou mayest cool thy parched tongue.' 'I swear by all the gods of Serendib,' rejoined the polonga, 'that I will not harm the infant.' 'Thou seest yonder hamlet; in front of it gushes forth a spring of water, that abates not during the intensity of the summer-heat.' The polonga wended his way to the spot, and there beheld a dark-eyed girl bathing in the rushing waters. Having quaffed the delicious liquid, he repented him of his oath touching the infant. His evil soul prompted him to kill her, and, as she lay beneath the shade of a leafy tamarind-tree, he approached and inflicted a mortal wound. As he retired from his dying victim, he again met the cobra, who seeing blood on his fangs, and perceiving the cause, thus addressed him. 'Hast thou forgotten the sacred oath thou swearest unto me? The blood of thy victim cries for vengeance. Thou shalt surely die.' And, darting his fangs into the body of the polonga, he slew him instantly."

There are many other venomous snakes, reptiles, and insects indigenous to the island, which we cannot notice; and, when the Kandians catch and kill any of these, they invariably suspend their lifeless bodies to the trees, we presume as a warning to their fellows. The only exception to this rule being the sacred naga, who, even if exterminated, is never subjected to so great an indignity.

The beautiful little creature, the ichneumon, is the declared foe to this snake, and is invariably the assailant: the animal springs upon the back of the snake and seizes the nape of the neck, and never uncloses its teeth until the snake is lifeless.

Those who have witnessed the battle say that the cobra always tries to escape, and that before commencing the fight the ichneumon runs to a particular plant and eats a portion, and this serves as an antidote to the reptile's poison. We are rather incredulous upon this latter point, but are quite certain that the ichneumon will assail the snake in the open air, and as scrupulously avoid doing so if in an enclosed space. We cannot say either if the antipathy of the ichneumon extends to other serpents, as all the encounters we have heard of took place with the cobra-capello.

The crocodiles of Ceylon grow to a great size, some of the full-grown males measuring twenty feet; but their average length is fifteen. The species found in the island differ materially in the formation of the head from the crocodiles of the Ganges, but they are equally ferocious, never leaving go of their prey, seizing alike men and animals; and a native told us he knew a man who was dragged out of his canoe and devoured by one of these monsters. In the tanks and streams of Putlam these reptiles swarm, being also found in small sheets of water that are met with in the flat and scantily-populated districts, and occasionally in a season of long-continued drought, crocodiles will be seen in the jungles, making their way from the dried-up tanks to the rivers. Europeans hunt these creatures, and consider it good sport, and the lives of many valuable dogs have often been sacrificed, as the crocodiles frequently seize the animals and drag them under the water. The only way to avoid this disaster is to ride close to the dogs, and fire as they approach the water.

Another method of destroying the crocodiles is the following, which, although efficacious, savours too much of slaughter in our estimation to be called sporting. Hooks, baited with flesh, are attached to about twenty thin, but strong strings, a piece of wood being fastened to the opposite extremity of the lines, to which a strong cord is attached. This apparatus is cast into the water by attendants, the float indicating when the bait has been seized; the men then pull the cord, and the numerous strings having become entangled in the wide-set teeth of the crocodile, the head is soon drawn above the water, and the sportsman aims a shot between the head and neck to break the spine; the creature is then hauled on shore and despatched with spears, or guns. We have heard of some men killing in this manner many dozens in the course of the year, but we again repeat, it is too like butchery to suit our taste.

In the districts infested with crocodiles, men calling themselves crocodile-charmers abound, and, as these cunning fellows know the habits and haunts of the reptiles, they generally succeed in conveying a party safely through, or across a stream. Crocodiles, although ferocious, are sluggish and cowardly if attacked, and the natives of Putlam will go in a large body into the water, and drag them on shore with strong nets. Those who drag the net keep their legs in constant motion, whilst others shout and strike upon the water with long poles; this disturbance appears to terrify and confound the crocodiles, who comparatively struggle but little when entangled in the net.

Men, armed with spears and fire-arms, remain on the banks of the tank, or stream, and so soon as the reptiles are drawn into shallow water they are speedily despatched. The natives in using the spear try to wound the reptile under the fore leg, as that is the most vulnerable part of the creature. And they prefer this mode to wasting powder and ball, as from the hard and irregular surface of the crocodile's skin, it is difficult for any, save a good marksman, to mortally wound the reptile.

The fecundity of the crocodile is proverbial, as the female lays from seventy to eighty eggs, which are larger than a goose's; these are deposited in the sand, being hatched by the heat of the sun, and numbers of the eggs fortunately never arrive at maturity. Those who have broken the mature eggs, and liberated the young crocodiles, state that they utter a sharp bark immediately on leaving the shell, and will snap and bite a stick, or any other weapon held near them.

It is impracticable to particularize many of the insect tribe, although Ceylon is as rich in these as she is in her ornithological and vegetable kingdom, and the brilliance and beauty of the fire-flies and beetles are proverbial, whilst the white ants are equally celebrated for their destructive propensities.

This small insect is dreaded both by Europeans and natives, as it will undermine houses, destroy furniture, devour clothing, and render provisions useless. And what is most extraordinary is, that the insect will eat away the interior of a beam, or leg of a piece of furniture, leaving the exterior apparently sound, and the first intimation you have of the work of destruction being commenced, is the beam falling down in particles of dust; or the table, bedstead, or chair giving way. At certain seasons they acquire wings, and possibly, to the dismay of the inhabitants, in a few minutes every article in the room will be covered with white ants, and the only way to entice them out of the dwelling is to have a fire kindled in the compound, as a brilliant light invariably attracts these insects.

The Cingalese call their nests "heaps of old boiled rice," and they are composed of various substances, so amalgamated as to bear a strong resemblance to a fine white honeycomb and grains of rice. We have heard of those who have broken off pieces of these abodes to examine them, and who have as a reward for their laudable spirit of investigation, we presume, been most severely bitten or stung by the inmates. A difference of opinion exists, as to whether white ants sting, or bite; we know not what means they employ, but we do know they can draw blood in one instant, and cause extreme pain when inflicting the wound.

CHAPTER IX.

Geographical position of Ceylon—Size, fertility, and produce—Mentioned by classical writers of antiquity—Hindoo and Cingalese records—Date of the submersion of the island, nearly coincides with the Mosaic—Indian conqueror, Wijeya—Aborigines—Island visited by the Romans—Cingalese ambassadors visit Rome—Account given in the sixth century by Comas Indicopleustes — Island first visited by the Portuguese in 1505—Native account—Dutch in Ceylon—Wars between the Portuguese and Dutch — Affecting historical anecdote — Battles — The Portuguese possessions in Ceylon obtained by the Dutch in 1658—List of the Portuguese Governors.

CEYLON is situate between 5° 56′, and 9° 50′ north latitude, and between 80° and 82° east longitude; and, from the shape and position of the island, it has, with no less beauty than truth, been compared to a pearl-drop on the brow of the Indian continent. Its length is about 276 miles, its breadth about 103, and its circumference is about 900. The superficial area is nearly 24,000 square miles, and the population is estimated (since the last census) under a million and a-half. The island is bounded on the north-east by the Gulf of Mannar, by which it is separated from the main land, and the Indian Ocean bounds its other shores.

The sea-shore presents great diversity of scenery; in some places studded with barren rocks, in others wooded to the water's edge with cocoa-nut trees, which skirt the island, presenting a scene of truly oriental beauty.

In the interior are mountains from 6,000 to 8,000 feet in elevation, which form a species of natural circular fortification, protecting the interior, by means of which the natives were enabled to defy European modes of warfare for more than three centuries. Many of these mountains are clothed from base to summit with primeval forests, and among the trees may be seen the cinnamon-laurel, but, when this shrub attains the dimensions of a moderate sized tree, it is useless for commercial purposes. It is on the slopes of these mountains that the soil best adapted for the cultivation of coffee is situated, and since 1835 the culture of

L 2

this shrub has so increased, that the produce of Ceylon alone, is nearly sufficient to furnish the supplies requisite for the consumption of Great Britain.

Although the breezes passing over the ocean and these lofty mountains are at times refreshing, the oppression produced by the heated atmosphere is frequently extreme; but the suffocating simooms experienced on the continent of India are here entirely unknown.

The Wellánee, the Mahawelliganga, the Guidora, and the Kalluganga, are the principal rivers; and the sources of these, together with those of some smaller and tributary ones, originate in the lofty mountains; and the fertility of this verdant isle may be attributed to the plentiful supply of good water.

The temperature of the island varies consider ably, as in the mountains, and at Newera Ellia, the thermometer will fall below freezing-point, whilst on the coast it will range from eighty-six to ninety-six of Fahrenheit.

From the earliest ages Lanka-Diva, or Ceylon, has been renowned for the wealth of its marine, vegetable, and mineral productions: the sea yielding costly pearls, and a plentiful supply of various and delicious fish, fit for the sustenance of man.

The vegetable kingdom teems with riches of another nature, equally valuable—the coffee-bush, from the berry of which the fragrant decoction is made; the cinnamon-laurel, the bark of which furnishes delicious spice, and from whose leaves a pure oil is obtained; the nutmeg-tree, with its aromatic spice; the clove-tree, with its fragrant blossoms; the sugar-cane, with its juicy pulp and spiral slender leaves; and the tobacco-plant.

The graceful cocoa-nut tree, which will spring into existence where there is scarcely soil sufficient to cover the root; the green fruit furnishing a cooling and delicious beverage, the ripened nut food, the shell fuel, the fibres are woven into coir, or rope, and from the old nut a pure oil is extracted; the leaves, when plaited, form a shelter from the elements; the trunk yields a juice from which, when fermented, a spirit is distilled, or sugar extracted; and the tree, when past bearing fruit, is cut down, and the beautifully-variegated timber is made into articles of furniture.

The Jack-tree, with its enormous fruit of an oval shape, measuring more than eighteen inches in diameter, affording nourishment; while its yellow trunk, when hewn, is made into articles for domestic use. The magnificent bread-fruit-tree, with its splendid foliage and fruit; the orange, pomegranate, lime, shaddock, and tamarind, with their luxuriant verdure, flowers, and delicious fruit; added to these, we find the Malay apple, cashew-nut, fig, papaw, jambo, almond, guava, custard-apple, rambatam, and mangoe trees, and nearly every other tropical fruit, all being distinguished for their size and umbrageous foliage.

Amongst the denizens of vegetation, we find the elegant banana, or plantain-tree, with its broad, young leaves, folded trumpetwise one within the other; the superb amethyst, bell-shaped flower, with yellow petals, and the pendant clusters of yellow, ripened, luscious fruit: the amber ananas, or pineapple, with its green crest, and the grenadilla melon with its mottled rind. Whilst amongst culinary vegetables are brinjal, yams, sweet potatoes, occus, a species of cucumber, pumpkins, and rice; whilst European vegetables and fruit, such as strawberries, peas, beans, potatoes, and cabbages, have been introduced into Kandy and Newera-Ellia since 1823.

In the forests are found, the noble talipat, ebony, calamander, banyan, areka-nut, suriya and many other trees, whose names are totally unknown to Europeans; but, were we to attempt to give an account of all the riches of the botanical produce of Ceylon, it would occupy volumes.

The fruitfulness of the earth's womb is here developed in the production of the ruby, emerald, sapphire, onyx, amethyst, opal, moon-stone, cat's-eye, jacynth, and topaz. The precious gems here enumerated are found at the present day; and we have been informed by a Kandian noble of high rank, that gold was formerly found on the island.

From the foregoing facts, it is apparent

> "What Heaven has done for this delicious land;"

and, by judicious and energetic government and management, the prolific and fertile isle might soon be rendered the most productive of our colonies, and the brightest colonial gem in the British diadem.

The Cingalese are extremely proud of the celebrity and antiquity of their isle; and the native historians assert, that thousands of years before the birth of our Saviour, the island was peopled by a race whose mental powers were highly cultivated, and of whom they are the descendants. Certain it is, that the Cingalese, for centuries past, have been retrogading in the arts and sciences; as the antiquarian remains of public buildings, tanks, and temples of vast magnitude, found in the interior of the island, indicate the existence of a nation, which had nurtured and brought to perfection the nobler arts.

These extraordinary remains will be noticed more particularly in a future paper devoted to the antiquities of Lanka-diva; but to proceed regularly, we must now glance at the early history of Ceylon, although the greater portion of it is involved in obscurity. Cingalese historians affirm that here was situated the garden of Eden; from the top of the highest mountain in the island, called Adam's Peak, they say that the progenitor of all mankind was expelled, and that from this mountain's top the trace of his footstep is to be seen.

We gather from Herodotus that the earlier Greeks had a knowledge of the countries and islands east of the Indus, but the first circumstantial account that we have of Taprabane, or Ceylon, is given by Onesiculus, the Macedonian admiral, who lived B. C. 329 or 30. Diodorus Siculus B. C. 44, gives a correct account of the size and situation of the island and describes the natives, customs and productions, with extreme fidelity, although a love for the marvellous is occasionally indulged in. Strabo states that Taprabane abounded in elephants, and that the contiguous waters teemed with amphibious creatures of an immense size. Dionysius, who flourished A.D. 36, confirms former accounts, saying, "And from thence the vessel's course being turned to the west, immediately in front of the promontory of Koolis, you will come to a large island, Taprabane, mother of Asia born elephants, and other strange animals." This celebrated geographer treats of the size and value of the elephants and their tusks, the gems and fragrant spices. Notwithstanding numerous other proofs have been adduced to prove that Ceylon is synonymous with the Taprabane of the ancient classical historians, a diversity of opinion has arisen among writers, as to the identity of the island; but, as it would be unprofitable to follow ancient or modern authors through their various disquisitions on this subject, we shall proceed to give an account of the presumed origin of the Cingalese. Ribeiro writes, in his "Historia de Ilgha de Zeilau:—

"The Chinese, from a remote period, were the masters of Oriental commerce; and some of their vessels were driven upon the coast of Ceylon, near the district which they subsequently termed Chilau. The mariners and passengers saved themselves upon the rocks; and, finding the island fertile, soon established themselves upon it. Shortly afterwards, the Malabars, having discovered it, sent hither their exiles, whom they denominated Galas. The exiles were not long in mixing with the Chinese; and from the two names was formed Chingalees, and afterwards Chingalais."

The other statement is, that the son of an Indian king, Wijeya Singha, of renowned warlike propensities, who, the native authors assert, conquered the island, and bestowed upon them his name of *Singha.* Why or wherefore the island is called Ceylon, and the people Cingalese, can matter little; but to us it appears evident, that the Chinese were neither wholly nor in part the aborigines of Ceylon, as those who are acquainted with the yellow skins, small elliptic eyes, broad faces, and flat features of that nation, will readily admit that the Cingalese differ from them completely, both in complexion and features. But there is great similitude in every way, between the person and complexion, of the Cingalese and Indian.

To us it seems that the only hypothesis to be drawn from the above is, that the Indian king, Singha, did conquer the island of Ceylon, at an early date, and that his followers mixed with the aborigines, and from them the present race is descended. Whether any of the aborigines, however, are now to be found in the island, whose blood is unmixed with Indian, it is difficult to prove, or whether the Veddahs, or wild men, of the present day, are descendants of the original inhabitants of Ceylon; but at this time they are a distinct race, and are only to be found in the interior, living in the jungle, in caves, or in rude huts built of the branches of trees, wandering from jungle to jungle in search of game, quitting each successively as food becomes scarce, and shooting their prey with rude bows and arrows; and these Veddahs will not hold intercourse, live in a town, or intermarry with the inhabitants. We have been informed that the language they speak is unintelligible to most other natives of the island. All these facts, therefore, strengthen our previously-stated supposition, that the Veddahs, are the aborigines of the island; and that the other inhabitants are the issue of the aborigines and the Indians.

It is distinctly proved by historical records that the island was conquered by Wijeya, B.C. 543, and Ceylon was then called, as it now is by Hindoos, Lanka-diva. It may not be irrelevant to remark, that both Hindoo and Cingalese chronicles agree in stating, that about 2387 B.C., the island was overwhelmed by the sea, and in this date there are but forty years difference between it, and the time assigned to the deluge by Usher, in his erudite chronology. The native writers state that this calamity was brought about by the wickedness of their monarch, Rawana, who then ruled the island, and the obdurate sinfulness of the inhabitants; and this also, is a remarkable similarity between the Mosaic and heathen reasons assigned for the flood.

Cingalese records state, "The foaming waves of the ocean overwhelmed the most fertile and extensive provinces, as well as the lovely capital of our pearl-like island, Sri-Lanka-poora, and since then the resplendent palaces, stately towers, seven concentric walls, and battlements of shining brass, are known only to the gods of the sea." Rawana was the sovereign of Southern India and Ceylon, and carred off the lovely wife of Rama, the king of Oude, into his "pearl-island kingdom," and bloody wars ensued which nearly depopulated the island. And the whole history is set forth in the Rama-yama, the oldest epic poem extant. Having thus glanced incidentally at the history of Ceylon before the flood, and the birth of our blessed Lord, we will proceed to the first century of our era.

Pliny affirms, that during the reign of the Emperor Claudius, a Roman vessel from the coast of Arabia, was driven upon that of Taprabane, or Ceylon; that the king of the country treated the Romans with hospitality and kindness during their sojourn of six months; and upon their departure they were accompanied by four ambassadors from the Eastern to the Roman monarch. Many modern writers treat this account as fabulous; but, in our opinion, Pliny is borne out in his statement by the fact, that Roman medals of ancient date were found, in the year 1574, at Mantotte, in Ceylon. We learn also, from Pliny, that a fleet, consisting of more than one hundred sail, went each year from the Red Sea to the coasts of Malabar and Ceylon, for the purposes of trade. Doubt has been thrown on this assertion, as writers state that it would have been impracticable for the ill-constructed vessels of that period, and with imperfect knowledge of navigation, for the Romans to have traversed the Indian Ocean; and although it must be allowed that such a voyage must necessarily have been a perilous one, still it was perfectly practicable to have sailed with one monsoon, and to have returned by the opposite, as is the custom, in the present day, with the unwieldy junks of Siam.

All writers agree that in the first century after

the Christian era, regular commercial intercourse was established between the inhabitants of Southern Europe and those of India and Ceylon. Gibbon, in his "Decline and Fall of the Roman Empire," writes:—"The objects of Oriental traffic were splendid and trifling; silk, a pound of which was esteemed not inferior in value to a pound of gold; precious stones, amongst which the pearl claimed the first rank after the diamond; and a variety of aromatics that were consumed in religious worship and the pomp of funerals." The articles here enumerated appear to have been the principal exports required by the wealthy and luxurious Romans; with the exception of the elephant's tusks, from which they manufactured articles of furniture, drinking-vessels, and personal ornaments, and this coveted-material Ceylon could supply most abundantly; therefore we may fairly conclude that the trade of Ceylon with Rome was considerable. About this time the Chinese began to trade with the Cingalese; and we find commerce gradually extending until the sixth century, when Ceylon was visited by Cosmas, who was surnamed Indicopleustes, during the reign of the Emperor Justinian; and he particularly treats of the precious gems and spices, which were conveyed to all parts of India, Persia, and the Arabian Gulph, from Ceylon.

We cannot trace, century by century, the course of the history or commerce of Ceylon, but will quote the words of Marco Polo, who visited the island, A.D. 1244. After describing its position and size, he writes:—

"Both men and women go nearly in a state of nudity, only wrapping a cloth round their loins. They have no grain besides rice and sesame, of which latter they make oil. Their food is milk, rice, and flesh, and they drink wine drawn from trees. The island produces more valuable and beautiful rubies than those found in any other part of the world; and likewise sapphires, topazes, amethysts, garnets, and many other precious and costly stones.* In this island there is a very high mountain, so rocky and precipitous, that the ascent to the top is impracticable, as it is said, excepting by the assistance of iron chains employed for that purpose; by means of these some persons attain the summit, where the tomb of Adam, our first parent, is reported to be found."

And yet this circumstantial account, with its veracity of detail, was stamped as fable, both by the contemporaneous writers, and those who followed, for a lengthened period, after the decease of the learned and truthful author.

* Samanella, or Adam's Peak.

In the year of our Lord, 1444, Nicola de Conte, a Venetian, gives a particular account of the tali-pot-tree, its leaves, size, &c., and describes the mode of preparing cinnamon, and the precious gems and pearls that were found in Ceylon. From the fourteenth to the sixteenth century, we have much valuable information given us by various authors, concerning the trade of the island; but as our principal business is connected with it after it came into the possession of Europeans, we will at once state, that, in 1505, the Portuguese, under Don Lorenzo de Almeida, visited the island, and were permitted to trade.

Previously to proceeding with the history of the country from the sixteenth century, we must take a retrospective glance at the ancient historical account of the government of Ceylon under its native rulers, or kings. From these accounts, it appears that the island was frequently in a state of warfare, either with the Malabars, or Moormen of the adjacent continent; that, with the fortunes of war, each would conquer alternately, and in turn be subdued, when ratifications of peace would ensue to be again broken, which, necessarily, produced fresh hostilities; and it is apparent that Kandy and the adjacent country became subjugated eventually by the Malabars, who placed a prince of their own nation on the throne, and maintained their position against the native kings of the south, the Portuguese and Dutch rulers, until dethroned by the force of British arms and valour in 1815. The island was divided into various principalities, each ruled by its own king, who would continually make incursions into the domains of a brother monarch, when war would result; the weaker party would become captive, and his kingdom would merge into that of the conqueror.

Notwithstanding these continued internal commotions, the wealth of the people appears to have been great; and arts and sciences were cultivated to an extent which would seem incredible, were the statement not borne out by historical and native writings of that period, and supported by the remains of ancient grandeur, which are dispersed throughout the island.

We shall now leave the ancient historical retrospect of Ceylon, and return to A.D. 1505, when the Portuguese obtained permission from the emperor of Ceylon to trade with his subjects, bartering the produce of Europe for the ivory, gems, and spices of their island. History asserts that it was chance, or rather adverse winds, which drove the Portuguese vessels on the shores of Ceylon, whilst in pursuit of some Moorish pirates whom they had seen sailing in the direction of the Maldives, and the winds proving adverse, they sought refuge in the Bay of Colombo. The Portuguese at that period were endeavouring to extend their trade, and obtain possessions in the east—Goa, on the Malabar coast, being their principal settlement, and the contiguity of Goa to Ceylon offered peculiar facility for bringing their policy into action. Francisco de Almeida, the governor of Goa, was a shrewd, crafty, wily politician, and one well calculated to carry his sovereign's schemes for the extension of his dominions into effect. Accordingly, we find that the vessels were scarcely anchored off Colombo, before he made overtures to the emperor to trade with the natives. From a curious antiquarian work in Cingalese, the following description of the Portuguese, their diet, and guns, is extracted :—

"And now it occurred, in the Christian year 1505, that a ship from Portugal arrived and anchored in Colombo. The race of men are exceedingly white and beautiful; they wear a covering to the feet and head made of iron, and they are always in motion. Their drink is the colour of blood, and they eat what looks like a white stone. They have weapons of warfare which make a noise like thunder when it breaks upon Jugandere Parivata, and a ball of iron shot from one of them, after flying some leagues, will break a castle of stone."

According to the Portuguese historian, Ribeiro, a treaty was made between the Portuguese and Cingalese monarchs, and it was stipulated that the emperor, Prackrama, should pay a tribute annually, to consist of two hundred and fifty thousand pounds of cinnamon, to the king of Portugal, on condition that the latter should assist in defending Ceylon from her enemies and invaders.

Although the trade of the island had been decreasing for centuries, still, in 1518, it must have been considerable; for, when the Portuguese monarch sent a fleet of nineteen sail to enforce the payment of the tribute, the commander of this expedition, Alvarengo, writes (according to Ribeiro):—"In the harbour of Colombo we found many ships from Bengal, Persia, the Red Sea, and other places, waiting for their freights of elephants' tusks and spices" Prackrama refused to pay the tribute, and hostilities were commenced by Alvarengo, who took possession of Colombo, and forced the Cingalese monarch to acknowledge himself tributary to the crown of Portugal. On the death of Prackrama, in 1527, the island was torn by civil war, which was carried on with more or less vigour until the year 1536 (during the whole of this period skirmishes continually took place between the Portuguese and natives, which invariably concluded by the success of the former), when the reigning monarch placed his grandson, and successor to his throne, under the protection of the crown of Portugal, sending an embassy to that court with the image of the young prince, and a crown of pure virgin gold.

Between the years 1518 and 1536, the Portuguese had introduced the form of Roman Catholic worship into Ceylon, and had endowed a monastery in Colombo, and Juan Monteira, the first Romish bishop of Ceylon, died at Colombo in the latter year.

In 1541, the effigy of the young prince, Dharmaa Paala, which had been sent to the court of Portugal, was crowned by John III., in the great hall of his palace at Lisbon, with extreme ceremony and rejoicings, the ambassadors from the Cingalese monarch, with a numerous retinue, being present on the occasion—the king of Portugal, by this public act, acknowledging that he had accepted the protection of the young prince, and that he undertook the charge confided to him by the grandfather of Dharmaa Paala, the then reigning monarch of Ceylon, who having been accidentally shot by a Portuguese gentleman in the succeeding year, the Portuguese raised Dharmaa Paala to the throne, thereby exciting considerable commotions amongst the natives, as the uncle of Dharmaa Paala laid claim to the crown, and was supported by numerous followers; and, in consequence, much bloodshed ensued.

Eventually the arms of Portugal were victorious, and Dharmaa Paala retained possession of the throne until he bequeathed the whole island, in 1580, to the crown of Portugal. It is about this time that a native historian writes :—" From this period forward, the women of the principal people, and also the women of the low castes, such as humowas and challias, *for the sake of Portuguese gold, began to turn Christians*, and to live with the Portuguese ;" and it is from this intercourse of the Cingalese women with the Portuguese, and subsequently with the Dutch, that the BURGHERS, or half-castes, have principally sprung. These Ceylonese, as they call themselves, in contradistinction to the Cingalese, possess all the vices of the natives, without the redeeming or ennobling qualities of either their European or Asiatic progenitors.

The Portuguese were not allowed to retain peaceable possession of the island, as Rajah Singha proclaimed himself king of Ceylon, and a long and bloody war ensued, which ended in the defeat and death of Rajah Singha, at the advanced age of one hundred and twenty years, which event occurred in the year 1592.

The Portuguese now resolved upon subjugating Kandy, which had remained to this period an independent state, and sent a large force thither for that purpose, which was defeated, suffering great loss.

It was in the year 1602, that the Dutch first turned their attention towards Ceylon; their possessions in the East Indies were vast and lucrative, and this island would open a new gate to gain, could they obtain a footing; consequently, in furtherance of their design, Admiral Spillbergen was despatched by the Prince of Orange and States General of Holland, with three men-of-war, fully armed and equipped, to open communication with the natives.

The fleet anchored south of Batticalloa on the 29th of March in that year, and the admiral immediately commenced a correspondence with the governor of Batticalloa, and finally despatched a messenger to the king of Kandy, Wimala Dharmaa, who received him with cordiality, and sent a letter to the admiral, written by himself, inviting the admiral to his kingdom. Accordingly, on the 6th of July following, Admiral Spillbergen, with his suite, set out for Kandy, and they were treated by the king with great attention and hospitality; every opportunity was afforded them to acquire information, and every public building opened to their inspection. The king appeared desirous to have the Dutch for allies, and offered every facility for carrying on trade between the two nations; endeavouring at the same time, with eager curiosity, to obtain insight into the laws, customs, and religion of Europe.

The admiral's mission proved a most successful one, as he obtained permission to build a fort on the sea-shore, and to carry on a free trade in cinnamon and pepper. Spillbergen sailed from Batticalloa on the 2nd of September, and, espying three Portuguese sail off the coast of Ceylon, he made for, engaged with, and finally captured these vessels, and sent them as presents to the king of Kandy.

In the following year, Schalt De Weerd was sent by the Dutch to Ceylon, and was received by their new ally, Wimala Dharmaa, in the most amicable manner, and an ambassador from the king of Kandy accompanied De Weerd when he sailed for Achen. De Weerd, however, subsequently exasperated the king of Kandy by breaking the treaty of alliance, and releasing four Portuguese vessels which had been recently captured by him. Wimala Dharmaa, upon the return of the Dutch squadron to the coast of Ceylon, remonstrated with the admiral upon this violation of the treaty and breach of faith; and the ambassador excited Wimala Dharmaa's suspicion, cautioning him against the treachery of his new allies.

Shortly afterwards, the admiral requested the king to visit him on board his ship; but this the monarch positively refused to do, fearing that he might be made prisoner, alleging, as his reason, that the queen was alone at Kandy, and that he must return to her. De Weerd continued to press his request with impertinent importunity, and concluded by saying, that the king need be in no hurry to return to the lascivious queen, as doubtless she had found some one to supply the king's place before this time: adding, that if his request was not complied with, he would not attack Galle, according to the articles of the treaty. Wimala Dharmaa immediately ordered his attendants to seize De Weerd, saying, "Seize that foul-mouthed pig!" A skirmish then ensued between the Kandians and the Dutch, as the former essayed to carry their monarch's orders into effect, and

De Weerd and many of his attendants were killed.

It is impossible to read of the conduct of Schalt De Weerd without loathing the character of the despicable, treacherous, coarse, Dutchman, who met the fate his insolence drew on his head; and, although historians endeavour to palliate his conduct, by saying that he was heated with wine; in the estimation of all right-minded men this excuse, if a correct one, only heightens the folly of the Dutch, in sending an admiral, addicted to drunkenness, to negotiate and carry out a treaty with an ally.

The following epigrammatic and terse note was sent by the king of Kandy to the second officer in command of the squadron:—

"He who drinks wine is worse than a sow. Buddha has executed justice. If you want peace, let there be peace—If war, then war."

It appears from history, that the Dutch allowed the death of De Weerd to pass unnoticed, as they did not declare war against Wimala Dharmaa, who died in 1604, and was succeeded by his brother, Senerat, who married the widowed queen of Kandy.

We find no further mention of the Dutch until the year 1612, when Marcellus De Boschouder arrived at Kandy, and entered into a new treaty with the Kandian sovereign, offensive and defensive; they were then granted the exclusive right of trading in Ceylon, and were allowed to commence building a fort at Cottiar. The Portuguese, already in possession of the island, viewed with jealous hostility the privileges granted to the Dutch; and immediately on the fort of Cottiar being commenced, despatched an army, consisting of more than 4,000 soldiers, composed of Portuguese, Cingalese, and Moormen, to attack the fort, which they took after a desperate resistance made by the Dutch, and butchered in the most barbarous manner the whole of the occupants, including women and children.

This massacre of his new allies, by the Portuguese, so exasperated Senerat, that he sent an army of 5,000 men in pursuit, who fell in with the invaders before they reached their own territories, and vanquished them, making many prisoners, from whom they demanded heavy ransoms. The king of Kandy now resolved upon expelling the Portuguese from Ceylon, and commenced war in a vigorous style against them, successfully; and, in 1614, we learn that an envoy from the viceroy of Goa proceeded to Kandy, and proposed a treaty of peace, which Senerat refused to accede to. From this date until 1635, we find the Kandians, assisted by the Dutch, at continued war with the Portuguese; the latter erecting forts at Trincomalee and Batticalloa, for the protection of the coast, but suffering constant and severe defeats; the Kandian army advancing as far as Colombo, in their attempts to expel the Portuguese from Ceylon: and it was only after a protracted and desperate struggle that the Portuguese succeeded in retaining possession of the fort of Colombo.

In the year 1635, Senerat died, after a brilliant reign of thirty years, and was succeeded by his eldest son, Raja Singha II.

Wijaya Paalaa, the king's brother, claimed as his right, that Matelé and the adjacent provinces should be formed into a separate kingdom, and he proclaimed their monarch; and endeavoured to enforce his demand by flying to arms, and calling in the aid of the Portuguese, who readily acceded to this request in the expectation that the commotion produced by civil war would aid their own designs.

Historians differ materially as to the number of the invading army—Ribeiro and Botelho stating that it was composed of seven hundred Europeans, and twenty-eight thousand Indians; while

M 2

Valentyn affirms that it consisted of two thousand three hundred Europeans and half-castes, with six thousand Caffres. But be the number what it might, it is certain that a large army, commanded by Don Diego de Melho, did penetrate into the interior, and, after ransacking Kandy, retired to Gannaruwa. Here Rajah Singha, the king of Kandy, surrounded them with his forces, putting all to death, either by the sword or barbarous modes of torture, and subsequently cut off their heads and piled them up in a pyramidical form, as a warning to all aggressors; and history asserts that only eight-and-thirty Europeans escaped this frightful slaughter.

In the year 1637, the Kandian monarch resolved upon calling in the aid of his Dutch allies to assist him in vanquishing the Portuguese, and driving them from Ceylon, and sent ambassadors to Batavia for that purpose, who were received with every mark of respect; and envoys from the Dutch were immediately despatched to Kandy. A treaty was entered into, whereby the Dutch agreed to furnish troops to the Kandian monarch upon the stipulation that the whole expenses of the war, on land and at sea, were to be defrayed by Rajah Singha. This the king consented to readily, but insisted that all the forts built by the

Portuguese, as they were taken, should be placed in his hands. All being now satisfactorily arranged, the envoys returned, and Admiral Westerwold was sent in command of a force of six hundred men and several pieces of cannon, who immediately attacked Batticalloa, wresting it from the Portuguese; and the king of Kandy, as a token of gratitude, sent two ambassadors to Batavia with presents to the General and Council of the Indies.

Trincomalee was taken from the Portuguese in 1639, and by the orders of Rajah Singha the fort was razed to the ground, and not one stone left standing on the other. The fort at Batticalloa had previously shared the same fate, so that the whole of the fortifications belonging to the Portuguese, on the eastern coast, were now destroyed.

In the year 1640, the war continued to rage with renewed vigour, success following the Kandian and Dutch troops. Negombo, a fortified town about eight leagues and a-half to the north, was taken by the Dutch after a faint resistance made by the Portuguese, as the spirits of the men were sinking under the continued prosperity that followed the Dutch arms. Immediately after taking Negombo, the Dutch marched to Point de Galle, and stormed the place, which was taken after a vigorous resistance had been made by the governor, Ferreiro de Bretto, who fought by the side of his men the whole night of the assault, and fell covered with wounds, and his life was only spared at the entreaty of his noble and heroic wife.

This affords us an opportunity of relating an instance of the devotion and courage of woman, where her affections are called forth, and which is recorded by Ribeiro, who states, the governor of Point de Galle, Ferreiro de Bretto, was married to a woman who was passionately attached to him, and that on the night of the assault she remained at his side on the batteries, animating and cheering him by her presence and courage. At length, after receiving five wounds, a blow with a musket levelled him, and the soldier was about to dispatch him when his wife threw herself between them, calling upon him as a man and a Christian to spare her husband's life. Finding the soldier hesitate, she implored him to take her life first, and thus save her the anguish of seeing her beloved husband butchered before her eyes, and threw herself on her knees, clinging to her prostrate husband. A Dutch officer, who was near, hastened to the group, desired the soldier to desist, raised the weeping lady, and had the gallant governor tended until his wounds were healed.

Admiral Koster, under whose command Galle had been taken, was now made governor of the place, and he immediately commenced building and repairing the fortifications; but finding the Portuguese were making preparations to retake Point de Galle, he deemed it necessary to call in the aid of the Kandian king, and proceeded to Kandy for that purpose. Rajah Singha received him with cold civility, and, although he promised to assist the Dutch admiral against the Portuguese, refrained from keeping his word, as he considered that were the Dutch to become masters of the south of the island he would only be exchanging his enemies.

The king now appeared to have awakened to the line of policy which had induced the Dutch to give him the aid of their troops to expel the Portuguese from Kandy, which was, that they might eventually become the masters of the whole island, as every place which had been taken by the Dutch had a large garrison left there to guard and protect it from the natives as much as from the Portuguese. Admiral Koster vehemently pressed the king for his aid, which was at last peremptorily refused. The admiral then accused the king's ministers of interfering to prevent Rajah Singha keeping his treaty with the Dutch. High words ensued, and the admiral quitted the king's presence in great wrath, setting out immediately for Galle, which he was never destined to reach, as he was murdered on the road between Kandy and Batticalloa, it is said by the king's orders.

The Portuguese appear to have been imbued with their former valour, as they retook Negombo, and there were constant skirmishes all over the island between them and the Dutch. In the year 1644, the fortune of war again placed Negombo in the hands of the Dutch, and they forthwith fortified the town, throwing up earthen bastions at every corner of the fort, and on these were mounted several pieces of cannon.

In 1646, a temporary pacification was entered into between the Dutch and Portuguese, which continued until 1654, and, during the intervening period a species of desultory war was carried on by Rajah Singha against the Dutch and Portuguese.

The Dutch authorities at Negombo, in 1646, carried off some of the king of Kandy's tame elephants, and slew them for the sake of their tusks and molar teeth. This act of wanton aggression naturally excited the anger and aroused the vengeance of Rajah Singha, who without loss of time surrounded the Dutch troops, took their commander, Adrian van der Stell, prisoner, caused him to be strangled, then cut off his head, and sent it enclosed in a silken wrapper to his countrymen who were stationed on the sea coast, with a message to the effect that thus he punished murderers and robbers.

In the year 1655, hostilities again recommenced between the Dutch and Portuguese, and Caltura was taken by the former in the October of that year. During the month of December following, the Dutch took prisoner the Portuguese governor of Jaffnapatam, as he was on his road from Manaar to Colombo, then the stronghold of the Portuguese. The Dutch now prosecuted the war against the Portuguese with renewed energy; and, marching up to Colombo, laid siege to that city, blockading it both by sea and land; and, after severe loss on both sides, and an obstinate resistance on the part of the Portuguese for seven months, it was surrendered by capitulation, the Portuguese stipulating that they should be allowed to retire unimpeded to Jaffnapatam.

The accounts given by Ribeiro of the sufferings

of the Portuguese during this siege are frightful. Reduced to starvation, they swallowed the most loathsome matter, resorting to the most revolting expedients to sustain life—maternal love being engulphed in the pangs of hunger, and mothers cutting the throats of infants at their breast, devoured their offspring to sustain life. These accounts are too horrible to dwell upon, and we willingly let a veil fall over them.

Not contented with the victory they had already obtained, the Dutch pursued the Portuguese to Jaffnapatam, thereby violating the articles of the capitulation; and, after a siege of four months, it was surrendered, and the inhabitants made prisoners of war. The Portuguese historian vituperates most bitterly the indignities offered to his nation by the Dutch—houses pillaged, plantations destroyed, wives dishonoured, and daughters ravished, are amongst the crimes that he attributes to the Dutch conquerors.

It is at all times fearful to contemplate the horrors of war, and its attendant misery to individuals, even of the victorious nation, but how much greater to meditate on the sufferings of those attached to the conquered country? But in no history do we find greater atrocities recorded than those laid to the charge of the Dutch after the surrender of Jaffnapatam, in 1658, and which terminated Portuguese dominion in Ceylon; but our own sentiments cannot better be expressed than in Fox's favourite maxim, "Iniquissimam pacem justissimo bello antefero."

We conclude the account of the Portuguese rule in the island, by quoting the following from Percival's "Ceylon:"—

"The improvements made in the cultivation of Ceylon by the Portuguese were by no means considerable—that people, when they first took possession of it, were rather warriors than merchants. Their continual wars with the natives contributed to keep up the same spirit; and their principal attention seems to have been directed to the fortification of a few stations on the coast, and the erection of some military posts to awe the natives. But the Portuguese appear never to have properly discovered the advantages to be derived from this island, either in a commercial or military point of view. Their dominion extended all around it, and no station could be pointed out more commodious for a depôt, either of merchandize or military stores. These advantages were overlooked by the court of Lisbon; and those individuals who were sent to the command at Ceylon, were more anxious to gratify their pride by conquest, and their avarice by extortion, than to pursue a plan of permanent advantage either to the mother country, or to the colony. The Portuguese, therefore, by their own misconduct, were deprived of this valuable island before they were aware of the benefits to be derived from it."

Although we do not coincide completely with the view taken by this excellent writer, still it is self-evident that the Portuguese paid but little attention to the cultivation of this prolific spot of earth, and we do not find amongst Portuguese records any statement of the proceeds of any pearl-fishery; so that we may conclude that comparatively little attention was paid to the commercial or agricultural capabilities of Ceylon. However, it must be borne in mind that the Portuguese had to contend against innumerable difficulties, being not only at war with the natives, whom they never entirely conquered, but continually harassed by skirmishes and war with their European enemies, the Dutch.

The following is a list of Portuguese governors and commanders in Ceylon, as given by Ribeiro:—Pedro Lopez de Souza, Jerome de Azevado, Francois de Menezes, Manuel Mascarenhas, Homen, Nunho, Alvares Perreira, Constandin de Sà y Noronha, G. d'Albuquerque, D. George d'Almeida, Diego de Mello, Antoine Mascarenhas, Philippe Mascarenhas, Francois de Mello de Castro, Antoine de Souza, Continho, under whom Colombo was lost. At Jaffnapatam and Manaar there were also Antoine d'Amarel y Menezes, the last of their captain-generals.

CHAPTER X.

Historical account continued from 1659 to 1795, when the Dutch surrendered, by capitulation, their possessions in Ceylon to the British—List of Dutch Governors—Summary of the effect of Portuguese and Dutch rule upon the Cingalese character—Philalethe's account of the same.

THE year succeeding the subjugation of the Portuguese by the Dutch in Ceylon, namely, in 1659, Captain Robert Knox, the first author who wrote an account of the islands, was taken prisoner at Batticalloa, the frigate Ann, which he commanded, having been wrecked off that coast, when the natives made him and several of his crew prisoners, who, by the orders of Rajah Singha II., were sent up to Kandy, and there held in captivity until 1679, when an escape was effected.

From "Knox's Historical Revelation," we learn

that the Dutch experienced great difficulty in retaining the possessions which they had wrested from the Portuguese, as Rajah Singha, the king of Kandy, was constantly at war with them, endeavouring to retake the various fortified places and strongholds occupied by the Dutch. Notwithstanding these continual skirmishes, the Dutch, wishing to retain a footing in the island, in furtherance of their commercial and political views, endeavoured to preserve an amicable course with the natives, and sent frequent embassies to the Kandian court, to assure the monarch of their anxiety and desire to be at peace with him. Rajah Singha was not to be appeased by assurances, or professions; occasionally, he would receive the embassies with toleration, while at other times he would detain their envoys, without assigning any reason for so doing.

In the year 1670, we find Rajah Singha detained an envoy, who was resolved to leave Kandy, or sacrifice his life in the attempt. This noble-spirited man, whose name we do not find recorded, but which ought to have been handed down to posterity as an example of dauntless bravery, presented himself before the king, as he sat on his throne giving audience to his court, fully armed and equipped for a journey, his personal attendants remaining outside the palace gates, saying that he had come to take leave of his Majesty, as he was about setting out immediately for Colombo. He bowed respectfully to the walls, in accordance with the etiquette observed at the Kandian court on taking leave, and quitted the palace without any attempt being made by the king to arrest his progress. On the contrary, Rajah Singha gave orders that he was to proceed on his journey unmolested, and to receive what aid he might require in so doing. We can fully appreciate the Kandian monarch's conduct—himself a noble brave character, he could well estimate the dauntless daring and courage, that would prompt such a course of action. And had the Duch invariably pursued an open, honourable course with Rajah Singha, they would not have met with the constant annoyance which they experienced from the king of Kandy.

No language of ours can so well explain the erroneous plan they pursued as that of Knox himself, at that time a prisoner at the Kandian court:—

"The Dutch, knowing his proud spirit, make their advantage of it by flattering him with their ambassadors, telling him that they are his Majesty's humble subjects and servants, and that it is out of loyalty to him that they build forts, and keep watches round about his country, to prevent foreign nations and enemies from coming; and that as they are thus employed in his Majesty's service, so it is for sustenance, which they want, that occasioned their coming up into his Majesty's country. And thus, by flattering him, and ascribing to him high and honourable titles, which are things he greatly delights in, sometimes they prevail to have the country they have invaded, and he to have the honour; yet at other times, and upon better consideration, he will not be flattered, but falls upon them at unawares, and does them great damage."

Events pursued the same monotonous routine, between the Kandian and Dutch, until 1672, when France directed her attention to Lanka-diva, and despatched a squadron, commanded by Monsieur de la Haye, which anchored off Cottiar, and immediately sent envoys to the Kandian king. Rajah Singha received them most amicably, and granted them permission to build a fort near the Bay of Trincomalee. Monsieur de la Haye shortly afterwards sailed for the Coromandel coast, sending in his stead Monsieur de Lanerolle, accompanied by a suite, to the Kandian court. Most unfortunately for the French nation, Monsieur de Lanerolle was ill calculated for a political mission—hot-headed and impetuous, absurdly vain of the power, grandeur, and customs of his own nation, he refused observance to the code of etiquette adopted at Rajah Singha's court, and treated the monarch with undue familiarity and insolence. This exasperated Rajah Singha, and, upon the return of Monsieur de la Haye, he found De Lanerolle a prisoner.

The Dutch, taking advantage of this position of affairs, gave chase to the French squadron, taking some of their vessels, and the fort near Trincomalee which they had built. So terminated the only well-arranged scheme concocted by the French to obtain a settlement or possessions in the island of Ceylon; and which, in all probability, would have been successful, had it not been for the insane, overweening vanity of De Lanerolle, which was as strongly characteristic of the French nation in the seventeenth, as it is in the nineteenth century—it being a national failing, and not an individual's foible. For vanity, and nought but self-sufficient vanity, *caused* the disastrous events, precursors of the downfall of the French empire, which occurred during 1848; and the *effect* has been the convulsion of Europe, shaking it to its very centre.

There is a paucity of interesting matter connected with the history of Ceylon, until the year 1679, when the Dutch governor of Colombo, Van Goen, sent an embassy to Kandy, requiring the king to abide by the articles of the treaty made between the two powers. To this the king promised adherence, his warlike propensities and energy having become subdued by age and infirmity, for at this time he was between seventy and eighty. In the month of October, in the same year, Knox effected his escape, after having been detained a prisoner at the Kandian court for twenty years.

Again, there seems to have been a cessation of historical events worthy of record, until the year 1685, when Rajah Singha II. died, after a protracted reign of fifty-one years, and was succeeded by his son, Wimala Dharma Suriya. Knox describes Rajah Singha, with whom he frequently conversed during his captivity, to have been a well-formed, portly, athletically-built man, of a darker hue than most of his countrymen, with keen shrewd eyes "that were always in motion, who bears his years well, being between seventy and eighty years of age, and though an old man, yet appears not to be like one, neither in countenance nor manners." He was abstemious in his diet, and chaste in morals, and punished severely any dereliction from morality that he discovered among his court. Knox writes—

"Many times when he hears of the misdemeanours of some of his nobles, he not only executes them, but severely punisheth the women, and he hath so many spies, that there is but little done which he knows not of; and often he gives command to expel all the women out of the city, not one to remain; but, by little and little, when they think his wrath is appeased, they do creep in again."

Rajah Singha possessed, in common with most satraps of the East, an inordinate fondness for dress and jewels, delighting to adorn his person with gaudy-coloured raiment, and ornaments studded with jewels. History affirms that Rajah Singha exhorted his son and successor, Wimala Dharma Suriya the Second, on his death-bed, to remain at peace with the Dutch, and allow them to retain possession of their territories; and, being of a tranquil temperament, he followed his father's counsel; consequently, during his reign, there are no accounts of a peculiarly interesting character.

In 1707, Wimala Dharma Suriya died, and was succeeded by his son, Narendra Singha. The following year the Dutch obtained possession of the island of Java, and, at the commencement of 1709, they banished the ex-king of Java, Susasan Mang Burat Mas, with his family and attendants, to Ceylon. There were many followers of this king who shared his exile, and thus it was that the Malays became residents in the island, where, as a natural result, they multiplied considerably.

In 1721, the queen of Kandy died, and the Dutch sent an embassy to Kandy to condole with the king, Narendra Singha, upon that event—the Dutch, preserving all external tokens of respect for the king of Kandy, who allowed them to remain in peaceable possession of their dominions in Ceylon. The letter of condolence sent by governor Rumph was to this effect—"To implore the Almighty to comfort his Majesty on the trying occasion of the demise of the high-born, excellent, and all-accomplished queen."

In 1723, some Javanese princes and chiefs, forty-four in number, that had revolted against the Dutch at Batavia, were banished to Ceylon, and thus more Malays were introduced into the island by the Dutch.

In 1729, Governor Vuyst (governor of Colombo) made an attempt to render himself an independent sovereign, and in the prosecution of that scheme had recourse to the most atrocious cruelties, and perpetrated crimes of the blackest dye. He was at last taken prisoner by his countrymen and sent to Batavia, tried, and convicted of high treason to his country, and was sentenced to be broken alive upon the wheel, his body to be quartered, and then to be burned to ashes, and those ashes to be collected and cast into the sea. It is revolting to humanity to read these loathsome details, savouring of the ages of barbarism, and, though Vuyst met a merited reward for his crimes, in having had sentence of death executed on his person—still breaking alive on the wheel, quartering the body, throwing the ashes into the sea, refusing them Christian burial, is almost past credence, as having occurred in the eighteenth century, and casts a stigma of disgrace upon the nation that would sanction torturing the living body, or wreaking vengeance on senseless remains.

In 1739, Narendra Singha died without issue, and was succeeded by his brother-in-law, Sreewijaya Rajah Singha. History says that the character of Narendra Singha was vile: he was most licentious, indulging his passions without restraint; prone to anger, he insulted his nobles, and was on the brink of losing his crown, through a rebellion which these injured nobles headed. Notwithstanding all this, he reigned two-and-thirty years, and during this period his Dutch allies retained peaceable possession, and employed the advantage offered to increase their maritime dominions.

During the reigns of the last two Kandian kings, the ordinances of the Buddhist religion had been considerably neglected, the priests having become lax and careless in the administration of the various rites thereof; and, in 1745, Sreewijaya Rajah Singha sent a deputation of his chiefs to Siam, to request that priests might be allowed to come to Kandy, to restore the neglected ordinances of Buddha. In compliance with this request, several *upasampada*, or high priests, returned with the chiefs, who set to work vigorously, immediately on their arrival, to fulfil the mission which had brought them from Siam. It appears that Sreewijaya Rajah Singha devoted the principal portion of his time to purify and restore the religion of the state, and Buddhism under this monarch was restored to all its former grandeur.

During this reign, hostilities were renewed between the Dutch and Kandians; and, although some of the maritime provinces were taken by the latter, they were eventually retaken by the Dutch; and, in 1747, Sreewijaya Rajah Singha died, and was succeeded by his brother-in-law,

Kirtisree Rajah Singha, who, in 1750, sent another deputation of chiefs to Siam, to procure priests of Buddha; and, in 1753, these chiefs returned to Ceylon, accompanied by some Siamese priests of the highest rank, and Wellewike, the chief priest, was placed at the head of the Buddhist establishment in the island, under the title of Sanga Rajah.

In the year 1761, the violent measures adopted against the natives by governor Screuder, occasioned an insurrection on the western coast; the Kandians aided the insurgents against the Dutch, and thereby involved themselves in fresh hostilities, (for there had been for a short period a cessation,) and skirmishes were constantly carried on until the following year, when the Dutch made themselves masters of Kandy, Matelé, Doombera, and Wallapana; but Kirtisree Rajah Singha retook this portion of the kingdom, after the Dutch had held possession for nine months, and the slaughter that ensued is hideous to read of.

From this period, desultory warfare was carried on between the contending parties, until the Dutch appear to have obtained the advantage; as, in 1766, a new treaty was entered into between the Kandian monarch and the Dutch, which ensured to the latter the unmolested possession of all the places on the sea coast; and the Dutch now might look upon themselves as conquerors, having brought the eastern potentate under subjection, as by this treaty they dictated the articles which were agreed to by Kirtisree Rajah Singha, and one of these was, that the various humiliating ceremonies which were exacted by the king, when an envoy from the Dutch went to his court, were to be for the future entirely dispensed with, and totally abolished.

We must now take a retrospective view of events, and return to the year 1763, when Mr. Pybus was sent by the Madras government as ambassador to the king of Kandy, to assure the monarch of the friendly feelings of the English towards him, and the anxiety of the government to furnish him with the means of carrying on the war against the Dutch, and offered to enter into a treaty. National events of importance, and the stirring incidents of the American war, called for all the attention and money that our government had to bestow, and to this only can be attributed the non-fulfilment of the treaty entered into with Kirtisree Rajah Singha; but the impression produced by this breach of faith, on the minds of the king and royal family, was most prejudicial to the honour and probity of England.

In 1781, Kirtisree Rajah Singha died, and was succeeded by his brother Rajadhi Rajah Singha; and in the following year a fleet, commanded by Admiral Sir Edward Hughes, and a body of troops, headed by Sir Hector Munro, were dispatched by Lord Macartney, then Governor of Madras, to Ceylon, to take from the Dutch their territories in that island; and our troops took possession of Trincomalee, which the French re-took for the Dutch in the August of the same year, during the absence of Admiral Sir Edward Hughes, who had sailed for Madras to have some necessary repairs performed to his ships. Mr. Hugh Boyd had been sent with the expedition as ambassador to the king of Kandy, and left Trincomalee in February, but did not reach Kandy until the beginning of March, owing to the badness of the roads; for, although Trincomalee is less than 180 miles from Kandy, the route was a most tedious and perplexing one, Mr. Boyd and his companions having at times to force their way through a dense forest, or jungle. Previously to quitting Trincomalee, the following letter was despatched by Mr. Hugh Boyd to Rajadhi Rajah Singha:*—

"To the king of Kandy, &c.

"I have the honour of acquainting your highness, that I am appointed ambassador to your Highness, Durbar, by His Excellency the Right Hon. Lord Macartney, the Governor, and the President of Madras; and that I am charged with a letter to your highness, from the governor, in order to explain to you their favourable sentiments, and assure you of their friendship. I suppose your highness has already heard of the great successes of the English against their enemies, particularly the Dutch, whom they have now driven entirely from the coast of Coromandel, having taken from them their last settlement, Negapatam.

"To carry on the victories of the English against the Dutch, Vice-admiral Sir Edward Hughes, commander in-chief of the king of England's ship and marine forces in India, is now arrived with the fleet and force under his command at Trincomalee, in conjunction with the troops of the English East India Company. He has already taken one of their forts from the Dutch, called Trincomalee Fort, with many prisoners, and with-

* This letter will be found in the "Miscellaneous Works of Hugh Boyd," vol. II.

out opposition; and he is proceeding with vigour, and with certainty of equal success against their only other fort, called Ostendburgh, which must also yield to the great superiority of the British arms.

"This will certainly have been effected long before your highness can have received this letter. But in the character with which I have the honour of being invested, as ambassador to your highness, I am desirous to take the earliest opportunity in transmitting to you these happy particulars, to assure you that it is only against their enemies, the Dutch, that the arms of the English are directed, and that the highest respect and attention will be shown your highness's rights and dignity, and that your subjects will be treated with the utmost kindness and friendship, according to a declaration which his excellency, Sir Edward Hughes, admiral and commander-in-chief, has already published. I am happy in communicating these matters to your highness, not doubting that it will give you pleasure to hear of the success and power of your friends.

"As many more English ships and troops are expected soon to be here, and, as some great further operations will probably be soon carried on by them for the destruction of their enemies, and the advantage of their friends, I am ordered by his excellency, the Governor of Madras, to communicate to your highness, as soon as possible, the letter from him, which I have the honour of being charged with.

"I shall be happy, therefore, to deliver it to your highness in person, with every explanation and friendly assurance which you can desire, as soon as I shall know, in reply to this, that you have sent proper persons to conduct me thither; and this I hope your highness will be pleased to do immediately, as there ought to be no delay in transactions of so much importance.

"I am also charged with a letter to your highness, from his Highness Walah Jah, Nabob of the Carnatic, which I shall be happy to deliver to you. I only wait to have the honour of hearing from your highness, as I have desired; I shall then immediately proceed to enter on all these important matters, on the most friendly and satisfactory ground to your highness.

(Signed)

"HUGH BOYD."

Upon the arrival of our ambassador at Kandy, he met with innumerable delays, and was received with distrust and suspicion by the Kandian court; the natural result of our former breach of faith, and which but ill-accorded with the British character for probity. "It is now twenty years since your ambassador arrived here, while we waged war with our Dutch enemies: we replied frankly, and accepted cheerfully your offered and promised aid; but since your envoy left, not a breath have we heard of your offered aid, nor promised assistance. As you are now at war, in your turn, with the Dutch nation, and are desirous to injure them, and obtain their possessions, you come to us, professing that it is only for our benefit that you desire to force them to quit our kingdom. We doubt the sincerity of your nation, as we have ever met with treachery from Europeans."

Our ambassador made excuses for the non-fulfilment of the former treaty, and referred to the high character borne by England for probity and truth; but all his efforts proved abortive, and he quitted Kandy the latter end of March, without having accomplished either of the objects of his mission—namely, to make a treaty, and form an alliance with the king of Kandy—and for some years we left the Kandians and Dutch in undisturbed possession of Ceylon.

In the year 1785, Governor Vander Graaff first introduced paper currency into Ceylon; and, in 1789, the same governor caused a census to be taken of all the inhabitants of the maritime districts, subject to the Dutch East India Company; and the statistical returns gave eight hundred and seventeen thousand inhabitants, of both sexes, and of all ages.

In the year 1795, the union of Holland with France took place, and war was declared by us; and Colonel, afterwards General Stewart, was sent by the Governor of Madras, with a large force, to reduce Trincomalee, to which he laid siege, and, after the lapse of little more than three weeks, the fort was surrendered by the Dutch commander, as our troops were preparing to storm it. In the September following of that year, Jaffna was taken by the same general; Colpentyn was surrendered to the British forces, under the command of Colonel Bowser, on the 5th of November; and General Stewart shorly afterwards took Negombo. Success now followed the British arms in Ceylon, and General Stewart resolved upon attacking Colombo, the seat of government then as well as now, and marched for that place with his Majesty's 52nd, 73rd, and 77th regiments, accompanied by three battalions of Native Infantry, and some Bengal Artillery.

The route to Colombo lay through dense jungle, and over rivers swollen by the late rains; but no ambush was laid by the Dutch to obstruct the progress of our troops, and they reached the river Kelany (about four miles from the Fort of Colombo), which was defended by a strong fort, and there halted to await the expected coming of the Dutch troops. At the conclusion of the second day, intelligence reached them that the guns were dismantled and spiked, and that the troops had abandoned the fort, and retreated to Colombo. Our men crossed the river with great caution, fearing surprise, but no ambuscade had been laid. Our encampment was then formed, the siege of Colombo planned, and our soldiers immediately afterwards marched for the fort, expecting a strong resistance to be made by the Dutch; but to the astonishment both of General Stewart and the troops which he commanded, the only attempt to defend Colombo was made by a body of Malays, headed by a French officer, who were sent to meet them, but quickly retreated, and very shortly after Colombo surrendered, by capitulation, to the British forces, who were commanded by General Stewart and Captain Gardiner, R. N. Within a short period, the whole of the forts and possessions in the island belonging to the Dutch were delivered up to our troops.

We should not have found Ceylon so facile a

conquest, had it not been for the want of discipline and subordination found amongst the Dutch troops—the men refusing to obey their officers' orders, and the officers almost devoid of bravery or energy to defend their country's rights. According to "Percival's Ceylon," p. 92—"The Dutch force consisted of two battalions of Hollanders, the French Regiment of Wirtemberg, with some native troops, forming in all a force equal to that of the invaders."

In taking leave of the Dutch as rulers in Ceylon, we give the names of those who were sent there as governors. The first, in 1640, was W. J. Koster, who took Galle; J. Thysz, J. Matsuyher, J. Van Kiltenstein, A. Vander Meyden, R. Van Goens, J. Hustaur, L. Van Peil, T. Van Rhee, P. De Rhoo, G. De Heer, C. J. Simonsy, N. Becher, T. A. Rumph, A. Moll, J. Hertenberg, J. P. Schagen, P. Vuyst, S. Versluzs, G. Wontersz, J. C. Pielaat, D. V. Domburg, J. Maccara, Baron Von Imhoff, W. M. Bruininch, D. Overpeck, W. M. Bruininch, D. Overpeck, J. V. S. Von Galnesse, G. Van Vreeland, J. De Joug, J. G. Saton, J. Schrender, Baron Van Eck, A. Mooyart, J. W. Falck, W. J. Van der Graaff, J. G. Van Angelbeech, under whom Colombo and the entire possessions of the Dutch were delivered over to the British.

Under the Dutch, their own mode of worship was introduced into Ceylon, and there were many *professed* converts among the Cingalese. This arose from a regulation of the Dutch, which prohibited any native from holding an office, however humble, under their government, unless he professed to belong to their church.—The Dutch encouraged agriculture to a great extent, and introduced the cultivation of coffee, pepper, cardamons, and cinnamon. It was under Governor Falck that the latter shrub was *first* cultivated. The pearl-fisheries were also lucrative and productive, under their management; consequently, it must have been a national loss of no trivial nature, when so profitable and promising a settlement was wrested from them by the British.

We shall wind up our summary by glancing at the effect produced upon the native character by the line of conduct pursued by the Dutch, who acted as if they believed that their responsibility as Christians and enlightened men, commenced and terminated by forcing nominal religion upon the natives—by making an external avowal of Christianity the only stepping-stone to patronage, or employment under government; and they neglected no opportunity or means whereby wealth could be amassed. Their public policy and private enterprise began and ended with the same goal in view—namely, the acquirement of riches. Thus the English commenced their rule in Ceylon, having the impressions to eradicate which had been produced upon the minds of the Cingalese, through the sufferings they had experienced under the military and religious oppression of the Portuguese, and no less oppressive grasping and religious despotism of their Dutch successors.

These fearful examples, set by professing Christians, have been too forcibly stamped upon the feeble and flexible characters of the natives; and European vices have thus become engrafted upon the effeminate, pusillanimous dispositions of the Cingalese who inhabit the lowland and maritime districts, thus forming a character of the most despicable description.

We subjoin the following extract from "Philalethe's History of Ceylon," in support of our previously-expressed views and sentiments:—

"The Portuguese were under the influence of a sentiment of bigotry, which, when it becomes a predominant feeling in the human heart, equally disregards the suggestions of caution, admonitions of prudence, and the higher considerations of humanity. It is a blind impulse, and it has all the effect of blindness, both visual and mental;

in the strange deviations which it causes from the straight path of virtue and truth, and consequently of the best policy, and most stable interest. The Dutch did not bend before the grim Moloch of religious bigotry; but *cent. per cent. was their faith, gold was their object, and Mammon was their god.* But the idol of the Dutch is as unfavourable to the growth of the loftier virtues, and to all that tends to humanize the exercise of power, as that of the Portuguese. Avarice is a cold, calculating feeling, and where it totally pervades the bosom, absorbing the affections, and concentrating the desires in a single object, it renders the heart as impenetrable as a stone to those moral considerations which are more particularly associated with a benevolent regard for the happiness of those who are placed in subjection to our will, or within the sphere of our influence. The insensate avarice of the Dutch proved as unfavourable to the happiness of the people of Ceylon, as the enthusiastic bigotry of the Portuguese."

CHAPTER XI.

Kandian character—Personal appearance—Cingalese of the lowlands—Character of the women—Native government—King's officers—Customs—Mode of smelting iron—British rule from 1795 to 1805—Governor North—First English governor—Supreme Court of Judicature established—Kandian war—Fearful massacre of British troops—Dastardly and disgraceful conduct of Major Davie—Extraordinary escape of two soldiers—Summary of political events—False policy of General Macdowall—Noble conduct of Captain Nouradeen—Bravery of Major Johnson—Sir Thomas Maitland succeeds the Honourable Frederick North—The judicious rule of Governor North.

Before we enter upon the history of Ceylon under the British, as the subjugation of Kandy forms a prominent feature of our rule, we will give a sketch of the character of the people, and the government of that nation under the dominion of their own sovereigns and rulers. All those authors who have written upon Ceylon remark, with great justice, the difference of character that is observable between the inhabitants of the mountainous and those of the lowlands and maritime districts. It is an insult to a Kandian to call him a Cingalese, as the Kandians hold the latter in contempt. The Kandians term only the inhabitants of the lowlands, Cingalese; and the natives of the latter, when speaking of the former, invariably make the same distinction—calling them Kandians, and not Cingalese.

The Kandians are a purer race, possessing much nobility of character—are daring, courageous, and generous; whilst the Cingalese are cowardly, servile, and mean: and the nobles of Kandy assert (and it was stated to us by a Kandian chief of high rank, and the highest caste) that the vices of lying and thieving, now so fearfully prevalent in Ceylon, were introduced into the Kandian provinces by the Cingalese, who had acquired these intolerably despicable vices from intercourse with the Portuguese and Dutch. Robert Knox, who passed twenty years in captivity at Kandy, thus writes of them, in the seventeenth century:—

"Of all the vices, they are least addicted to stealing, the which they do exceedingly hate and

CINGALESE MAN.

abhor; so that there are but few robberies committed amongst them. They do much extol and commend chastity, temperance, *truth in words and actions;* and confess that it is out of weakness and infirmity that they cannot practise the same, acknowledging that the contrary vices are to be abhorred."

After making this statement, he gives the following one, which is somewhat contradictory, as regards their propensity to *lying.* But great allowance must be made for the position in which Knox was placed; as his protracted captivity for so long a period (during which time he had received many promises relative to his release) would not predispose him to place much reliance on their veracity, or enable him to give an unprejudiced opinion as to the national character. Notwithstanding, there is much truth to be found in the succeeding quotation, which gives, on the whole, a fair estimate of the Kandian character:—

"In understanding, quick and apprehensive; in design, subtle and crafty; in discourse, courteous, but full of flatteries; naturally inclined to temperance, both in meat and drink, *but not chastity;* near and provident in their families—commending good husbandry; in their dispositions, not passionate—neither hard to be reconciled when angry; in their promises very unfaithful—approving lying in themselves, but disliking it in others; delighting in sloth—deferring labour till urgent necessity compel them; neat in apparel; nice in eating, and not much given to sleep."

For the bravery, which we deem inherent in the Kandians, and their love of country, no better proof can be offered than the determined, vigorous, and protracted resistance opposed to the attempted subjugation of their country by the Portuguese, Dutch, and British. And this dislike to the imposed yoke of a foreign power exists to no small extent at this moment, as the recent insurrection proved; whilst the Cingalese have tamely submitted to foreign rule for more than a century and a half. The difference of person apparent in the Kandians and Cingalese, is as marked as their mental dissimilitude. The bearing of the Kandian is haughty and erect; the complexion, bright bronze, or brown; the eye large—meeting the observer's fixedly and undauntedly; the brow high—nose, well formed and prominent; and the expression of the face intelligent. While, on the contrary, the deportment of the Cingalese is servile and crouching; their complexion of a yellower brown; the eye, although of good size, seldom fully opens, and endeavours to avoid looking fixedly on the observer; the brow low, the nose less prominent, and not so well formed, as that of the Kandian; and the expression of the countenance has a character of servile, low cunning.

Although it is affirmed by writers that the Kandians and Cingalese are both descended from the same parent stock, we disagree with them materially, as the Kandians have all the distinctive marks of a nobler race, and purer blood—being, in our opinion, the offspring of Malabars, who had intermarried with the Veddahs, or aborigines of Ceylon, whose blood has remained pure, owing to non-admixture with foreign conquerors; as Kandy remained a free, warlike, and independent state long after the lowlands had experienced the yoke of numerous conquerors, of various nations: whilst the Cingalese are the descendants of the followers of the Indian King, Wijeya, who conquered Ceylon long anterior to the Christian era. But the latter race has deteriorated, both physically and mentally, by constant admixture with the various tribes and nations who have conquered, colonized, or visited the lowlands and maritime districts.

Although Buddhism inculcates the practice of chastity and continence more than any other heathen religion, yet in no part of Asia is the observance of these virtues less practised than by the followers of Buddha, and more especially in Ceylon, where the want of chastity in woman, which pervades all classes, beginning with the highest and descending to the lowest caste, is lamentable in the extreme. This appears to have been a national failing, from the earliest records of the island; but in a work intended for general perusal it would be unadvisable to quote *verbatim et seriatim* from Knox on this topic, who expatiates fully and strongly on the total disregard evinced by the women for chastity. We shall, therefore, confine ourselves to the following extract from that author:—

"Whilst a woman would flee from the contact of a man of a lower caste than herself, so would she desire and seek it most anxiously with one of her own caste, or of a higher one."

At this time it is the crying sin of the natives, even among women professing Christianity; and many murders arise from the excited jealousy of husbands and lovers, who come unexpectedly, and find a paramour with the women; when the ever-ready knife, or any other weapon that is near, is seized hold of, and bloodshed ensues.

The government of Kandy was an absolute and

CINGALESE WOMAN.

despotic one, the king having unlimited power over the lives and property of his subjects: in fact, the Kandian nation being the slaves of the monarch—slavery was permitted, and practised to a great extent throughout the kingdom. But the king was not only lord paramount of the soil, the whole produce of which he could claim, if it pleased him so to do; but he claimed and enforced equal ownership over the persons of the cultivators.

The men of the next rank to the monarch were the two adikars, or prime ministers; and these adikars also acted as judges, and to them an appeal could be made, should a suitor feel dissatisfied with the decision of the governor of his province—and from the adikar a final appeal lay to the king in person; but the king reserved to himself the power of inflicting capital punishment, and human life was constantly sacrificed in the most wanton manner, and on the most puerile occasions. These adikars were appointed by, and held office during the king's pleasure. After the adikars came the dissaaves, or governors of provinces. A certain number of this body were appointed to the command of the king's troops; and these held a superior rank to their fellows, whose business it was to receive and pay into the royal treasury the tribute to the king, and maintain peace and order in their provinces. The dissaaves, like the adikars, received their appointment from the king, who would disgrace them, depriving them of their offices, and putting them to death, or torturing them, as caprice dictated.

The next in rank and power were the ratramahatmeers, who acted as deputies to those dissaaves, who commanded the king's guards, or troops, by preserving proper order in their provinces during the disaaves' necessary absence from their districts, whilst on duty at court. Under these ratramahatmeers were many inferior officers, who obtained their posts either by bribery or from the patronage bestowed by their superior. When the dissaave, or ratramahatmeer, travelled through his province, to administer justice, he was attended by the whole of his inferior officers. Before the dissaave, or ratramahatmeer, was borne a long whip made from the fibres of the talipot palm, which was the emblem of their official rank, and also used by them as an implement of punishment. This whip was constantly kept in motion when borne before these officials; and the sound produced served to warn all travellers or passers-by to clear the road, and leave a free passage, and also to apprize those who had complaints or charges to

RATRAMAHATMEER.

prefer, that the dissaave, or ratramahatmeer, was at hand.

When a complaint had been substantiated, which, in the estimation of the official, called for corporal punishment, the criminal was straightway stripped, tied to the first tree, and flogged with the whip which a short time previously had given notice of the judge's approach. This business concluded, the dissaave would resume his way, to enact the same scene elsewhere. Fines, imprisonment, and torture were the other punishments inflicted by the dissaaves and ratramahatmeers, in the course of these periodical visitations, which were conducted with great state, ceremony, and parade; and were also very lucrative, as the dissaaves and ratramahatmeers were bribed to decide in the briber's favour, and consequently whoever could or would administer the largest bribe almost invariably gained his suit. But on the reverse of this pleasant picture stood a despotic monarch, who, from the merest whim, would take from them their rank and wealth. Knox, after referring to the above facts, writes :—

"But there is something came after, that makes all the honour and wealth of these great courtiers not at all desirable—and that is, that they are so obnoxious to the king's displeasure, which is so customary, that it is no disgrace for a nobleman to have been in chains—nay, and in the common gaol, too; and the great men, too, are so ready, when the king commands, to lay hold on one another, as he to command them, and glad to have the honour to be the king's executioners, hoping to have the place of the executed."

In the foregoing quotation is found a summary of the uncertain tenure of place and power, when held from or under a despotic monarch, who even dictated what description of dwelling his subjects were to build or inhabit. It may appear almost paradoxical that a nation should have suffered *one* man to tyrannize over their persons, actions, and properties, to the extent which the Kandians permitted under their own kings, and should yet rebel against the mild rule of the British government. But such is the anomaly presented by human nature, that we will cheerfully and willingly endure what we voluntarily submit to, or our forefathers have borne before us, however intolerable it may appear to others; whilst the supposition or knowledge that we are to be forced into a particular line of action, dictated by a novel or foreign power, who rules with its own laws, although the administration of those laws may be equitable, and for our benefit, produces a feeling which causes us to consider ourselves aggrieved; and we rebel against the foreign yoke This is not only a national feeling predominant amongst the Kandians, but will be found in every quarter of the globe, and is applicable to the inhabitants of every country.

Knox, after describing the various modes adopted for building their dwellings, says:—

"For they *are not permitted* to build their houses above one story high; neither may they cover them with tiles, nor whiten their walls with lime; but there is a clay which is as white, and that they use sometimes. The poorest sort have not above one room in their houses—few above two, unless they be great men; *neither doth the king allow them to build better.* The great people have handsome and commodious houses. They have commonly two buildings—one opposite the other, joined together on each side with a wall, which makes a square court-yard in the middle. Round about against the walls of their house, are banks of clay to sit upon. Their slaves and servants dwell round about without, in other houses, with their wives and children."

This author speaks of the ancient remains of grandeur which were found in Kandy, and these will be noticed in a chapter devoted to the antiquities of Ceylon. In writing of their cultivation of rice, the staple commodity of food for the nation, he tells us that their ploughs consisted of "a piece of wood, shod with iron [these primitive ploughs are used in the interior at the present day, and to them are yoked buffaloes, or bullocks] proper for the country." He describes minutely the Oriental custom of treading out the grain from the husk, "and this is a far quicker and easier way than threshing; at reaping also they are excellent good, just after the English manner." He also states, "their rents were brought to the king thrice in each year, and were generally paid in the produce of the soil, and not in money." Besides these, however, whatsoever is wanted in "the king's house, and they have it, they must, upon the king's order, bring it"

Knox describes the state of learning in the Kandian dominions, to have been in a fearful state of degradation, to what it had been in former times; and it is certain that for centuries, the inhabitants of Ceylon had been retrograding in learning, arts, and sciences, more particularly since the Portuguese and Dutch had obtained a footing in the island, "Their learning," says Knox, "is but small; all they ordinarily learn is, to read and write, but it is no shame to a man if he can do neither—nor have they any schools wherein they might be instructed in these or any other arts." The Kandians polished the precious stones found in their dominions by a species of grinding-stone, still in use among them, and which is very similar to an European one. They smelted the gold found in their rivers, in furnaces, formed of a species of white clay, found inland, and they fashioned the precious metal into ornaments for the head, nose, ankles, fingers, and toes; and in the gold were frequently set precious stones and gems. We subtract the succeeding lines from Knox, as giving a most accurate and interesting account of the mode adopted by the Kandians to obtain iron from the ore. He commences by saying, that the ore was found throughout the country, and that it generally lay about five or six feet below the surface of the earth:—

"First they take these stones and lay them in a heap, and burn them with wood, which makes them softer and fitter for the furnace. When they have so done, they have a kind of furnace, made with a white sort of clay, wherein they put a quantity of charcoal; there is a back to the furnace, behind which the man stands that blows.

Behind the furnace they have two logs of wood placed fast in the ground, hollow at the top like two pots; upon the mouths of these two pieces of hollow wood they tie a piece of deer's skin, on each part a piece, with a small hole, as big as a man's finger, in each skin. In the middle of each skin, a little beside the holes, are two strings, tied fast to as many sticks stuck in the ground, like a spring, bending like a bow—this pulls the skin upwards."

He then describes minutely the process of blowing, and continues:—

"As the stones are thus burning, the dross that is in them melts, and runs out at the bottom, where there is a slanting hole made for the purpose. Out of this hole runs the dross-like streams of fire, and the iron remains behind, which, when it is purified as they think enough, they drive through the same slanting hole; then they give it a chop half way through, and so fling it into the water: they so chop it that it may be seen that it is good iron, for the satisfaction of those who are minded to buy."

The state of religion observable among the Kandians, anterior to, at the period of, and subsequent to Knox's captivity, will be noticed hereafter; and we will for the present bid adieu to the ancient Kandians, and resume our history subsecutively, from taking possession of the Dutch settlements in Ceylon by the British, in 1796.

Mr. Andrews was sent as ambassador to the Kandian court, by the Madras government, to obtain Rajah Singha's ratification to the preliminary treaty, and to negotiate a definitive one on more enlarged principles, by which the Kandian nation was to have enjoyed privileges and advantages which they had not possessed in tranquillity for more than two centuries. Ten armed vessels were to have been placed at the king's service, entirely free from our superintendence, to carry on foreign and home trade; and the *seways*, or salt-marshes at Putlam, then most profitable, and which had been in the possession of the Dutch, from whom they had passed into our hands, were to have been given up to Rajadhi Rajah Singha. Our ambassador could not succeed in bringing matters to a termination, as the king of Kandy required various alterations to be made in the proposed treaty, to which Mr. Andrews was not authorized to accede.

The first pearl-fishery, under our government, took place during this year, and yielded upwards of sixty thousand pounds. The proceeds of the several fisheries under the Dutch and English will be given in a portion of this work devoted to the produce of Ceylon.

In the year 1797, an insurrection was caused by the employment of Malabar Duboshes, or collectors of the revenue and other duties; these offices had been formerly filled by the Cingalese aratchys, or headmen, but the Madras government had displaced them, substituting natives of the Malabar coast in their stead. These trivial disturbances were speedily quelled, and entirely subsided, when the Cingalese were reinstated in their official appointments.

The king of Kandy, during this year, made overtures to us for a renewal of the negociation, and conclusion of the treaty; but, before a definitive arrangement was entered into, Rajadhi Rajah Singha died, after a tolerably tranquil reign of seventeen years. Although he had five legitimate wives or queens, as well as concubines, he did not leave any male issue; and he bore the character of an indolent, voluptuous man, "addicted to love and poetry, and to nothing else, and who ruled his subjects with an easy yoke." The following is the personal description of Rajadhi Rajah Singha, given by Boyd in his "Miscellaneous Works:"—

"He is about thirty-six, or thirty-seven years of age, of a grand majestic appearance, a very large man, and very black, but of an open, intelligent countenance, as I found afterwards on a nearer approach. On the whole, his figure and attitude put me in mind of our Harry the Eighth. He wore a large crown, which is a very important distinction from the other princes of the East."

In the following year, 1798, Ceylon was made a King's Colony, and the Hon. Frederick North, afterwards Earl of Guilford, and a worthy successor to his learned and philanthropic progenitor, was appointed governor of the island, and arrived there in the month of October.

Historians differ, as to whether it was a nephew of one of the queens, or a son of a sister of one of the concubines of the late king, that Pilimi Talawe, the first adikar or prime minister, raised to the throne of Kandy, under the title of Sri Wikrama Rajah Singha, to the exclusion of the royal family; as Prince Mootoo Sawme, the chief or first queen's brother, was the legitimate heir to the crown. This step was taken by Pilimi Talawe to further his own ambitious views, as Sri Wikrama was but an automaton on the throne, whose actions were directed by the first adikar, Pilimi Talawe, who imprisoned the chief queen of the late monarch Rajadhi, and several relatives of the royal family; whilst Prince Mootoo Sawme, with his adherents and followers, made their escape from Kandy, and placed themselves under the protection of the British government at Colombo.

During the following year, the importation of slaves was prohibited, and torture and barbarous modes of punishment abolished in our possessions in Ceylon. In the month of February, Governor North granted an interview to Pilimi Talawe, and the prime minister appears to have been most cautious in his mode of proceeding with our government, as this interview was merely a complimentary one; but in a subsecutive one, in September, he offered to assassinate the monarch, Sri Wikrama, whom he had raised to that dignity, if the English would assist him to ascend the throne, that he, Pilimi Talawe, would govern Kandy as the English would dictate. This ignominious proposition was rejected in the manner it merited, and the governor made Pilimi Talawe understand, that neither the monarch, nor nation, which he had the honour to represent, either aided or abetted murder, or assassins; but, undaunted by this prompt and determined refusal of Governor North to aid him in his criminally nefarious project, Pilimi Talawe made many after-communications of the same nature, which were rejected with the scorn and contumeliousness they merited.

The first English seminary was established at Colombo, for the instruction of natives within the year; thus we find that immediately after Mr. North held the reins of government, and when naturally in a new colony, there were many important political, and commercial subjects to engross the governor's attention and time; that gentleman had been employing his leisure hours in endeavouring to ameliorate the sufferings, and improve the condition of his sable fellow-man. Governor North abolished the importation of slaves, torture and barbarous modes of punishment, and established a seminary for the instruction of the ignorant and benighted natives, and that within the space of twelve months. Noble conduct of this nature needs no comment or praise, and each one in reading this may apply the following text to himself, "Go and do thou likewise."

In the following year, 1800, Governor North agreed to send an ambassador to the king of Kandy, as the first adikar, Pilimi Talawe, had made overtures of an honourable nature, in the name of Sri Wikrama, in his official capacity of prime-minister. The Rev. Mr. Cordiner writes:—

"In order to elude the arts of the adikar, the governor promised that Major-General Macdowall should be sent as ambassador, if the consent of the king were previously obtained to his carrying with him a sufficient military force to maintain his independence. It was at the same time proposed, that if the king should approve of it, he should transport his person and his court for greater safety to the British territories, there to enjoy all his royal rights, and to depute to Pilimi Talawe, the adikar, the exercise of his power in Kandy."

The king of Kandy consented to the requisition, and General Macdowall started for Kandy on his embassy, escorted "by the light company, and four battalions of his Majesty's 19th foot, five companies of the second battalion of the 6th regiment of coast sepoys, five companies of the Malay regiment, a detachment of the Bengal artillery, with four six-pounders and two howitzers." Now, the utility of the caution evinced by Governor North in sending an ambassador, with a powerful escort, was displayed, as on the road the deputation met with opposition from the natives, and several skirmishes resulted, not without suspicion that Pilimi Talawe had secretly instigated the rebels to this contumacious mode of proceeding.

Our ambassador and his escort finally reached Kandy, where a series of lengthened interviews ensued between Sri Wikrama and General Mac dowall, which terminated in the general returning to Colombo, without having been able to effect a new treaty, or alter the position of affairs then existing between the British and Kandian governments.

Events of an historical nature remained in *statu quo* during the year 1801, but the following year was fraught with circumstances of interest, as well as with those of deep importance in a political point of view. The Supreme Court of Judicature was now first established, and vaccine innoculation was introduced. At the beginning of the year, the king of Kandy sent his second adikar as ambassador to our government at Colombo, when a satisfactory treaty was entered into, which ensured the safety, and permission to carry on commercial intercourse, to the subjects of the two powers. Shortly after the new treaty was ratified, it was violated by the Kandians, who committed the first act of aggression, by plundering some British subjects, who had purchased Areka-nuts in the Kandian dominions. Governor North demanded that restitution should be made of the stolen property, or that the parties should be reimbursed to the full value of their merchandize. This demand Pilimi Talawe, in the name of his sovereign, promised to comply with, but postponed the fulfilment of his promise, and after repeated demands had been made by our government for the required compensation, which were constantly met by puerile evasions, Governor North threatened the king of Kandy with hostile proceedings, if the demanded and promised restitution was not forthwith made.

War was declared against the Kandians in the January of 1803, and General Macdowall, at the head of a considerable force, marched for Kandy. These troops consisted of "two incomplete companies of Bengal artillery, with the usual proportion of gun-lascars, two companies of his Majesty's 19th regiment of foot, the entire of the 51st regiment (625 strong,) one thousand Ceylon native infantry, one company of the Malay regiment, and a small corps of pioneers." Colonel Barbut also set out for Trincomalee, commanding "one company of the Madras artillery, five companies of the 19th regiment, the greater part of the Malay regiment, and a necessary proportion of lascars and pioneers." These divisions, in their respective marches, did not meet with the slightest resistance, and, although each had pursued different routes, arrived almost simultaneously at the Kandian seat of government, which they found undefended and deserted, and our large army, which consisted of more than three thousand men, took undisturbed possession of Lanka-diva's capital, the palace of which had been fired before the retreat of the Kandians, and was partially destroyed; but in some of the apartments were found "pier glasses, statues, particularly those of Buddha, sets of glass and china-ware, and a few golden cups adorned with silver filagree." In the arsenal, or what was used for the store-house for their warlike weapons, a large quantity of arms of various descriptions were found by our troops, and appropriated.

Mootoo Sawme was now proclaimed king by Governor North, and he was crowned with all due ceremony at Kandy. This prince was the legitimate heir to the Kandian throne, as he was the brother of Rajadhi's chief queen, and he had placed himself under the protection of the British government, when Pilimi Talawe placed Sri Wikrama on the throne, after the decease of Rajadhi without male issue. A treaty was ratified by Governor North and Mootoo Sawme, to the effect that the British merchants and soldiers should be indemnified for losses sustained previously to, and during the war, that a portion of land was to be given up for the purpose of constructing a road from Colombo to Trincomalee, that the province of the Seven Korles, which is a tract along the western coast, should be made over for ever to the British, that the king should not form any alliance without the concurrence of his Britannic Majesty, and that an European force should be kept in Kandy, for the preservation of order. To all these considerations, Mootoo Sawme readily agreed.

A force was now sent to Hangrenketty, about sixteen miles from Kandy, commanded by Colonel Barbut, in pursuit of the fugitive Sri Wikrama, which was nearly drawn into an ambuscade, but, owing to the caution of the colonel, a timely retreat was effected, although the object for which the troops were sent remained unaccomplished. Pilimi Talawe evinced much penetration in the mode of warfare which he adopted with our troops, being fully conscious of the inferiority of the Kandian soldiers if opposed to them in regular engagement. He harassed them by hovering about the capital, cutting off supplies, and all communication between Kandy, Colombo, and Trincomalee. A detachment of our men were nearly taken by Pilimi Talawe, which had been sent out to commence a negociation with some chief in the vicinity, and our soldiers barely escaped annihilation, and were necessitated to retreat into Kandy precipitately. A reward of ten rupees was set on the head of each European, and five rupees on that of any of the native troops in the service of the British.

This harassing mode of warfare was beginning to make inroads on the health of our troops, when a negotiation was opened with General Macdowall by Pilimi Talawe. The adikar proposed to surrender the person of the deposed monarch, Sri Wikrama, into the hands of the British, on the condition that he, Pilimi Talawe, should have supreme authority in Kandy, under the title of Octoan Komarayan, or great and supreme prince, and that Mootoo Sawme should retire to Jaffnapatam, receiving a pension from the Kandian government.

Unfortunately for the honour of Britain, this degrading proposal was acceded to by General Macdowall, who returned to Colombo, withdrawing a large body of the troops, leaving Kandy under the command of Major Davie, with a garrison of only one thousand men. Pimili Talawe having found that his nefarious scheme for obtaining power, aud raising himself to the highest dignity had succeeded, now resolved upon attempting to obtain possession of the person of Governor North, and for this purpose requested a conference might take place at Dambadiva, about fifty-seven miles east of Colombo, and which had been a royal residence. Governor North being most anxious for peace, and to avoid bloodshed, acquiesced most readily to Pilimi Talawe's proposition.

A day having been fixed upon for the conference, namely, the 3rd of May, the governor went to Dambadiva, attended by a numerous suite and guards, whilst a detachment of three hundred soldiers met Governor North at that place. These precautions were necessary to guard against the treacherous designs of the perfidious Pilimi Talawe; and, had it not been for this armed force accompanying the governor, in all probability he would have been made prisoner, as the adikar *had a body* of armed men awaiting the governor's arrival, but he *had not* any proposal, or fresh negotiation to enter into. Finding it impossible to seize the person of Governor North in the face of his escort, Pilimi Talawe broke up the conference, after a nominal ratification of the former treaty.

General Macdowall returned to Kandy, and took the command of the garrison on the 16th of

May, and most unfortunately for the sake of humanity, and of Great Britain's honour, he was taken seriously ill, and compelled to leave Kandy on the 11th of June following, leaving the garrison under the command of Major Davie. Our pen almost refuses to perform its task, and record the horribly sickening details of the fearful massacre and sacrifice of human life, brought about, and entailed on his victims by the cowardice and pusillanimity of one man, who dishonoured and disgraced the country that gave him birth, the king he served, the commission he held, the uniform he wore, and the sword which he ought to have wielded. So long as there is power in language, or truth in history, the name of *Major Davie* will be execrated and loathed, as denoting all that is vile, despicable, dastardly, treacherous, and mean—

"Veritatis simplex oratio est;"

Therefore, we resume our history.

From concomitant circumstances, we are induced to believe, that Pilimi Talawe only waited for the absence of General Macdowall to attack the weakened garrison of Kandy; the power of the troops was diminishing daily, either by desertion, or sickness. They were under the command of Major Davie, a creature unworthy the name of man, who had neither the courage nor ability for an office which placed in his keeping and power the honour of his country, and the lives of his fellow-creatures.

Within a few days after the general was forced to leave Kandy, Pilimi Talawe besieged the garrison, and Major Davie surrendered by capitulation; and it was stipulated that Kandy should be delivered up forthwith, with the whole of the military stores, and that the British troops should retire to Trincomalee, being allowed to retain their arms. Before sunset on the day the surrender had been made, our garrison had evacuated Kandy. Major Davie, marching at the head of our troops, *leaving* 150 *sick Europeans in hospital*, who had not been named in the articles of capitulation, and for whom no provision was made, to be dealt with as their savage, barbarous enemies might choose.

Our troops, consisting of seventeen officers, twenty British soldiers, two hundred and fifty Malays, one hundred and forty gun lascars, accompanied by Mootoo Sawme and his attendants, reached Wattapolawa on the Trincomalee road, when their progress was intercepted by the river Mahavelliganga, at all times a rapid stream, but at that season much increased by the late rains. Major Davie in vain attempted to get the men across; and no mention had been made of this river in the articles; therefore their enemies, the Kandians, were not bound to provide them with canoes, or rafts; and they now stood on the surrounding heights, jeering at the position our troops were placed in. Mootoo Sawme, Major Davie, and the officers, with their followers, remained on the banks of the river during the night, and their attempts to procure rafts the following morning proved abortive. Observing their irresolution, some Kandian chiefs opened a communication with Major Davie, and his perplexed followers, and these chiefs offered to provide boats, *on the condition that Mootoo Sawme was delivered into the power of the Kandians.* Major Davie for a short time hesitated, *but finally agreed to this dishonourable, base, infamous, atrocious proposition,* and communicated his determination to the unfortunate prince, or rather king, Mootoo Sawme.

"Is it possible," he exclaimed, "that the triumphant arms of England can be so humbled, as to fear the menaces of the Kandians?"

But his expostulations were lost upon the dastardly, cowardly Davie, and Mootoo Sawme was delivered to his enemies—a living holocaust, presented by British officers to the demons of disgrace and cowardice.

No language is sufficiently powerful to express the dishonour brought on the name of Great Britain by this infamous act. The law of nations, as well as those of good faith and honour were violated: Mootoo Sawme fled to us for protection, placed his person in our keeping, confiding in our honour; we accepted the trust reposed—nay more, caused him to be crowned king in his own dominions, and entered into an alliance with him; then broke our faith with him, by listening to, and accepting the overtures of a rebel, thus deposing the monarch whom we ourselves had crowned. He retreated with our troops, still trusting in British probity, when he was shamelessly handed over to his enemies, by one of that nation to whom he had confided the safe-keeping of his person. And the man who was guilty of this atrocity was a *soldier*, and one who ought to have guarded the honour of his country, and the persons of those who placed themselves under the protection of Great Britain. Shame on the name of Davie!—dishonoured it is, and will be as long as time shall endure, and we spurn the name from our pen, as we would a loathsome reptile from our path.

Mootoo Sawme was taken before the usurper, Sri Wikrama and his adikar, when Pilimi Talawe put the following question to him :—

"Was it proper for you, being, as you are, of the royal family, to fly to the English for protection, and join them in fighting against your country?"

"I am at your mercy," the unfortunate Mootoo Sawme meekly replied.

Some further questions were put, and received humble replies, when this wretched prince was ordered to suffer the most barbarous tortures, and be impaled alive, thus meeting death in his most terrific and agonizing form. This sacrifice of Mootoo Sawme did not appease the insatiate Kandians, who, finding that their former demands had been agreed to, now refused to provide the promised boats, insisting that the British troops should lay down their arms, and return to Kandy. No attempt at resistance was made by Major Davie to this unprecedented demand—no expostulation used as to the breach of faith now exhibited by the Kandians; all they required was readily agreed to, and Major Davie, with his officers, were separated from their men, and the arms of the whole party taken from them. The men were then marched into a narrow pass, strongly guarded by their armed Kandian escort, and ordered out, two by two, and the question put if they would serve under the Kandian king? When a negative was given, these poor fellows were taken some distance from the main body, and butchered in the most horrible manner by their savage enemies. At the conclusion of this revolting slaughter of the soldiers, the officers shared the same fate—but three European and one Malay officer being spared. The names of these were, Major Davie, Captains Rumley, Humphreys, and Nouradeen. The first three lingered out their lives in a wretched captivity among the Kandians, but Captain Nouradeen's fate merits more particular and honourable notice.

The Kandians, not yet glutted with blood, returned to Kandy, and murdered the whole of the hundred-and-fifty sick European soldiers in hospital. What must have been the agony of these men, whilst this revolting massacre was taking place? Left unprotected, in a hostile country, by their commanding officer, whose duty it was to have provided for their safeguard, prostrated by sickness or wounds they had received whilst fighting under their country's banner, and in her monarch's cause, unprovided with arms, prostrated by bodily infirmity, prevented thus from availing themselves of the means of self-defence, with which nature had provided them, their mental sufferings must, indeed, have been most terrible. Nor can we be surprised, if, in their dying agony, they forgot their duty as Christians, and cursed the man whose cowardice, want of firmness, and humanity, had left them to meet death, inflicted by the hands of barbarous enemies.

Two of our men most miraculously escaped from the fearful slaughter; the first was Corporal Barnsley of the 19th regiment, he received a deep sword-cut on his neck, and had his head laid open by blows from a club, but he contrived to extricate himself from the heap of slain, and roll over a bank into a paddy-field, where he lay concealed until night. He then swam across the river, and received assistance and food from some kind Samaritans, who followed the precepts of Buddha, succouring the sick and needy, although the suppliant was not one who believed in their god. After much suffering and difficulty, the poor fellow reached our garrison at Matelé, and finally recovered from his wounds.

The other soldier was in hospital at Kandy, was torn out of his bed, had a blister pulled off his chest, and was knocked on the head with the butt end of a musket, and thrown with his murdered companions into a deep pit. He made his way from among the dead bodies, and crawled into a neighbouring drain, from whence he was dragged in the morning, and hung to a tree: the rope broke, and he was again suspended, and left to die, but strange to say the rope again gave way, and he contrived to secrete himself in a neighbouring cave for ten days, during which period he subsisted upon the grass that grew from the sides.

A Kandian who had seen him twice hanged accidentally found him, and was so astonished at his preservation, that he determined to inform the king. The superstitious tyrant declared that the soldier must be under the especial protection of the gods, thus to have escaped with life, and ordered him to be provided with food, raiment, and a dwelling, and eventually he, as well as Barnsley, had the gratification of being restored to their families. We believe if these accounts were read in a work of imagination, they would be declared to be beyond the bounds of probability, so true it is—

"That truth is *strange*, stranger than fiction."

The wretched being, Davie, died in 1810, and it is

asserted that in appearance and dress he had become essentially Kandian—and that he cohabited with a low caste woman, by whom he had a family, and it is said that grandchildren of his are now in Kandy. Military men affirm that our government tried to ransom this contemptible creature, but as the Kandian king demanded a seaport to be given up in consideration for his liberation, it was impossible to accede to such terms, and Davie was left to linger among a people who with all their faults are not cowardly; consequently, they must have despised him for his want of bravery.

It is the bounden duty of an historian to be impartial, and draw notice to the conduct of those placed in responsible positions; therefore we deem it necessary to animadvert upon the line of policy adopted by General Macdowall. In the first place, it was a decided breach of faith, and violation of our treaty with Mootoo Sawme, *the monarch whom we had crowned*, to enter into a negotiation with Pilimi Talawe, and agree that he should be the viceroy of Kandy, thereby deposing Mootoo Sawme, and promising that he should retire to Jaffnapatam. The overtures of the crafty, Pilimi Talawe, had not the excuse of being made in the name of the king, whom he acknowledged, and whose prime minister he was, namely, Sri Wikrama, but were made in his own name and for his own benefit, as he consented to deliver the person of his monarch into the hands of the British. General Macdowall evinced but an imperfect knowledge of human nature, *even* in *listening* to, *much more* in acceding to, the propositions of a man who was alike a rebel and a traitor to his king and country. He who was faithless to the country which gave him birth, and the monarch whose confidential servant he was, could not be relied upon, or be expected to keep faith with the British, whom he only availed himself of to use as a step in ascending the ladder of his ambition.

In the second place, General Macdowall is to be censured, for prematurely withdrawing so large a body of troops from Kandy, leaving only one thousand men in garrison, in the midst of a hostile, treacherous nation, who could, from the natural defence of the country, cut off all communication and supplies; added to which, this small body of men was left under the command of an officer totally incapable and unfit to have so important a trust reposed in him. The fearful consequences attendant upon the whole of the mistaken line of policy pursued by General Macdowall in this disastrous business, has been seen in the fatal results recorded in previous pages.

No attempt at palliation can be made for Major Davie's misconduct; and, for the credit of Great Britain, such transgressions of the laws of honour and humanity are rare. The result of Davie's pusillanimous cowardice, in acceding to all the unconscionable demands of his Kandian enemies, met with awful retribution in his own person, and those of his brother officers; but their sufferings could not restore to life the hundreds of slaughtered men who had fallen victims to the savage brutality of the Kandians. To a well-regulated mind, death is always preferable to dishonour, and this feeling is generally deeply imprinted on the heart of the British defender of his country; and fortunate it is that the contrary sentiment is rarely met with among Britain's sons; for, were it otherwise, and conduct such as Major Davie's of frequent occurrence, we should become a byword among the nations of the earth, instead of being honoured and respected where the name of England is known.

We expressed our intention of noticing the heroic conduct of Captain Nouradeen, whose life was spared at Wattapolowa by the Kandians. This officer was a Malay, then commanding the

Malay regiment; and Pilimi Talawe had used every persuasion during the period our troops occupied Kandy, to induce Captain Nouradeen to leave our service, and enter that of the Kandian, promising him high rank and riches. All these offers were steadfastly refused; and, when he was made prisoner, Pilimi Talawe renewed them, tempting Captain Nouradeen with life, rank, and riches, if he would serve Sri Wikrama; but the answer he received was, "that he (Captain Nouradeen) was already the servant of a mighty king, whose uniform he wore, and that he could not serve two masters." Finding all entreaty and persuasion useless, threats and tortures were essayed; but these proved alike futile, in inducing Captain Nouradeen to become traitor to the country which he served; and this noble, heroic fellow was put to death by Pilimi Talawe. The contrast presented in the character and conduct of Nouradeen and Davie needs no concluding comment.

In August, desultory warfare and ravage commenced between the British and Kandians, when Sri Wikrama, stimulated and intoxicated by his late successes, threatened to attack Colombo, but refrained from doing so; and, in September, he besieged Hangwelle, a fort of little importance, in our possession, and suffered a severe defeat.

At the commencement of the year 1804, the Kandians prepared and attempted a general invasion of the British settlements, but were repulsed on all sides; great havoc was made among their troops, and the losses they sustained were considerable. Shortly after this, Pilimi Talawe again made overtures of an amicable nature to our government; but the severe punishment the British had met with previously, after listening to his treacherous propositions in 1803, were too vividly impressed on their minds to permit them to hold further intercourse of a friendly description with so treacherous a man; and, therefore, the overtures made by Pilimi Talawe were rejected with the contempt they called for.

In the month of February of the year 1805, the Kandians again invaded the British territories; but the result was the same as that which they experienced the preceding year, viz., that of loss and defeat. A body of our troops, consisting only of three hundred men, followed by numerous coolees and servants, and commanded by Major Johnson, were ordered to the interior. This brave officer fought his way from Batticalloa to Kandy, and was there surrounded by the troops of Sri Wikrama. Nothing daunted, he cut his way through them, and proceeded in his road to

Trincomalee, although constantly harassed by the Kandian troops, who opposed the progress of this undaunted body of men. This small army, headed by Major Johnson, reached their destination with comparatively small loss, having had to pass through a hostile country, and constant skirmishes having taken place between them and the Kandian troops—thus showing what energy and bravery could perform when commanded by an officer possessing firmness and valour. The war was carried on with much determination and bravery on both sides; and the king of Kandy proposed a cessation of hostilities, which was agreed to by the British, although no formal treaty was entered into, and peace continued till 1814.

In July of this year, 1805, Governor North was relieved by Sir Thomas Maitland, who succeeded to the appointment of Governor of Ceylon. Governor North returned to England with the good wishes of all the natives and British subjects of that island; and certes, Great Britain is indebted to the abilities of the Hon. Frederick North, the first English Governor of Ceylon, for retaining this bright colonial gem in the British diadem. Governor North left the colony in a comparative state of tranquillity, no fresh hostilities having been renewed with the Kandians until 1814; and he found it a scene of disorder, warfare, and bloodshed. Mr. North left Lankadiva's verdant shores with the satisfactory conviction, that he had done much to ameliorate the condition, physically and morally, of the benighted inhabitants of Ceylon.

CHAPTER XII.

From 1805 to 1844—Sri Wikrama's tyranny—First Adikar family murdered—Affecting account of the execution—Heroic conduct of the wife and son—Babe taken from the mother's breast to be decapitated—Rebellion in Kandy—Martial law proclaimed—Tranquillity restored—Dalada relic—Death of the King of Kandy—Governor Sir Colin Campbell—His policy—Bishopric of Colombo constituted—The first Bishop Dr. Chapman—His exertions and character—Rebellion in Kandy—The Priests causes of dissatisfaction—New taxes and first disturbance—Pretender proclaimed — His progress — Rebels enter and destroy the public buildings at Matelé—Troops march from Kandy—Conflict with rebels—Martial law proclaimed—Reward offered for Pretender—Destruction of Kurnegalle—Observer newspaper exciting discontent—Alarming meeting of natives near the seat of Government—Attack of the police—Mr. Elliot addresses the mob—Reinforcements sent to Kandy—The Commandant takes possession of the Dalada relic—Pretender's brother shot—Result of

Courts Martial—Special sessions of Supreme Court—The Chief Justice's charge—His recommendation to mercy—Lord Torrington's reply.

ALTHOUGH there was a cessation of hostilities between the British and Kandians, we were not uninterested observers of the political events occurring in Kandy, which were most important, as the monarch, Sri Wikrama, was no longer the weak, supine youth—a mere automaton, placed on the throne by Pilimi Talawe, and whose actions were subservient to, and dictated by, his adikar, or prime minister. The footing upon which Pilimi Talawe had been with Sri Wikrama, during the first part of his reign, when the Kandians were engaged in war with the British, could not subsist during peace. The authority of Pilimi Talawe gradually declined, as the monarch held more securely the reins of government, and felt himself seated fastly on the throne. Sri Wikrama now exhibited his real character, which was that of a despotic tyrant, and he evinced his determination to govern, as his predecessors had ruled Kandy, with absolute power; whilst Pilimi Talawe, on his side, was in like manner resolved to retain, and maintain, his influential hold over the Kandian monarch and his court.

Mutual distrust between the monarch and his

adikar existed for years, until 1812, when Pilimi Talawe excited the jealous fears of Sri Wikrama, by requesting that the illegitimate daughter of the last king, Rajadhi, might be given in marriage to his son. Sri Wikrama was highly incensed at this presumptuous proposal of the adikar, as he viewed it as a covert attempt to be enabled to claim affinity with the royal blood, and summoned the whole of his chiefs to court, and preferred various charges of misconduct, and arrogant assumptions, against Pilimi Talawe.

The chiefs listened with becoming gravity to the complaints made by their king, and Pilimi Talawe was condemned by Sri Wikrama, with the concurrence of the assembled chiefs; when, to the surprise of all, the king pardoned the adikar, declaring his reluctance to punish so old a servant, and reinstated Pilimi Talawe in his office of adikar.

It is difficult to fathom the motive which actuated Sri Wikrama: it must have been dictated either by the most noble generosity, or by the most subtle cunning; but Pilimi Talawe enjoyed his position as adikar only for a short time after he had been reinstated in his office, as his conduct again excited the king's displeasure, who banished him to his province, forbidding him to leave it without his (the king's) permission, and depriving him of his rank and honours.

Scarcely was Pilimi Talawe in his province, before he hired Malays to murder the king. This conspiracy was discovered by Eheylapola, formerly the second adikar, but whom the king had made first adikar when he disgraced Pilimi Talawe; the conspirators were taken, tortured, and condemned to be trodden to death by elephants, trained to that purpose; whilst Pilimi Talawe and his nephew were tortured and beheaded.

The demons of cruelty and suspicion now reigned lords paramount in the breast of Sri Wikrama; he condemned his chiefs to death without just cause, and feared rebellion to exist in every breath his subjects drew. Eheylapola, who at that time was devoted to his king, Sri Wikrama, regarded with distrust: province after province the king declared to be in a state of rebellion, although Eheylapola vouched for their allegiance; nevertheless, Sri Wikrama fined some of the inhabitants, imprisoning, torturing, and mutilating others. In some districts, the king ordered the priests and Moormen to quit, forbidding all women, except natives of those districts, to remain in them. The domestic wretchedness this edict caused is well described by Dr. Davy, who was in Ceylon at the time.

"Wives were separated from their husbands; mothers from their children; the young bride and the aged parent—all indiscriminately were torn from the bosom of their families, and driven from their homes, producing scenes alike of distress and anger, which might well shake the firmest loyalty."

Thus we see how Sri Wikrama contrived to goad into rebellion his stanchest adherents and subjects. In the year 1814, for some trivial neglect of duty, Eheylapola was ordered to his district of Saffragam, and thither he retired, in obedience to the king's command; but as Eheylapola was beloved sincerely by the inhabitants of Saffragam, they exhibited every demonstration of joy at the return of Eheylapola. This Sri Wikrama chose to construe into an act of rebellion, and proclaimed Saffragam to be in a state of insurrection, and despatched troops there, to make Eheylapola prisoner, and bring him to the capital, alive, or dead; and these were commanded by Molligodde, formerly the second adikar, but upon whom Sri Wikrama had bestowed the place of Eheylapola. This nobleman, however, with several chiefs, took refuge in Colombo, placing themselves under the protection of the British government, whilst Molligodde took prisoners many of his adherents, and returned triumphantly to Kandy, carrying with him the adherents of Eheylapola.

The fury of the king at the escape of Eheylapola knew no bounds, and he wreaked his vengeance on the victims within his grasp. Executions, tortures, impalements, mutilations, confiscations, and imprisonments, were now the daily—almost hourly—occurrences. The place of torture and execution flowed with human gore —the air was filled with the shrieks of victims, under the hands of the torturer, and Kandy was now one vast slaughtering-place.

As Sri Wikrama could not get the person of Eheylapola into his power, he determined to obtain possession of his wife and children. Accordingly, they were made prisoners, with Eheylapola's brother and his wife, the tyrant resolving to wreak his vengeance on all. They were, forthwith, brought to Kandy, condemned to suffer death for being the wife, offspring, and relations of a rebel, and were to be executed publicly in the market-place of Kandy, in the presence of the whole court and population.

The day appointed for this horrible butchery

arrived, and the wife of Eheylapola, with his four children (the eldest boy being but eleven years of age, and the youngest an infant of a few months old, sucking at its mother's breast,) were led to the place of execution. The wife, a woman of majestic mien and noble deportment, attired in her court-dress, and adorned with all her jewels of state, befitting her high rank and station, advanced boldly to meet her fate, declaring her husband's integrity, and expressing her hope that the life which she was about to give up might be of benefit to him. She was ordered to stand back, as it was the king's command *that she was to die last*—to stand by and see her children butchered. She uttered no remonstrance, but embraced her eldest boy, telling him to submit to his fate as became Eheylapola's son. The child hesitated, and terrified, clung to his mother for protection, when his brother, two years younger, stepped forward boldly, embraced his mother, and told his brother not to disgrace his father by such cowardly conduct, and that he would show him how to die as became Eheylapola's son; advanced with firm step to the executioner—one blow—a lifeless trunk, deluged in blood, falls to the earth, and the young noble spirit had taken its flight.

But the refinement of barbarous cruelty was not to terminate in compelling a mother to stand and see her offspring butchered; the trunkless head was thrown into a paddy-pounder, the pestle placed in the mother's hand, and she was ordered to pound the head of her child, *or she should be disgracefully tortured.* The mother hesitated; but the feelings of innate delicacy implanted in the high-born woman's breast prevailed—every mental anguish would be preferable to the public exposure of her person—she lifted up the pestle, closing her eyes, and let it fall on the skull of her dead child.

This hideous scene was enacted with the two other children, and the wretched mother had to endure the same mental torture. At last, it was the infant's turn to die, and it was taken from its mother's arms, where it lay sleeping, and smiling, in tranquil unconsciousness. Eheylapola's wife pressed her babe convulsively to her bosom; then, in mute agony, allowed the executioner to take her last child from her. In a moment the little head was severed from the delicate body. The milk that had been drawn a short time previously from the mother's breast, was *seen distinctly flowing*, and *mingling with the sanguine stream of life.*

The Kandian matron then advanced eagerly to

meet death. With a firm step, she walked towards the executioner, but with caution, to avoid *stepping in the blood, or treading on the lifeless, mutilated bodies of her children.* Her face was calm—almost wore an expression of satisfaction —the worst had happened—*she had seen her children slaughtered*—they were out of the tyrant Sri Wikrama's power. The hand of the executioner is laid on her, to lead her to her watery grave.* She thrusts him aside, telling him not to pollute a high-born Kandian matron with his touch; to remember that she was Eheylapola's wife, and had stood calmly to see her children murdered; would she therefore shrink from meeting them in death? Bade adieu to her brother-in-law, telling him to meet death as became his birth; called to her sister-in-law not to unman her husband by useless wailings, but to follow her; then walked towards the tank, (contiguous to Kandy,) two executioners following and preceding, carrying large stones.

They have arrived at the tank; Eheylapola's

* Eheylapola's wife and sister were condemned to be drowned; the brother and children to be beheaded. The details of this tragedy and attendant circumstances were described to the writer by a Kandian chief, who was an eye-witness to this horrible butchery.

wife gazes fixedly on the tranquil water, whereon the sunbeams glitter sportively in millions of rays; the sister weeps as the executioner commences attaching the heavy stones to her slender throat. It is firmly secured; the weight bears her fragile form to the earth; and the executioners are compelled to carry her to the tank. She shrieks wildly as they near the tank; they hold her over the waters—more piercing screams rend the air. A sudden splash—then the waters close over a tyrant's victim, serenely unconscious of the atrocity perpetrated.

Eheylapola's wife had stood motionless during this period, a slight expression of scorn passing over her features, as her sister's shrieks filled the atmosphere. 'Tis now her turn to die. The executioners advanced towards her, carrying the ponderous stone. She motions them off. They still advance—are quite close to her; the cords that are to attach the weight to her throat already touch her person; she asks them to desist, assuring them that she will not make any resistance, or attempt to save her life. The executioners refuse, stating they must adhere to their orders, and one lays his hand roughly on her shoulder. She shrieks, and eludes his foul touch, for with a bound she darts towards the tank, and leaps into the water: they close over her form in eddying circles, and her spirit has flown for ever. The executioners depart, palm-trees droop gracefully over the waters, and the sunbeams glitter sportively in millions of sparkling rays, as the stream murmurs a requiem over the murdered wife and sister of Eheylapola.

The butchery in the market was not completed when Eheylapola's wife quitted it, for her husband's brother was still to die. The headsman advances towards him, sword in hand, lays his blood-stained hand on the chief's shoulder, attempting to raise his head. The chief, with an indignant exclamation, throws the audacious hand off his person, plants his feet firmly on the earth, draws himself up to his full height, standing with majestic dignity, and scornfully desiring the executioner to fulfil the tyrant's command. Has the chief's stern gaze unnerved the headsman? A blow was struck! a stream of red blood gushes forth!—but, horrible! the head is not wholly struck off! The sword is again poised in the air—a flash of light falls on the glittering weapon of destruction: it descends on the muscular, manly throat; the sword is now reeking with red blood!

A headless trunk falls to the ground, whilst the head, with glaring eye-balls, rolls along the earth, and is thrust aside rudely by the executioner's foot. The bloody tragedy is finished!

Before the temples of the gods Nata and Vishnu, and opposite to the queen's palace, was this fearful scene enacted. Sri Wikrama laid all feelings aside save those of revenge; for, by the Kandian laws it was forbidden that human blood should be shed near a temple; also to wound or shed the blood of a woman was considered a heinous crime, and one of the innocent children of Eheylapola was a girl.

During the time this revolting butchery was going on, women shrieked, closing their eyes to exclude the terrific reality; men groaned in mental torture, burying their heads in their hands; whilst many of the noble Kandian youths, in anguish rolled on the earth, their mouths pressing close to the sod to stifle their cries. We will wind up this fearful account by quoting a contemporaneous author:—

"During this tragical scene the crowd, who had assembled to witness it, wept and sobbed aloud, unable to suppress their feelings. Palihapaul Depaaul was so affected that he fainted, and was expelled his office for showing such tender sensibility. During two days the whole of Kandy, with the exception of the tyrant's court, was as one house of mourning and lamentation, and so deep was the grief, that not a fire, it is said, was kindled, no food dressed, and a general fast was held."

We believe the savage cruelty of this barbarous tyrant to be unparalleled in ancient or modern history: the crimes imputed to the Roman emperors, Nero and Caligula, were trivial, when compared with those constantly practised by Sri Wikrama, and our astonishment is extreme that any nation—more especially a warlike one, such as the Kandians—should have submitted for a lengthened period to the cruel tyranny exercised by their monarch. Sri Wikrama spared neither age nor sex—the sucking infant, children, old and young women, were all alike condemned to be tortured in the most revolting, disgusting manner, mutilated and executed, if they or their relations incurred his displeasure, or from the caprice of the instant. We can comprehend man viewing with apathy the destruction of his fellow-man; but we cannot understand how men could permit the slaughter of the delicate woman, or the helpless child—every feeling implanted in our nature rebels against the bare supposition that the creatures whom, from very instinct, we feel ourselves bound to protect, should be slaughtered before our eyes, for no crimes which they had committed, but simply for being the wife of the bosom, and the offspring of a man who had incurred a tyrant's displeasure. It is an enigma how this debased specimen of human nature, Sri Wikrama, escaped assassination by the hands of his subjects; but the scourge of retribution was near, hovering in his path, although the punishment he met with in this world did not equal his deserts.

At the end of this year, Sri Wikrama cruelly tortured ten native traders (British subjects) who had gone into his territories for merchandize. They made their escape from Kandy, coming to Colombo in a mutilated condition, some without ears, others without eyelids—the remainder either noseless, footless, or handless—and made complaint to the Governor-general, Sir Robert Brownrigg. On the 10th of January, 1815, war was declared against the King of Kandy, not against the Kandian nation, "but against that tyrannical power which had provoked, by aggravated outrages and indignities, the just resentment of the British nation, which had cut off the most noble families in the kingdom, deluged the land with the blood of its subjects, and, by the violation of every religious and moral law, had become an object of abhorrence to mankind."

The British troops entered the Kandian territories on the following day, and fighting commenced. The Kandians gave battle, not as men fighting for liberty and their land, but as mercenaries in the service of a tyrant, who, for gold, fought against the British, who were disposed to befriend them ; and skirmish after skirmish ensued, and war was carried on by the Kandians without spirit, or energy. Mollégodde, the successor of Eheylapola, at this critical period, deserted his cruel master, Sri Wikrama; and, as he was the only efficient commander whom he possessed, and one whose place it was impossible to refill, the loss Sri Wikrama sustained was irreparable. Mollégodde had been long disgusted with the tyrant's service, and awaited the opportunity of joining the English, which had been only deferred until he could get his wife and children from Sri Wikrama's court. The tragical execution of Eheylapola's family warned Mollégodde what would be the fate of his wife and children, if he abandoned his office of adikar, leaving these sacred ties in the clutches of the savage king. But no sooner had he effected the withdrawal of his family from the Kandian territories, than he offered his aid to the British, to assist in dethroning Sri Wikrama.

On the 14th February, Sir Robert Brownrigg established his head-quarters at Kandy; but the king had made his escape from thence a few days before, and it was reported that he had fled to Doombera, about twelve miles from Kandy; and as part of our troops, which were advancing to the capital, had fallen in with two of the king's wives, a quantity of jewels and treasure which were captured, the report bore every appearance of being a correct one. Sir Robert Brownrigg lost not an instant in forming plans to ensure the capture of Sri Wikrama. Detachments from Colonel O'Connell's, Majors Kelly and Rook's divisions, were ordered to scour the country round, making every possible search for the tyrant, to cut off all retreat.

Energetic and efficient as these officers were, their search was fruitless; and, in all probability, the English never would have succeeded in capturing Sri Wikrama, had not his own subjects aided them. Eheylapola's followers were looking with lynx-eyed vengeance, for the wretch who had butchered the wife and children of their beloved chief. They sought him with unwearied perseverance, found him; and, although the

Malabar escort which surrounded the tyrant, Sri Wikrama, fought nobly in defence of their blood-stained monarch, captured the fugitive king, bound him hand and foot, reviled him with the atrocities he had committed, and the murders he had caused, spat upon him, telling him that it was Eheylapola's slaves—the slaves of the woman he had butchered—that thus treated him, in revenge for his savage brutality; that they now intended to drag him to a neighbouring village, that he might be execrated by the multitude as he went along. Curses loud and deep were showered on the head of Sri Wikrama, by his own subjects, as he passed along the road; almost each inquired of him for a murdered or mutilated relation or friend; curses and missiles were hurled at him; he was subjected to every species of ignominious reproach; and, finally, was handed over a prisoner to the British.

Sri Wikrama, the last king of Kandy, was taken prisoner at Galleehewatte, in Doombera, on the 18th of February, 1815, being exactly four days after Sir Robert Brownrigg had established his head-quarters in the capital of his dominions. Some historians, with a misplaced, maudlin sensibility, have deprecated the treatment that Sri Wikrama met with at the hands of Eheylapola's followers. Although Christianity teaches us to forgive our enemies, and those who have inflicted injuries upon us, the best Christian finds it a most difficult precept to follow. Can we, then, wonder at the reproaches and ignominy, which these men showered on one, who had condemned the innocent children and wife to a cruel death, solely because he could not lay hands on the person of their chief?—more especially as these men did not profess Christianity, but were heathens, followers of Buddha. On the contrary, these men are to be commended for the forbearance they exhibited in placing Sri Wikrama alive, untortured and unmutilated, immediately after they had made him prisoner, in the hands of the British.

The personal appearance of Sri Wikrama was not unprepossessing, except when he was excited, then his eye gleamed with the fire of a demon, and the face wore an expression of malignant cruelty. He was tall, well-made, slightly *enbonpoint*; the features of the face good, and the expression intelligent; the complexion of a clear, rich, dark brown; the head well formed, (although the animal organs predominated over the intellectual,) with are dundancy of long, thick raven-black hair. He took great delight in adorning his person, and wore a profusion of costly jewels at all times; but on state occasions, the cap and dress in which he habited himself glittered with gems of inestimable value. We need only say of his character, "*Ex uno disce omnes.*"

On the 2nd of March, Sri Wikrama was finally and formally dethroned; and a convention concluded between Sir Robert Brownrigg and the Kandian chiefs, together with the chief officers of the Kandian territories. The official notice published on the occasion states:—"This day a solemn conference was held in the audience-hall of the palace of Kandy, between his Excellency the Governor and Commander in-chief of the Forces, on behalf of his Majesty, and of his Royal Highness the Prince Regent, on the one part, and the adikars, dissaaves, ratramahatmeers, and other principal chiefs of the Kandian provinces, on the other part, on behalf of the people, and in presence of aratchegays, coraals, vidhans, and other subordinate headmen from the different provinces, and a great concourse of inhabitants. A public instrument of treaty, prepared in conformity to conditions previously agreed upon, for establishing his Majesty's government in the Kandian provinces, was produced, and publicly read in English and Cingalese, and unanimously assented to.

The British flag was then, for the first time, hoisted, and the establishment of the British dominion in the interior was announced by a royal salute."

The second article of the treaty stated—" Sri Wikrama was, by consent of his subjects, formally declared to be deposed, his family and relations for ever debarred from ascending the throne, and all the rights and claims of his race to be extinguished and abolished."

The two succeeding articles were devoted to minor political arrangements.

The fifth article declared—"That the religion of Buddha was inviolable; its rights, ministers, and places of worship were to be maintained and protected."

The sixth and seventh articles were of an immaterial nature.

By the eighth and eleventh it was declared—"That the laws of the country were to be still recognised according to established forms, and by the ordinary authorities, and that the royal dues and revenues were to be levied, as before, for the support of the government."*

* We have merely given the outlines of the treaty, and what we considered most probably would interest the general reader.

In the month of January following, Sri Wikrama, and all the members of his family, were banished to Madras, and our government in Ceylon were well pleased to be rid of the onerous duty attendant upon the safe-keeping of the ex-king's person; as they apprehended either his escape, or that some Kandian, to benefit his country, might assassinate him, to prevent the possibility of his regaining the throne of Kandy.

From this period, until the 10th of September, 1817, the government of the British was submitted to with tranquillity; but at this date some Kandian chiefs of Welasse rose in rebellion, resolving to struggle to regain the independence which they prized so highly, and for which their various conflicts with Malabars, Malays, Moors, Portuguese, Dutch, and, finally, their voluntary subjection to the English, had failed to eradicate from their breast. The conduct of the chiefs, in heading and exciting the inhabitants of their districts to revolt, was inexcusable, as they had voluntarily sought the aid of the British to assist in dethroning their king, Sri Wikrama, had entered into a treaty with, and sworn allegiance to, the government of Great Britain—the treaty which had been entered into by us with the Kandians, had been most rigidly adhered to—and they had not the shadow of an excuse for rebelling against the government, whose aid they had sought, and to whom they had voluntarily subjected themselves. Mr. Wilson, the government-agent of the district, went to meet the rebels, and endeavoured to quell the revolt, but most unfortunately did not succeed in his object, although his life fell a sacrifice, having been killed by the rebels.

The pretender to the throne of Kandy was a priest of Buddha, who had thrown off the yellow robes of his office; the chief who principally aided the pretender was a man of great influence in his district, Kapittipola, and brother-in-law to Eheylapola, and who brought many followers with him to join the pretender. Pilimi Talawe, the son of the former adikar, also joined the rebels, with many other chiefs. Considerable alarm was now felt by our government, for, in less than six months from the commencement of the revolt, every district of any importance was in a state of rebellion; in the various skirmishes which took place, we lost many officers and men; the rebels also skulked about our encampments, waylaid, and murdered our soldiers.

On the 21st of February, 1818, martial law was declared in the Kandian provinces, and the sacrifice of human life was terrible on both sides. Our soldiers were now beginning to sink under the effects of the unwholesome atmosphere of Kandy, and, day by day, events assumed a more gloomy aspect for the British, whilst the Kandians grew bolder, and held a grand meeting at Deyabetmewala, at which the pretender and chiefs were present. Dr. Davy, in his "Ceylon," writes:—

"During the three following months our affairs assumed a still more gloomy aspect. Our little army was much exhausted and reduced by fatigue, privation, and disease; the rebellion was still unchecked—all our efforts had been apparently fruitless—not a leader of any consequence had been taken, and not a district subdued or tranquillized. This was a melancholy time to those who were on the scene of action, and many began to despond, and augur from bad to worse, and to prophesy that the communication between Colombo and our head-quarters at Kandy would be cut off, and that we should very soon be obliged to evacuate the country, and fight our way out of it."

These gloomy forebodings were not destined to be realized: disunion of a serious nature now manifested itself among the chiefs, and the pretender was taken prisoner by an adverse party, who set up a chief of their own selection. Kapittipola, their most able general, was defeated in several engagements, and, in October, was taken prisoner, with Pilimi Talawe, by the British; one by one, the chiefs were taken, tried, convicted of high treason, and beheaded. Notwithstanding these stringent, but necessary measures, a spirit of rebellion still continued to manifest itself, and it was not until February, 1819, that the administration of martial law in the Kandian provinces ceased.

We purposely omitted mentioning the capture of the Dalada relic, which they say is a tooth of their god Buddha, and which they hold sacred, until this page. This relic was taken, towards the end of the late rebellion, and, trifling as this incident may appear at the first glance, we believe we are borne out by facts, that it is owing to the circumstance of having given up the possession of the Dalada relic to the charge of the priests, which has, in a great measure, occasioned the late insurrection in Ceylon, 1848, the full particulars of which will be given subsequently. The Cingalese tradition is, "That whoever obtains possession of that sacred relic, obtains with it the government of Ceylon;" and no sooner was it made known that the Dalada was in the possession of the British, than the followers of Buddha returned to their allegiance, district after district laid down their arms, and acknowledged the sovereignty of Great Britain. A new convention was now entered into with the chiefs, by which it was stipulated—

"That all personal services, excepting those required for making and repairing roads and bridges, should be abolished, and that all taxes should be merged into one, a tax of one-tenth on the produce of the paddy-land. That justice should be administered by the board of commissioners at Kandy, and by the agents of government in the different provinces, aided by the native Dissaaves, who were henceforth to be remunerated, not by the contributions of the people, but by fixed salaries."

In January, 1820, a man of the second caste assumed the title of king of the Kandians, and collected some few of the Veddahs, or aborigines, at Bintenne, and created new disturbances; but, as the self-elected king of the Kandians was apprehended immediately after his assumption of that dignity, his followers quickly dispersed.

The Dalada relic was placed in the keeping of the government-agent of the Kandian provinces, and was publicly exhibited to the priests and people, for worship, at stated periods. Whether it was consistent with our character as a Christian nation to have aught to do with, or sanction the heathen worship, of a piece of yellow ivory, we will not enter upon here.

The island was now in a state of tranquillity; for

although trivial disturbances took place amongst a few, which were quelled as soon as they arose, the nation appeared to be satisfied with our government. Attention was directed to the formation of schools of instruction for the natives, both by our government and by the missionaries, and attempts were made to induce them to embrace Christianity. Literary and agricultural societies were formed; means of communication, by the formation of roads from one part of the island to the other, were planned and commenced; bridges were thrown over rivers; and every facility offered for the transit of passengers and merchandise. In short, we tried to convince the natives of Ceylon, by every honourable means, that we were not a nation of warlike bigots, or of grasping adventurers; but wished to improve their moral condition, and contribute to their happiness, whilst they conducted themselves as loyal subjects of the crown of Great Britain, to whom they had sworn allegiance.

The political horizon of Ceylon remained unclouded for years; the colony gradually improved under our management. In 1832, the ex-king of Kandy died at Vellore, of dropsy; and until 1835 no event occurred worthy of especial remark. In the January of that year, Mollégodde, the first adikar, and Dunewille Looko Banda, who was related maternally to one of Sri Wikrama's queens, with several others of lesser note, were charged with high treason, and for having conspired against our government. A mass of contradictory evidence was gone into; and, although they were acquitted, little doubt remained on the minds of many that a conspiracy had been concocted, but which had been frustrated before the plot had ripened. Regular lists were found, appropriating the various places held under our government to the Kandian chiefs. This the officials did not approve of, and still less did they admire the list whereon the names of *their wives* were inscribed, each lady being allotted to some particular chief, and to those of the highest rank, two of England's matrons were apportioned.

The conspirators tried to prove that these documents were forged; and did so to the satisfaction of the jury, who acquitted them. Mollégodde lost his rank as first adikar, another chief being appointed in his stead; but he was reinstated in his office in March, 1843, having given proofs, during the intervening period, of his loyalty. Dunewille Looko Banda was also taken into the service of our government; and in this year died the son of Sri Wikrama, in exile.

From the year 1835 until 1848, no attempt at revolt, or rebellion, agitated Ceylon. Since the colony had come into our possession, various charitable, scientific, scholastic, literary, and agricultural societies were established; a legislative council was formed, and a supreme court instituted. In short, Ceylon enjoys all the advantages of our most flourishing colony; and by many political economists is considered the most promising colony we possess.

In justice to the late efficient governor of Ceylon, Lieutenant-General Sir Colin Campbell, who assumed that appointment in 1841, we must state what his exertions have done for that colony. He found it a burthen to the mother country. The valuable land sold at five shillings per acre; and government servants enriched themselves at the expense of the country, by purchasing this land, turning it into coffee and sugar estates, and neglecting their official duties, (to discharge which they were paid by their country,) they devoted their time to the cultivation and improvement of these estates. Governor Sir Colin Campbell prohibited, by a government minute, the sale of crown land under the sum of twenty shillings per acre; and at this advanced price found numerous and ready purchasers, and frequently a much higher sum was realized. By the unbiassed representations of the Governor to the home government, civil servants were forbidden to purchase or retain land for agricultural purposes, and were required to devote their whole time and attention to the duties of the respective offices which they held under government.

Sir Colin Campbell met with most determined opposition on this point from the colonial corps; and vituperation of the most disgraceful nature was heaped upon his head, by those members of it who were amassing large fortunes by these agricultural pursuits, to the neglect of their official duties. Undauntedly, however, did Sir Colin Campbell pursue the straight path of honest duty to his sovereign and country, and was rewarded by his own conscience, and by the approbation of all right-minded men. Sir Colin Campbell used every exertion in his power to have the salaries of the Ceylon civil servants increased, and was successful in his efforts; thus benefiting the men who had so lavishly censured him for performing, to the best of his ability, the duties of his office as Governor of the colony, by insisting that the paid servants of the crown should perform those duties that required their undivided attention, and for which they were remunerated.

In 1845, Ceylon was constituted, by letters patent under the great seal of England, an episcopal see, by the title of the Bishopric of Colombo, as previously it had been included in the see of Madras; and the Rev. Dr. Chapman was appointed the first bishop. The bishop arrived in Colombo in 1846. We believe that the exertions of this truly pious, benevolent man, have done more towards the conversion of the heathen, since his arrival, than had been effected during the previous centuries, that nominal Christians had formed settlements in Ceylon.

Every part of his diocese is visited constantly by Dr. Chapman; unwearied in his duty, undaunted by the fear of contagion, he visits hospitals, jails, and the unwholesome jungle—sedulously learning the native language, whereby he may be enabled to communicate with and preach to the Cingalese, without the aid or intervention of an interpreter. He has made the natives understand that his is not to be a temporary residence, but that it is his intention to pass his life among them. No words can express his resolve so beautifully as his own, and which he addressed to a native congregation, shortly after he entered upon the duties of his sacred office—"I have come to Ceylon to live among you, and learn your language; with God's blessing to benefit you, and with his permission to die in your country." Possessing great piety, learning, and humility, Dr. Chapman is blessed with great eloquence, fluency of language, facility of expressing ideas, extreme urbanity of manner, unbounded benevolence, a most prepossessing exterior; and devotes the whole of his time and attention to the arduous duties of his office.

In conclusion, we can only say, that Dr. Chapman is a worthy, though humble, follower of his Great Lord and Master; that his appointment as bishop, and residence in the colony, are calculated to benefit professing Christians, as well as the benighted heathen, for the force of his *example*, coupled with his precepts, must influence and counteract, to a great extent, the effect which the lax morality practised by many Europeans in Ceylon, has had on the hearts and minds of the rising generation, both of English and Cingalese.

Nothing worthy of remark occurred until 1848, when the rebellion broke out which has drawn so much attention to the colony; to understand the events connected with it clearly the reader must remember, that Ceylon is the stronghold of the purest and most enthusiastic Buddhism, and the priests of this religion have long been dissatisfied with a government over which they have no control, but with which until lately they might have considered themselves in some measure connected. This connection was severed when our government surrendered to the priests the custody of the tooth of Buddha, which had ever been regarded as the palladium of Cingalese sovereignty. The abandonment of this sacred charge on the part of the government has been regarded by its present sacerdotal guardians, not only as a breach of faith, and a mark of great disrespect, but also as an exhibition of political weakness; in reference to the ancient tradition before referred to, namely, that whoever possessed this sacred relic should govern the island.

In 1842, the priests fomented rebellion, and succeeded in raising a puppet-pretender to the Kandian throne, who with many of his adherents were tried and convicted of high treason; and the former made a full confession of his guilt, as well as the manner in which he had been induced to lend his name to the rebels. The flame of rebellion thus raised was only smothered, and the priests availed themselves of the dissatisfaction expressed by the people at certain financial regulations introduced in 1848, known as the road-tax, gun-tax, dog-tax, and slop-tax, to refan the smouldering combustibles.

In this effort the chiefs were not inactive, and early in July of the same year Gonegallegodde Banda, stated to be a descendant of Rajah Singha, who had been previously sojourning in the house of a native, following the occupation of a *wederala*, or doctor, resided for five days in Kandy, acting as the chief leader of the malcontents. While there, he was an inmate of the Dalada Maligawa, whose priests maintained him. He had figured in two previous rebellions, and was tried for high treason in 1843, and acquitted.

On the 6th of July a large concourse of people, amounting it is said to four thousand, assembled from various districts in Kandy, stating that they desired to have an interview with Mr. Buller, the government agent; this gentleman, on receiving intelligence, went to meet them at the Cutcherry, but owing to their violence he was obliged to retire to the Maligawe. Here he attempted to address the multitude without effect. Many of the crowd became excited with ardent spirits, and their violence increasing, the police attempted unsuccessfully to disperse the mob and arrest the ringleaders.

The civil authorities were met by the people with determined resistance, and the latter becoming more and more irritated, armed themselves with branches of trees, and knocked down and injured some of the police. A company of the 15th regiment was then called out, who assisted the police to disperse the people. The apparent object of the crowd was to extort a promise, that the obnoxious tax ordinances should be repealed. It is a remarkable fact, that none of the headmen or chiefs were present on this occasion; and there can be but little doubt, that having stimulated the people to take this step, they abstained from implicating themselves publicly with the demonstration, while they anxiously awaited the result of the movement.

The local authorities now took effective measures to inform the people, that the colonial secretary, Sir Emerson Tennent, would receive the chiefs and small deputations from the various districts, at the Pavilion, on the 8th of July.

In the meantime every precautionary measure, which was practicable, was adopted to preserve the public peace. Special constables, both European and Malays, were sworn in, notices were posted at the various entrances to the town, and at the ferries, intimating, that no persons bearing arms would be permitted to enter. As evil-designing persons had circulated a list of thirty articles, on which they asserted the government were about to levy taxes, the government agent issued a notice contradicting it, and giving correct information, relative to the new taxes.

It having been intimated to Sir Emerson Tennent in the early part of the day on the 8th of July, that the people, who were assembling in the Esplanade, were principally composed of the inhabitants of Upper and Lower Doombera, he sent for the Ratra-mahatmeers of those districts, who stated that they had failed to counteract the false reports, or induce their people to remain quiet. On hearing this reply, Sir Emerson Tennent informed them, that as they had lost control over the people, they had forfeited the confidence of the government, and he accordingly suspended them from their respective offices.

In the afternoon of this day, the colonial secretary entered the Pavilion, which was crowded with the chiefs and their followers. He addressed the meeting at considerable length in favour of the new ordinances, applauding the chiefs, who had supported the government, and expressing the dissatisfaction which must inevitably follow an opposite course. After the meeting had broken up, the chiefs and their attendants dispersed among the crowd, about two thousand in number, which gradually disappeared, and the town was restored to perfect quiet.

When the people withdrew from Kandy, Gonegallegodde Banda retired for a day into a jungle called Danha Galla, where he received the homage of a large body of Kandians as their king. From thence he proceeded to the forest of Dambool, from which he was escorted by an armed body of men, sent by Golla-bella Ratra-mahatmeer, to a cave in the forest of Dahe Yatte Madda Gallinna, to await reinforcements. Here the pretender was joined by four hundred followers well armed and provisioned, and an ola was written by his order to Golla-bella Ratra-mahatmeer, desiring him to state why he had not forwarded clothing for his use; on the 26th of July an answer was sent, accompanied with various articles for the pretender's use, stating that they were for "My Lord the King, until such time as you shall pass Ballacadua, where I shall join you with the Maha Nilime and clothes for five kings."

The following day, the pretender came with his armed escort to Dambool Vehara, and at half-past eleven o'clock A.M. he was invested with the sword of state, and proclaimed King of Kandy.

The morning of the 28th, the whole body marched to Selleman Galla, where a palanqueen was brought, volleys were fired, and other rejoicings took place. From this place the pretender proceeded in his palanqueen with an increased retinue to Pallaputwelle, where they halted for the night. On his arrival on the following day at Wariapulla, the pretender abandoned his palanqueen, and proceeded during the night with four of his attendants to Doomborka Owelle, to visit Ettepulla Banda, leaving the command of his small army to his prime minister.

It was not until the 27th, however, that a report reached the authorities at Kandy, that the people were assembled at Matelé "with swords and fire-arms," and that a king had been crowned at Dambool the preceding night at the fortunate hour. It was further ascertained that the post-office communication was stopped on the Trincomalee road, and crowds of armed people were assembling in all directions. On the 28th, Mr. Buller proceeded in person to Matelé to ascertain the true state of affairs, and was met a short distance from Kandy by the police magistrate of Matelé, who was hastening to Kandy for assistance. This gentleman brought the intelligence that four thousand armed men were in the neighbourhood of Matelé, who had entered the town at noon on that day in a riotous manner, beating tom-toms and blowing horns, drove out the police stationed there, destroyed the public buildings, including the magistrate's residence, and burnt down the Bazaar.

Mr. Buller hastened back to Kandy accompanied by Mr. Waring, and at ten o'clock the same night a detachment consisting of one captain, two subalterns, four sergeants, one bugler, and one hundred rank and file of her Majesty's 15th regiment; and one captain, four subalterns, four sergeants, and one hundred rank and file of the Ceylon Rifles, under the command of Captain Lillie of the Ceylon Rifles, an old and experienced officer, well acquainted with the country, and accompanied by the government agent, and deputy Queen's advocate.

The progress of the troops was veiled in darkness, until their arrival at the Rest-house of Balla-cadua, when the day broke. After the detachment had marched nine miles and a half, a shot was fired within a few yards of them, which did not take effect. Two shots were fired half a mile further on the road, close to the rear of the troops, which possibly were only intended as signals. Another shot was fired half way down the pass from a gingal gun with the same object in view. A mile from Matelé, some armed natives were observed on the side of the Matelé road, and on that leading to Wariapoola. Those in front seemed disposed to parley, and some of the troops went up to them unmolested; while some were ordered to move on their flank to get to their rear; a few of the rebels escaped, but most of those in front were taken prisoners. The insurgents who were concealed in the jungle on the side of the hill, now commenced firing, by whom one man of the 15th regiment was slightly wounded.

The Rifles now entered the jungle on the flank of the rebels; a conflict ensued, in which the latter were completely routed, with the loss of six killed and several wounded, and eight of the latter were taken prisoners. The 15th regiment remained on the high road in reserve. The jungle was cleared by the Rifles, after which it was ascertained that the insurgents had possessed themselves of a bungalow on the Wariapoola estate, about half a mile from the high road. Captain Lillie marched with the Rifles to attack them, under the guidance of Mr. Adams, a volunteer civilian. The natives, however, forsook the house as soon as the party came in sight; the latter pursued them, and were fired upon by a party of rebels stationed in the jungle on their flanks, most happily without effect.

Here the palanqueen of the pretender was found, and broken in pieces by the Malays, before Captain Lillie could save it. Some thirty pounds of gunpowder were also discovered; and in the verandah of the bungalow, Mr. Baker, the superintendent of the estate, was found tied by his legs and arms to the railing, suffering great agony from the tightness of the ligatures and the position he was kept in by the ropes: on being released his skin was found to be quite discoloured; he was then removed to Matelé for medical aid.

Captain Lillie returned the next day to Kandy with the detachment of the 15th regiment, leaving that of the Ceylon Rifles under the command of Captain Watson, to protect Matelé.

On the 29th of July, a proclamation was issued offering a reward of £150 for the apprehension of the pretender, and placing the Kandian districts under martial law. On the 28th, an urgent application was made for military assistance from Kurnegalle, which is about twenty-five miles from Kandy, but owing to the troops which had been dispatched to Matelé, Colonel Drought was unable to accede to it.

On the following day, however, one of the magistrates came in person to seek assistance, when thirty men and two officers of the Ceylon Rifles were dispatched; on their arrival after a forced march, they found Kurnegalle already in possession of the insurgents. The Cutcherry had been entered and plundered, all the records and papers were being burnt or torn, and the mob were in the act of breaking open the treasure-chest, when the troops advanced upon them. The Court House had been plundered and its records destroyed, the gaol had been broken open and the prisoners liberated, while the bazaar was burnt down, and nearly every building more or less damaged.

The Rifles opened a fire upon the armed mob, who attacked them in return as they approached, but soon after took to flight: twenty prisoners were taken, and six-and-twenty bodies of the insurgents were afterwards buried. Notwithstanding this loss, the rebels, amounting to four thousand strong, made a second attack upon the town two days later, and after suffering loss were again driven out by the Rifles; and on the same day they made another equally unsuccessful attempt, with some further loss, but no casualty occurred on either of these occasions to the Malay troops.

After the affray at Wariapoola, the Pretender proceeded to Eleadua with a few followers, where he remained until he received an ola and provisions from Dulledewe Maha Nileme, when he immediately started for Kurnegalle, at which place he arrived in time to lead on the second attack. After the defeat, he turned towards Dambool, but for some unknown cause he altered his course and entered the forest of Madaoelputta, where he remained for some time in concealment, being closely pursued by various detachments sent out in search for him.

We must here break the narrative of events in Kandy, as they occurred in chronological order, and request our readers to accompany us to Colombo, to enable them clearly to understand the *causes* of the late rebellion.

A newspaper, called the "Observer," is published in Colombo, whose editor for several years has endeavoured to excite a spirit of opposition, amongst the Burgher and Cingalese community, against all the measures of the local government, and of jealousy against the European inhabitants. This newspaper has a large circulation therefore amongst that portion of the community to whom it is particularly addressed, and especially the Burghers, to which class, almost all the proctors and notaries belong. On the 3rd of July, 1848, a letter was published in the "Observer," in the Cingalese language, purporting to be translated from the English, and signed "an Englishman," which was prefaced by certain observations of the editor; we subjoin a literal translation of both.

"We have pleasure in publishing a letter written by an English gentleman, who is kindly disposed to men, without distinction of colour or race, concerning the injustice of the new taxes lately imposed by government. The Cingalese people should consider, that to all persons, subject to the English government, there is a legal right of making known their pleasure, before they expend money in paying taxes. Therefore, those persons who say, that to Cingalese men there is not understanding enough to establish in Ceylon a council including natives to represent the inhabitants, should consider the present constitution of the council of France, and its results. Certainly the Cingalese people are not more unlearned or foolish than the greater part of the individuals, who elected members for the French council. Certainly the Cingalese men are not more unlearned or foolish than the Tamul men of Pondicherry belonging to France. It is now appointed that a Tamul man of that country should represent the inhabitants in the French council. If the men of this country wish to be freed from paying improper taxes and other wrongs, let them request a council, where they may be able to discuss their affairs, not nominally, but in a right manner.

"In order to show the wrongs inflicted on the inhabitants of this country, and the justice which they should receive, we translate this letter into Cingalese, and publish it.

(Signed) "We the Persons who publish
the paper called the
'Colombo Observer."'

"*To the Gentlemen publishing the 'Colombo Observer.'*

"GENTLEMEN,

"By residing in an out-station, and constantly conversing with the natives by privilege, I have an opportunity of knowing the great displeasure that is stirred up among the inhabitants concerning the new taxes lately imposed upon them, and also their thoughts and words on the subject. Further, if the government dare by forcible means to collect these taxes, I can think that the displeasure among the inhabitants will be much more increased, and from this many serious consequences will follow. Although there are many reasons on account of which the people should resist the government appointed from time to time, still up to this time they, without manifesting an opposition, have been obedient. However, if they should pay the money required for these taxes, so unjust, and impossible to be borne, lately imposed by government, obediently, and sit quiet without imposing their whole power, the Cingalese people will not only be considered a race of slaves, obedient to everything, just or unjust, done by government, but the world will not regard them as a race of men of good mind, and submitting to justice, and not to injustice (i. e. to justice only). No person says that it is not right for government to collect taxes for the protection of the people, but should not this collection of taxes be according to the ability of the rich and the poor inhabitants?

"Many persons are displeased on account of the taxes * collected from the people of England, and it is not proper to impose such taxes unless the government be very poor; however, we can-

* By this tax we mean a portion of the annual income of the English people paid to government.

not say that it is altogether unjust, since they are collected according to the circumstances of the rich and the poor. In England they are not collected from hundreds of thousands (lacs) of workmen and poor. They collect *7d.* on each £1 of the yearly income of the rich only, but, according to the taxes lately appointed in Ceylon, the poorest men will have to pay the new tax of 3*s.* in the £1.

"Is there a greater injustice than this? All persons know that there are thousands of inhabitants in this Island, who do not possess three or four cocoa-nut trees, or the fourth or fifth part of a field, and who do not receive into their hands 10*s.* in the year. However, according to the new taxes, such people are bound to pay 7*s.* or 8*s.* yearly to government. A gun is a very necessary thing for the protection of their crops. By some poor people the gun is the only valuable article possessed. To rear a dog is also necessary; and for these 4*s.* must be paid, together with the 6*d.* paid for writing the certificate; the gun-tax is 3*s.*, and for the dog 1*s*; and again 3*s.* are collected yearly from each person for making roads. If there be more than one dog, there is another charge.

"In this manner, a poor person will have to pay 7*s.* or 8*s.* to government. This sum is sufficient for the maintenance of one person for two months. If other persons were to pay in this manner, a European who receives £300 annually must pay £50, or two months' pay, for new taxes; he who receives £600 must pay £100. An English padre (clergyman) receiving £700 a year, must pay £116, and a little more; an agent receiving £1000, must pay £166, and a little more. The gentleman, Emerson Tennent, Great Secretary, must pay about £500, and the Governor £1500.

"Some may say that 7*s.* or 8*s.* are not sufficient to maintain a single man for two months, but I know very well that to the poor people in the Galle and Jaffna districts this sum is quite sufficient for two months. Very well; let us say that 7*s.* or 8*s.* are sufficient for the expense of one month, yet, according to this, what a great and unbearable sum goes to the government yearly!

"What European is there who submits to this payment? Even when there is a war-rumour, or when the government is heavily poor, no European will submit to such an unjust payment. But these taxes are imposed, not only at a time when not only is there peace, but when the people should be relieved as much as possible from other heavy taxes paid to government. What, then, is the intention of the Governor, since he lays such a heavy burthen upon the poor, and delivers the rich from it?

"The saying that the collection of this tax is

imposed by the unanimous vote of the legislative and executive councils of this island, is not a true saying. The government is trying to make even those gentlemen of the Legislative Council, not belonging to government, to agree to any thing that is done; those gentlemen of that Council who are under government cannot oppose government on account of this. Though there is a saying that this matter is sanctioned (appointed) by the Council, it is not a true saying.

"The government of Ceylon is doing injustice, like the government of Russia. I see no difference between those two governments except in name. It is now understood and acted upon by many countries in the world, that when people pay taxes to a government, they must consider whether it is a tax that can be borne by the people, and that they must have the privilege of expressing their opinion to government, and also whether the money raised by the tax is vainly spent, or whether it is spent to the advantage of the people. Not long ago millions of the people received this right: some Cingalese people who understood things right to be done, expected that they would receive a part of this right; but, according to circumstances, it now appears that in proportion as other races are delivered from injustice, more and more injustice is coming upon the inhabitants of this country.

"Now I say, is it proper that the Cingalese

people should submit to such severe injustice? Will they do so? It is altogether improper to submit. I hope they will not act so. I think the Cingalese people will show they are not a race of slaves, without doing (not doing) such severe things as Europeans lately did in order to be delivered from injustice. Justice will be done to them if the reasons against injustice are rightly expressed by petitions to the great Legislative Council, called the Parliament of England. I think the Cingalese people know this, and I have no doubt they will believe it. Petitions should be written, and sent to the different districts of the Island, and signed by all collectively. Let all the inhabitants of Ceylon demand of the English government to be delivered from injustice, and to have justice done.

"Gentlemen, who print newspapers, I request you will publish to the Cingalese under the payment of taxes like a burthen, that the government is doing injustice, and that you will inform the people of high office, that injustice, as a devil (or demon of injustice) driven from the place where he formerly was, will not be permitted to come and live in this Island, If you do so, Cingalese people are not an ungrateful race.

"I am,

"An Englishman."

The foregoing was not confined to the circulation of the "Colombo Observer," but they were struck off on slips of paper, which were extensively distributed amongst the people even in the most remote parts of the country, by political agitators; and in Kandy they were known to have been explained, and enlarged upon, to the natives by dissatisfied or disappointed Europeans, connected with the coffee estates. We must bear in mind that the publication of the letter took place three days before the disturbances broke out in Kandy, and such a document, with its notes and comments, must have been calculated to excite the minds of the people, upon whom it had a more injurious effect from their belief that it was penned by an Englishman.

An ordinance had been passed about the same time with those already complained of, which was intended "to provide for the registration and license of certain traders," to resist which an attempt was made by the wealthier shopkeepers, by whom a combination was formed to intimidate their more necessitous brethren, to force them to close their shops, and to prevent the sale of the necessaries of life. The fear of this event enabled these wealthy conspirators to effect a rapid sale of all their own stock at exorbitant prices. Eventually the poorer class of shopkeepers were suffered to continue their trade uninterruptedly, while the conspirators, to whom the payment of one pound per annum could not be an object, contented themselves with presenting a petition to the Governor, praying the suspension of the law, which of course could not be acceded to.

At the same time, a large number of copies of a petition purporting to be addressed to the House of Commons, mis-stating and exaggerating facts, calculated to inflame the minds of the people, were secretly circulated among the natives in the vicinity of Colombo, as well as in more remote districts, by agents employed to obtain signatures. The substance, expressions, and misrepresentations, contained in it, so very closely corresponded with a letter, which subsequently appeared in the "Colombo Observer," bearing the signature of Mr. Elliott, the editor, that he has been generally considered as the author of the document, and the instigator of its circulation. The following is also the translation of a document, copies of which were circulated with great activity throughout the villages for many miles round Colombo.

"NOTICE.

"His Excellency the Governor has, for the present, enacted several taxes to be levied from the inhabitants of this island, viz. :—

"Upon fire-arms, dogs, men, boats, and boutiques (shops); and, in addition to this, it is also enacted to levy, in a few months more, a tax upon trees, lands, cattle, and all useful quadrupeds. We, the inhabitants of several villages, have consulted and agreed upon a petition about the matter.

"It is therefore kindly requested, that the inhabitants (both great and small) of all the villages will assemble at seven o'clock in the morning of Wednesday, the 26th instant, prepared for the same."

The authors of this movement most cautiously kept themselves out of view. In the meantime, precautionary measures were taken by the government, and, amongst the rest, a circular was addressed to the headmen, reminding them, that they would be held responsible for the conduct of the people.

On the morning of the 26th, the people poured in large numbers towards the town from the neighbourhood and from distant villages, and assembled at a place called Borellæ, a spot where several roads met, close to the Wellicadde gaol, about a mile from the town. The mob having collected, marched upon the police, who were drawn across the road to prevent their approach to the town. Their intention was evidently to force a passage through the civil force, the superintendent was struck down, and several of his men more or less injured. In the midst of the contest, Mr. Elliott arrived, and holding up hands was recognised by the mob, many of whom were intoxicated, and his influence became immediately apparent, as they were soon tranquillized, and listened with great attention and satisfaction to his harangue. In the midst of this proceeding, the Governor, accompanied by the major-general and some troops, arrived, but finding the excitement of the people quelled, the Governor and military soon after returned to Colombo.

The ostensible object of this meeting was to petition, and before the crowd dispersed a great number of signatures were obtained on separate sheets of paper, which were undertaken to be presented by Mr. Elliott, along with a document in Cingalese previously prepared; indeed it has been stated that these signatures were all attached to the petition at the office of the "Observer" previously to the meeting. This gentleman is reported to have demeaned himself upon the occasion, in such a manner as to induce a belief, that he was accidentally present; but he is stated to have shown that he had such influence over those who guided the mob, that little doubt was entertained of his being the instigator of the movement.

Some of the paragraphs of this petition, which was afterwards presented to the governor by Mr. Elliott, recapitulate much of the substance contained in the letter of the "Englishman," and concludes with the following sentence: "But if your Excellency will not mercifully give us a favourable reply, we certainly will *not obey* any of these new laws."

Lord Torrington states, that had he been aware of the concluding paragraph, he would have declined to receive it, and would have held Mr. Elliott responsible for the presentation of such a document. The editor of the "Observer" excuses himself on the grounds that the petition being in Cingalese, he had only an imperfect and general knowledge of its contents, and his own name was not appended to it. This defence must be admitted, by the most prejudiced mind, to be a criminal admission by Mr. Elliott that he had omitted a public duty, by neglecting to inform himself fully of the opinions and wishes of those whom he volunteered to support.

The government having been informed that other meetings would be attempted, under the plea of petitioning the Governor, the following notice was issued :—

"Information having been received that the inhabitants of the interior, and of some of the Korlls in the neighborhood of Colombo, are, under the advice and encouragement of evil-disposed persons, assembling in large numbers, under pretence of presenting petitions to the Governor. Notice is hereby given, that his Excellency the Governor, although willing at all times to receive and consider petitions from any of the inhabitants, if presented in a proper manner, will not allow large assemblages of the people for this purpose, and he will take strong measures to prevent meetings of this nature, which can tend only to cause breaches of the peace.

"By His Excellency's command,

(Signed) "W. Morris,

"Acting assistant Colonial Secretary.

"Colonial Secretary's Office, Colombo,
July 28, 1848."

The government took active measures, by posting police and military in the vicinity of those places where meetings were proposed to be held, and by this means the peace of the western province was preserved.

But, to return to Kandy. Reinforcements marched to the proclaimed districts from Colombo; the military pensioners, of whom there are about three hundred in the Island, were called out; two divisions of road-pioneers were brought in to assist the troops and escort the baggage, while the "Lady Mary Wood" steamer was despatched to Madras, and returned with three companies of her Majesty's 37th regiment and a large supply of ammunition.

It must have been also gratifying to the government to find, that all the respectable inhabitants of the town and neighbourhood of Kandy placed themselves at the disposal of the commanding officer, for the protection of the town; by which means he was enabled to send out detachments to various localities, where their presence was urgently required, both as a protection to the Europeans and peaceably disposed amongst the natives, against rebels and plunderers, and as an encouragement to the Malabar coolees, who, it was feared, through terror might be driven from the coffee-estates. Ammunition was distributed amongst the planters, and most fortunately, wherever the coolees received moderate encouragement, they were found to resist all intimidation on the part of the Kandians. Thus, although nearly all the estates about Matelé were recklessly injured and plundered, in all other districts, wherever the proprietors or superintendents remained at their posts and encouraged their coolees, the properties have remained uninjured.

Knowing the great importance that is placed by the Kandians in the possession of Buddha's tooth, and fearing that it might be made use of as a great stimulant to, if not inspire confidence in, the rebels, the commandant demanded the keys of the temple from the priests, and examined the shrine in the presence of the government agent. The object of superstitious worship had not been removed, but the commandant, deeming it prudent to secure integrity on the part of the priests, kept possession of the keys. This step was soon followed by an order prohibiting the beating of tom-toms, and the collecting of crowds in the temples.

Several prisoners, who had been captured since the proclamation of martial law, were tried and shot; and amongst them one of the most desperate robbers in the island, who had, on more than one occasion, broken prison, and for whose apprehension a reward had long previously been offered. This individual was the most active agent of, and an attendant upon, the pretender; he died exclaiming, "If the king had had three men about him as bold and determined as myself he would have been master of Kandy."

On the 4th of August, Dingeralle Hanguranketty, who called himself the elder brother of the pretender, was, with several of his followers, taken prisoner by a party of the Ceylon rifles, in the neighbourhood of Kurnegalle. Amongst these was one Calle Banda, an ex-ratramahatmeer, who acted as adigar to Dingeralle, who had assumed the title of king in the district of the Seven Korles. This aspirant to royalty was shot on the following day, under the sentence of a court-martial. It is said to have been the intention of the two brothers, who were playing the parts of kings, to have united their followers at Kurnegalle, which was frustrated by the unexpected arrest of Dingeralle.

We find that happily the disturbances were entirely confined to those districts where they first broke out, and that the loss of life was also limited to the unfortunate rebels. Several hundred prisoners were taken, of whom one hundred and twenty were tried by courts-martial: eighteen of these were shot, twenty eight transported for various terms; four were imprisoned with hard labour; twenty-nine suffered corporal punishment with imprisonment; thirty-three suffered corporal punishment alone, and eight were acquitted.

The Governor having excluded in the proclamation of martial law that portion of the town of Kandy wherein the Court House is situate, a special sitting of the Supreme Court was opened on the 28th of August, by the Chief Justice, Sir A. Oliphant. Of eighteen prisoners who were arraigned for high treason, eight were convicted, and the Queen's advocate abandoned the trials of a similar number of prisoners on the same charge, holding them over for minor offences to be tried at the regular sessions, or gaol delivery. We have much pleasure in giving the following extracts from the Chief Justice's address in discharging the jury at the close of the special sittings, breathing as it does that humane spirit which ought to be predominant in the breast of every British judge. His Lordship having observed that the crown prosecutor had informed him that there were no more prisoners to be tried on that occasion, said,

"It is now my duty, and I must say it is a pleasant one, to thank you in the name of the country, and of the court, for the unwearied and patient attention with which you have listened to the court, the bar, and the witnesses, during the investigation of these trials. Your verdicts *have invariably been those of men of sound sense and discretion*; and, while you have thought it your duty to support the laws and uphold the government of this country in the proper discharge of your functions, you have considered it also incumbent upon you to make recommendations to mercy, which will be backed by me, and I hope they will be allowed to have their due weight in the proper quarter.

"I am myself determined to recommend all the prisoners to the merciful consideration of the government, and thus go a step even further than the jury have done. I have attended to all the cases brought for trial, which perhaps some of you may not have been in a position to do, from not having sat upon the trial of all the cases; and I think I can perceive with tolerable clearness the cause of this rebellion, and I venture to express my belief, that the origin of it is the feeling remaining in the minds of the people that they are a conquered nation. It may not be the immediate cause, and the feeling may principally exist amongst the local and petty headmen, who are discontented because they have not a government of their own—the original government. They have not arrived at a participation of our feelings, and do not see the superiority of our government, nor the benefit of our free institutions; but, on the contrary, would restore their old laws and institutions.

"It is quite possible that the imposition of new taxes fanned the flame, and precipitated them into the commission of this crime. The petty headmen availed themselves of this opportunity, to revive old feelings; which in fact had never been lost sight of, but I trust this will never occur again; indeed, I may say I feel confident there will be no more rebellions of this sort.

"The people must see that any attempt against the British government is now a hopeless one, and, as a witness said yesterday, 'that thereby they will only lose their lives.' For, as deposed to by Lieutenant Annesly, only eleven men marched out of Kurnegalle, and of these only two had shewed themselves, when the three or four thousand Kandians assembled in their front ran away; there can therefore be little fear for future occurrences. But we must not teach our subjects to fight, war is an art too easily learnt.

"The legislature, I am confident, will only enact, in a paternal spirit, such laws and regulations as will prove beneficial to the subject; and I trust they will send the schoolmaster amongst the people, who will educate them in the arts of peace, and teach them the sin and folly of taking up arms against lawful authorities. The duty of the governing and governed is mutual, the one paternal, and the other allegiant.

"There is a large portion of this country, whose wants and circumstances are quite unknown, where no European has been seen for thirty years, except upon some hunting expedition. It is not only expedient but necessary for us to teach the inhabitants of these districts, that the white man has been sent here, not only to impose and collect taxes, but to elevate the moral and intellectual character of the people. . . .

"The duty of a juror is a most important one to the community. It is the bulwark of justice and liberty; and upon it depends the due administration of justice. The prisoner's counsel will sometimes press hard upon the jury for the acquittal of his client, and the counsel for the crown will, on the other hand, urge them for a conviction, while the judge may very often take an improper view of the case, for he is not exempt from human infirmity.

"It is then to the sound sense of the jury alone that the country must look for discrimination.

All rests with the jury. It is for them to weigh the guilt and innocence of the prisoner; and I can only express in conclusion my own hope, that all future juries in this country will weigh the cases which may be brought before them, with the same care and attention, as you have bestowed upon those which have been tried during the present sessions."

In conformity with the opinion expressed by his lordship, the Chief Justice addressed the following despatch to the Governor:—

"Colombo, September 23, 1848.

"My Lord,—I have the honour to transmit herewith notes of evidence, sentence of the court, recommendation to mercy by the jury, and certain petitions, in the case of the Queen v. Penelebodde Kuralle and others, and marked No. 2.

"Also notes of the evidence, sentence of the court, and recommendation to mercy by the jury, in the case of the Queen v. Tunamalua Kekooa Banda Karale, and another, marked No. 3.

"Also notes of the evidence, sentence of the court, recommendation to mercy by the jury, and certain petitions, in the case of the Queen v. Kandapulle Banda and others, and marked No. 4.

"Also notes of the evidence, sentence of the court, and recommendation to mercy by the jury, in the case of the Queen v. Wijayasoondere Mudianselay Appoohamy and others, and marked No. 5. All cases of high-treason tried by me at the sessions lately holden at Kandy, for the special purpose of trying persons implicated in the late rebellion.

"I have to report to your excellency that the several convictions in the said cases respectively were obtained in due course of law. I have also to state that I recommend as fit and proper objects for your excellency's clemency, as far as regards the punishment of death, not only all the persons recommended by the jury for the reasons given by them, but also all the prisoners who have been found guilty.

"The most culpable of these appear to me to be Penelebodde Keerale, Warapitia Ettapolla Banda, Kandapulle Banda, Wannenayeke Mudianselagey Punchiralle, Wijaysoondere Mudianselay Appoohamy, and Kolambulamulle Mohattelay Appohamy; and under different circumstances, I should have recommended your excellency to have executed such three or four of those last mentioned as should, after minute investigation into their respective cases by the law-officers of the crown, have appeared to have been most guilty.

"To have carried out the last penalty against these would have been necessary for the vindication of justice, order, and good government, and for an example to others. But I find that that example has been already made. I learn that some twenty persons have been already shot for their share in this rebellion by the courts-martial; I therefore think, when it is considered that no one European has been put to death,—that one soldier only has been wounded by the rebels,—that no persons have appeared in warlike array against the troops since the outbreaks at Matelé and Kurnegalle,—that the blood which has been already spilt is sufficient for all purposes, whether of vindication of the law, or for example.

"I advise that the prisoners last above mentioned be transported for life, that the others, not recommended to mercy by the jury, be transported for fourteen years; and that those who have been recommended be imprisoned and kept to hard labour for such short periods as, after consideration with the crown-lawyers, may be deemed due to them respectively. I have, &c.,

(Signed) "A OLIPHANT, C. J.

"The Right Honourable Viscount Torrington."

It is with deep regret that we feel ourselves called upon to supply the reader with the answer of the Governor to the foregoing recommendation of the Chief Justice; conceiving it as we do so much at variance with that spirit of justice tempered with mercy, which should be the characteristic attribute of the crown, or the crown's representative.

"The Queen's House, Colombo, September 25, 1848.

"Sir,—I have the honour to acknowledge your letter of the 23rd instant, transmitting the notes of evidence, and sentences of death passed on the prisoners convicted of high treason at the last session of the Supreme Court held at Kandy for the special purpose of trying persons implicated in the late rebellion.

"I have given to this communication, not only the respectful attention becoming your high authority, but that painful and anxious consideration inseparable from the solemn question of life and death, suggested by your recommendation of all the prisoners for a commutation of punishments. But, after soliciting the advice and opinions of the Executive Council, it is with reluctance, that I feel myself unable to concur with you in the propriety of that course towards some of those men, convicted in due course of law, and whose guilt has been so clearly established, that the strict line of your duty, uninfluenced by other considerations, would have led you, as you state, to recommend to me to inflict on them the last penalty of the law, in vindication of justice, order, and good government.

"These considerations, I must observe, are unconnected with the judicial question on which it was properly within your province to assist me with your advice; but, irrespective of this, I am compelled to say, that neither they nor the reasoning founded on them, which has induced you to adopt a different line in recommending these parties to mercy, has produced the same result in my mind; whilst at the same time such publicity has unfortunately been given to your opinions on this subject, as would involve the government in embarrassment were I to set aside your recommendation to mercy, and leave these individuals for execution.

"On the other hand, I foresee much practical inconvenience likely to result from this summary review of all the proceedings of the highest civil tribunal in the Island, followed by a sweeping modification of its judgment upon men convicted of the gravest offences known to our laws.

"Upon a deliberate calculation, however, of the comparative evils of either course, and feeling strongly the disadvantage at which I am placed in acting on my own judgment, I have deemed it best to lean to the side of mercy, and to adopt so much of your recommendation as regards the commutation of all capital punishments, substituting transportation for life in the instance of those convicts, who have not been recommended to mercy by the juries, and transportation for fourteen years in all the other cases. I have, &c.,

(Signed) "TORRINGTON.

"The Hon. Sir A. Oliphant, Kt., C. J."

END OF VOL. I.

20, *Great Marlborough-Street,*
April 1, 1850.

MR. SHOBERL'S NEW WORKS.

I.

THE RIFLE RANGERS; or, Adventures of an Officer in Southern Mexico. By Capt. MAYNE REID. In 2 vols. small 8vo. with Illustrations.

II.

Dedicated to Lady Franklin.

A NARRATIVE of ARCTIC DISCOVERY, from the Earliest Period to the Present Time. With the Details of the Measures adopted by her Majesty's Government. For the Relief of the Expedition under Sir John Franklin. By JOHN J. SHILLINGLAW. In small 8vo. with Maps of the Arctic Regions, and Portrait of Sir John Franklin.

III.

NEW HISTORICAL ROMANCE.

ROYALISTS AND ROUNDHEADS; or, the days of Charles the First. In 3 vols. post 8vo. (Just ready.)

IV.

THE NEW WORK ON HUNGARY.

SCENES of the CIVIL WAR IN HUNGARY, in 1848-9. With the Personal Adventures of an Austrian Officer in the Army of the Ban of Croatia. Third Edition, 7*s.* 6*d.* bound.

"A book of deep excitement—of soul-harrowing interest."—*Naval and Military Gazette.*

V.

THE NEW MILITARY NOVEL.

COUNTRY QUARTERS. By the COUNTESS of BLESSINGTON. With a Portrait and Memoir by Miss POWER. In 3 vols. post 8vo.

"A perfect delineation of life and manners."—*Messenger.*

"Will be more keenly relished upon a second than upon a first perusal."—*John Bull.*